ॐ

For Mother, Her children are everything.
Mother's heart will become full when
She sees each child growing spiritually.

– Amma

My First Darshan
A collection of Stories from around the World

Published by:
Mata Amritanandamayi Mission Trust
Amritapuri PO, Kollam Dt., Kerala,
India 690525
Website: amritapuri.org
Email: inform@amritapuri.org

First Edition: January 2003 – 1,000 copies
July 2003 – 2,000
July 2004 – 2,000
July 2005 –   750
July 2007 – 1,000
July 2011 – 1,000

MY FIRST DARSHAN

A Collection of Stories from around the World

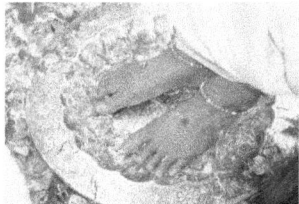

Kameshvari Jaganmatah Saccidanandavigrahe
Grhanarcamimam Pritya Prasida Paramesvari

Oh Ruler of Desire, Mother of the Universe
Embodiment of Truth-Consiousness-Bliss
Please accept this offering with Love
Oh Supreme Divinity, be pleased!

Contents

Who is Mata Amritanandamayi?

Mata Amritanandamayi also known as Amma or Mother was born in 1953 in a small fishing village in Kerala, India. From Her tender childhood, She sought out God even without the guidance of a Guru. At the age of twenty-one, She outwardly manifested Her state of God-Realization and began to initiate aspirants into spiritual life. By the age of twenty-seven, She had established the spiritual headquarters of Her mission in the house of Her birth.

In 1987, Amma made Her first world tour in response to invitations from Her children in America and Europe, inspiring and uplifting many people. Fifteen years later, Her children now number in the hundreds of thousands and reside on every corner of the earth. Amma's birthplace has become the location of an ashram that draws visitors from around the world, and from where She travels worldwide to impart Her blessings to people.

Amma individually meets every single person who comes to Her by hugging each one. Dubbed as "the hugging saint" by the western media, it is not uncommon to see Her greeting visitors with hugs for ten hours a day or even more, day after day.

Although born into a Hindu tradition, Amma does not advocate any religion, nor does She differentiate between religions. Her message is simple and is the same as that of all great religions – to love and to serve others selflessly, seeing ourselves in them. Amma teaches that selfless service is an important part of spiritual practice. It is an act of worship and an expression of love and reverence to the Divine which manifests as Nature and as all Beings.

Amma is the embodiment of all that She teaches. She devotes every moment of Her life to the service of Her children. Her message has taken the form of a growing charitable mission that reaches out in many different ways to help the poor and the suffering.

Swami Amritaswarupananada, one of Amma's senior disciples, describes Her with these words, "Amma is a mystic accessible to anyone and everyone, with whom you can converse and in whose presence you can feel God. She is humble but firm as the Earth. She is simple, yet beautiful like the full moon. She is soft like a flower and hard like a diamond. She is Love, She is Truth and She is the embodiment of renunciation and self-sacrifice. She not only teaches but does. She is the giver of everything and the receiver of nothing. She is a great Master and a great Mother. Such is Mata Amritananadamayi."

It is left to you…to decide who and what Amma is…through the intuition of your own heart…

An Offering of Love

My First Darshan is an offering of love to souls everywhere. This book is a collection of short stories written by fifty-four of the hundreds of thousands of people blessed to have received darshan from Mata Amritanandamayi Devi, their beloved Mother and Guru. Writers share their heart warming and deeply moving experiences with Her in these stories. This book is their offering at Her Divine Feet.

Many of Amma's "children" regard Her as a divine incarnation, not unlike Christ, Buddha, or Krishna. Teachers, students, business owners, corporate employees, physiotherapists, healers, yoga instructors, artists — Amma's children are from all walks of life. They come from countries across five continents. They range from young boys and girls to old grandfathers and grandmothers. Some are from traditional religious households while others had no spiritual or religious training prior to their meeting Amma. Together, their stories beautifully showcase Amma's love, which transcends all barriers of culture, nationality, language, religion, and age.

The stories in this book are from people who have only met Amma once as well as from those who have known Her for nearly two decades. About half of the stories are from those who were already on a spiritual path when they first met Amma. Others met Her serendipitously but still felt drawn to Her.

About the Stories

The stories follow a similar format. The writer briefly shares his or her spiritual background, if any, prior to meeting Amma and then describes events leading up to the first darshan with Her. This first meeting is described in detail and is followed by a brief description of the writer's journey with Amma over the years. Sometimes, however, this brief description of the latter journey is not so brief. But knowing how Amma's children love Her stories, we did not have the heart to prune them down. Perhaps *How I Became Amma's Child* would have been a more fitting title for some stories instead of *My First Darshan*. We trust that our dear readers won't mind this sweet indulgence.

The stories in the book represent nearly thirty different countries. A quick way to tell the country of residence of the writer is to look at the sidebar quote, which includes both the writer's name and country. In general, one to three stories are included from any one country. A fourth of the stories are translated from languages other than English.

Amma's words appear in italics at the start of every chapter and every story. These teachings of Amma relate to a theme in the chapters and the stories and are taken from Her books and talks. Amma's words also appear throughout this introduction as italicized text.

Names and short biographies of the writers are included to make the stories more personal. These are real experiences that happened to real people. In many cases, writers allowed the use of their birth names instead of their spiritual names given to them by Amma so that readers new to Amma and unfamiliar with Sanskrit names and Vedic traditions might relate to the stories more easily.

A chapter includes stories from Amma's younger children. It is deeply moving to read about the manner in which Amma's love is molding these young ones. Blessed indeed are they for coming to Amma so early in their lives and for making such a whole-hearted attempt to live in tune with Her teachings.

The final chapter includes stories from Amma's renunciate children who live in Her ashrams. Especially powerful journeys of transformation, these stories are filled with rich lessons and deep insights.

"Inconsistencies"

In order to preserve the regional flavor of the different countries of our writers, we have not changed spellings and other usages to make them consistent throughout the book. It is our belief that these "inconsistencies" add a certain richness.

As Amma's spiritual children, we capitalize pronouns to refer to Her. In the stories, however, small letters are used for Amma during the first darshan and perhaps beyond to accurately reflect the writer's feelings during those times.

The Power of Amma's Love

If the stories in the book are all testimony to one thing, it is to the unmistakable power of Amma's love. A love that expresses itself in the simple language of the heart and is easily understood by another heart that is open. A love that knows no barriers and sees no differences. A love that heals and purifies on all levels – physical, emotional, and spiritual.

It is the power of this Divine Love that draws Amma's children to Her. Amma totally and unconditionally accepts and loves each and every person who comes to Her. It is not a coincidence that the words *Love* and *Heart* appear in more story titles than any other words.

> *Even if all the beings in the whole world loved us, we would not experience an iota of the bliss we feel from a moment's taste of the Love of God. So great is the bliss we feel from God's love that there is nothing to compare with it.*
>
> *– Amma*

While Amma blesses Her children with many gifts on the material level, the greatest blessing is in the transformation that Her love brings about. It is not uncommon to find evidence of material benefits in the lives of Amma's children. She knows exactly what gift to give and when to give it. If the stories in this book, however, do not focus on such gifts, it is because Amma's children realize, sooner or later, that these gifts are mere trinkets when compared to the Divine Grace that Amma showers – the Grace of leading one closer to God.

All who have experienced the transformative power of Amma's love in their own lives attest to the fact that She is the best teacher.

Amma teaches the lessons we need to learn for our spiritual growth with deep love and unending patience. She advises not just with words but also by Her divine will the right opportunities are some-how created for us to learn. We may fail again and again, yet She never gives up on us. How this process unfolds is difficult to explain or understand; it can only be experienced.

> *Children, the mother who gave birth to you may look*
> *after matters relating to this life. But Mother's aim is*
> *to lead you in such a way that you can enjoy bliss in all*
> *your future lives.*
>
> *— Amma*

Often Repeated in the Stories...

It is impossible to describe in words ... I burst into tears ... felt like I was home at last...

Amma's infinite Grace blesses Her children with glimpses into the true nature of Reality known as Sat-Chit-Ananda (Truth-Consciousness-Bliss). This Reality is something far, far beyond our common day-to-day experiences and impossible to describe in words. This may be one of the main reasons why many writers find it...*impossible to describe in words...*

Amma says that in the presence of a great Master, the closed bud of our heart opens up. Deep down our soul knows that we have come home even though the intellect may not comprehend. Tears of love, joy, and bliss may pour down our eyes even as our rational minds may wonder at what is really happening...

This may partially explain why, upon meeting Amma, some immediately recognize Her as a Divine Being. Others, however, take a long time to open up to Her. Amma says that the intellect cannot possibly understand a true Master, the heart is needed for this understanding.

The mind projects its perceptions on everything one sees and hears – projections that may have nothing to do with reality. The stories in the book powerfully demonstrate this deceptive nature of the mind.

For example, while the writer in one story feels amazed at Amma's simplicity and the lack of a red carpet or a throne or any special lights, in another story, the writer sees Amma's chair (the same chair) being adorned with flowers and wonders at the pomp and circumstance about Her. Many people see Amma as a loving mother who embraces each one as a dear child when they first set eyes upon Her. Yet, to others, the same Amma appears as a charlatan who encourages followers to come up to Her on their knees.

Coming to Her and Becoming Her Child

How do Amma's children come to Her arms? The stories illuminate a great truth taught by scriptures from around the world. God is ever-present and waiting at the doors of our hearts. However, He cannot come in unless we open the doors and invite Him in. His very nature does not allow Him to force His way through if the doors are tightly shut. We must call out before He can respond. Hearing the very first call, He will come rushing to the aid of His little one.

> *The Guru is like the sun. The Guru cannot be otherwise. The Guru just shines. Whoever keeps the doors of their heart open receives the light.*
>
> *– Amma*

Another common theme that emerges from the stories is that no matter how deeply moving a writer's first darshan experience is, it is by remaining connected to Amma even during the times that She is physically away that the relationship with Her is strengthened. Whether by reading Amma's books and trying to follow Her teachings or listening to Her bhajans or attending satsang, it is this effort on one's part that is required.

> *What meaning do our lives have if we cannot set aside at least one hour a day out of twenty-four for thinking about God? Think how many hours we spend reading*

the newspaper, gossiping, and doing other useless things.
Children, we can definitely set aside an hour for sadhana
if we really want it. That is our real wealth. If we can-
not spare a whole hour at a stretch, keep apart half an
hour in the morning and again in the evening.

— Amma

The Greatest Grace

Amma travels for nearly eight months of the year meeting Her children in all corners of the globe and individually blessing them. A look at Her grueling tour schedule would perhaps make even the most hardened road-warrior wince. Out of Her compassion Amma chooses to travel like this, so that many, many more people can come to Her and be blessed. The fact that She individually meets every single person who comes is the rarest and greatest gift of Grace that She offers.

Mother does what she does because she cannot do other-
wise. To love is her nature, to serve is her nature.

— Amma

Meeting Amma, opening our hearts to Her, and letting Her love transform our lives is something that can only be experienced. There are simply no words to describe this miracle of Grace.

Reading this Book

Reading this book is rather like eating dessert, to borrow words from a famous compilation of short stories. One cannot eat or read too much at one time. One should perhaps not attempt to read all the stories in a single sitting. The unique flavor and joy in every story will be lost.

Reading the stories slowly, taking the time to savor each one, and reflecting on the beautiful insights and lessons within will help more in enjoying this book. We invite you to immerse yourself in these uplifting stories and wish you happy reading!

1

The Power of Love

The holy river Ganges springs forth from the lofty Himalayan peaks and flows down through the valleys into the plains, purifying whoever comes to have a dip in her, be it a leper or a healthy person, beggar or millionaire, man or woman, sinner or saint, without any distinction whatsoever. Mother Ganges receives everyone with equal love and concern. She doesn't resent anyone. She only has the noblest feelings towards all, whether or not they come to bathe in her sacred waters. It is Mother's wish to be like the Mother Ganges.

– Amma

Mutham Kodu Mone

*Love just happens. Nobody thinks about how
to love, or when and where to love. Love is a
sudden uprising in the heart. There is no logic
in this. It is beyond logic.*

— Amma

In 1997, I was working and living in Kuwait with my wife and our
three sons. I am a Hindu by birth, but I had no special knowledge
about our religious scriptures. Kuwait has no temples, so we were
in the habit of praying at a Catholic Church every Friday evening.
I would pray to Mother Mary at the Church. I believe that there
is only one God who is known by different names, so there was
no problem with praying at a Church. This had been our regular
practice for many years.

In January or February of that year, I was severely infected
with the chicken pox virus. There is a belief among Hindus that
chicken pox is a sign of Devi Vilayattam and that it helps to purify
and increase the resistance power of one's body. I don't know if
this is true, but it was shortly after that I first learned about Amma.
Perhaps my body was going through some kind of a purification
process before my first meeting with her.

In mid-1997, a weekly documentary program about Amma was
shown on T.V.; the series lasted several weeks. My wife recorded
all the programs and after watching them, I felt that there was
something supernatural about Amma. I became eager to learn
more about her.

Luckily, there was a Balakendram of Amma in an apartment
close to my home, where children were taught about spirituality.
I also learned that monthly bhajans were being conducted at the

Indian Embassy. I soon started sending my children to the Balakendram and attending bhajans with my wife. However, within two or three weeks, the Balakendram stopped due to some problems.

> *Before chanting the Ashtotharam every morning, I would give a mutham (meaning kiss, in Malayalam) to Amma's photo.*
>
> **– Mohanan Mavilakandy, Bahrain**

At this time, I felt we could start the Balakendram in my home. This turned out to be a blessing because it made us all more involved with Amma's activities in Kuwait and also gave us a chance to learn more about her. Soon, I started the practice of reciting the Ashtotharam every morning. Before chanting, I would give a mutham (meaning kiss, in Malayalam) to Amma's photo. But I would do this with a little reluctance because in my spiritually immature mind, Amma was a woman. Still, the practice continued.

In September or October of that year, at about 3:00 a.m. one morning, my youngest son, who was only three years old at that time, had a sudden attack of convulsions. Nothing like this had ever happened before and my wife and I became very alarmed. We called out to Amma to help. We took him to the hospital but by the time we arrived, he had already become quite normal. The doctors examined him and admitted him for one day but no sign of illness was found. I felt that this was truly a miracle performed by Amma! We had cried out to her from our hearts and she had responded.

The Balakendram classes and bhajans continued. In January 1998, Swamiji Amritaswarupananda visited Kuwait and we had a chance to meet him. Slowly, I became eager to see Amma. We were building a new house at that time and I wanted to take Amma's blessings before the house-warming ceremony. Every year we travelled to India in July or August when the boys' schools closed for the summer and at first, I thought we could see Amma then.

But, my longing to see her increased. Finally in April, when I could not resist it any longer, I decided to fly to Cochin to see Amma. I couldn't afford to take the rest of the family with me since five plane tickets would be too expensive. Only my family knew that I was travelling to India just to see Amma. Our friends were told that I was going on a business trip and that I intended to visit Vallikkavu once the work was over.

I started praying to Amma constantly. "May I be blessed by your darshan and may I be able to kiss your lotus feet."

On Tuesday evening, April 7, 1998, the day finally arrived. I flew from Kuwait and reached Cochin. I arrived in Amritapuri around 3:00 p.m. the next afternoon. I first went to the reception to get a room. Bombay Acchan, the man in charge, asked me whether I had taken Amma's darshan. When I said that I had not, he told me to go quickly because darshan was coming to an end.

At first, I hesitated. I had come from a long journey and felt that I was not clean. But Bombay Acchan persisted. He told me that it did not matter whether I was clean or not. Upon hearing this, I ran towards the darshan hall. There were very few people there. I joined the queue.

As I waited with an overfull heart, I watched Amma give darshan. I was finally fulfilling my ardent desire for her vision. I couldn't believe that I was standing in front of Amma herself! I couldn't control my tears. Suddenly, a brahmachari came to inform everyone in the queue that the canteen was about to close and that those who had not eaten lunch yet, should go to the canteen immediately. I am slightly diabetic and I had not eaten, but I was quite all right. To me, darshan was more important than anything else. I remained in the queue.

It took only around twenty minutes to come near Amma. She was sitting cross-legged and her feet were under her sari, not to be seen. A deep sorrow struck me as I thought that I might not be able to kiss her divine feet. My eyes filled with tears. But just before my turn, I beheld something unbelievable. As if in answer to my prayers, Amma slowly changed her position so that her feet were now on the floor! Amma looked at me and smiled so lovingly!

"My son" she said.

Amma held me and drew me towards her. She placed my head on her shoulder and whispered something into my ear. At first, I didn't understand anything. But soon I realised that she was saying "mutham kodu, mone, mutham kodu, mone," which means "kiss me, son, kiss me, son" in Malayalam.

I turned my face towards Amma's neck and showered her with *muthams*. This was a supremely blissful experience. I burst into tears again and couldn't say a word. The house-warming ceremony was totally forgotten. Amma gave me prasadam and asked me to sit nearby. I bent down towards her lotus feet, caught them with my hands and deeply kissed them. Words cannot describe the wonderful experience I felt at this moment. My mind was in a different world controlled by a divine power.

While sitting near Amma, I remembered that I used to give a *mutham* to Amma's photo but always with some reluctance, not knowing whether this was right or wrong. Today, Amma herself had asked me to give *muthams* to her. In doing so, she had cleared my doubts and my ignorance. She had also known my heartfelt desire and had given me an opportunity to kiss her holy feet. This realisation made me again weep like a child. I felt like the most blessed person on this earth.

After Amma's darshan was over, I walked out of the hall. I was just walking casually, without any purpose. I wasn't looking for the canteen because its closure notice had already been given some time back. To my surprise however, I saw a brahmacharini walking towards me with a plate of rice and curry. She asked me if I had eaten my lunch yet. When I said no, she gave me the plate. This was my first lunch from Amma. Amma had shown me again that she knew our needs and would take care of them.

In the evening, I attended bhajans. I don't know why but I kept crying throughout. When I left Amritapuri the next day, I felt like a child departing from its mother. The departure was really tough and there was only one prayer on my lips.

"Amma, may I be lucky enough to come back again soon and have your darshan. And may I be able to bring my wife and boys with me this time."

This two-day visit to Amritapuri remains as the sweetest memory of my life. On the way back to Kuwait, I waited at the airport with pain and sadness. Only thoughts of Amma were with me. Suddenly just for few seconds, the entire area was filled with a fragrance, the same divine smell that I had experienced on Amma's lap. I felt Amma's presence and looked around, but...

In August that year, during our annual vacation in India, my family was able to meet Amma for the first time. Amma showered Her endless love on all of us.

Amma's teachings have heavily influenced all aspects of my life. My behaviour has changed and my previous habit of having a hot temper has improved. I now have a greater awareness of my words and deeds. Every moment, Amma performs miracles with our lives. She shows, in so many ways, that Her children are always in Her eyes. I pray that the light of Amma's unconditional and divine love is always with all Her children, leading us steadily in the right direction. I offer these words at Her Lotus Feet.

Mohanan Mavilakandy lives in Manama, Bahrain with his wife and three sons Anirudh, 12, Akhil, 10, and Vaishnav, 8. He is of Indian origin and was born and brought up in Kerala. He spent 13 years in Kuwait before moving to Bahrain. Currently he works with Ericsson-Bahrain as their Finance and Administration Manager.

I Want to Play with You

When my children are sad, Amma longs to give them peace.

– Amma

I had been on the spiritual path for many years. In 1993 I had a dream that I can never forget. In the dream, I was walking toward the town square of an old European city. Many people were gathered around an Indian lady. I did not know who she was, but I felt very attracted to her. I could sense that this was no ordinary person.

Before I could reach her, she suddenly got up and walked away briskly. The crowd dispersed as I tried to follow her cautiously. When I caught up with her, I stepped in front and asked the one question that really concerned me.

"Will I be able to bear children in this lifetime?"

She smiled and replied, "Get a thorough examination from your doctor."

Saying this, she continued walking forward. I tried to follow, but lost sight of her in the maze of alleyways. Finally, I saw her again. She was in a medieval church, wearing a blue gown, looking just like Mother Mary.

For many days, I pondered the significance of the dream. My husband and I wanted to have children but I had not been able to conceive for many years. I did not really know whether to pay any attention to the answer the lady had given in the dream. For some time, I did nothing. A few weeks later, I went to a specialist for an examination. He determined that we could not have children without using artificial means.

> *I looked at her face, mesmerised. It beamed like a thousand suns and her eyes twinkled with joy and love.*
> *– Karin Nirmala Iser, Switzerland*

Towards the end of that year, a palm-reader read the lines on my hand and told me that my life was about to completely change as a result of an important person coming into it.

"Hmm…A new relationship?" I wondered. This idea did not appeal to me at all because I was very happily married.

"My own child?" I hardly dared to think of this possibility. "Would my long cherished wish to be a mother really become true?" The very thought warmed my heart.

Early the next year, my husband and I visited India where we first heard about Amma. When I saw her picture, I realised that this was the same lady I had seen in my dream! I was stunned! I learned that she had an ashram in Kerala. I really wanted to visit but our vacation time was almost over and we had to return to our jobs in Switzerland. We learned that Amma visited Switzerland every summer, and felt happy knowing that we could meet her then.

On our way back home, I read Amma's biography and felt very touched. The idea of a female avatar fascinated me. I thought that perhaps Amma was the teacher I had long been searching for. I impatiently awaited her visit.

On August 13, 1994, we made our way to Schweibenalp to meet Amma. On that first evening, I stood with many other people in a meadow in the Alps singing *Amma Amma Taye*, against the backdrop of the setting sun, waiting for Amma to come. I felt very happy clapping to the rhythm of the song even though I did not know the words.

After about half an hour of our singing, Amma's car drove up. She got out of the car easily and greeted everybody with her palms folded together over her head. Then she walked towards us at a fast pace. I looked at her face, mesmerised. It beamed like a thousand suns and her eyes twinkled with joy and love. Her skin appeared almost black.

As she came near me, I stretched out my hand like everyone else to touch Amma's hand. Amma touched my hand gently and very softly. Her blossom-white sari left behind an aroma of roses as she walked past. I gazed after her, the aroma now coming from my own hands.

"What a special person she must be…!"

The next day was Amma's first darshan program. I sat in the tent by myself observing the colourful event. The whole thing seemed like a festival. Amma was receiving everyone with a hug. From the loudspeakers came the devoted singing of the monks. The air was rich with incense.

Soon I spotted my husband. He had been experiencing many conflicting emotions since the previous day and had escaped briefly for a hike up the mountains. He seemed to be in a better mood and we decided to go for darshan together.

We joined the line. I watched Amma and how she took everyone in her arms. The closer we got, the more nervous I became, but when our turn came, I forgot everything and burst into tears in Amma's arms. It was as if time stood still. Like I was a ship and had arrived at a long-awaited port to finally rest.

Right after darshan, my husband left to go to our room. When I learned that we could ask Amma questions, I jumped for joy. "Really? We can ask God questions? Finally I can clarify all my questions!" I joined the question line.

I wrote out my question on a piece of paper and when it was my turn, handed it to the translator. I asked Amma about the spiritual path I should follow. Amma smiled at me while the translator read my note to her.

"Pray to the Divine Mother very fervently and deeply. Take Amma as your Guru. Amma will guide you," she said.

The answer shot through me like a bolt of lightening. I felt paralysed. I understood the seriousness of Amma's answer. There was no going back now. A deep feeling of bliss flowed through me and my heart pounded with joy. I did not know whether to laugh or cry. I lingered in the hall briefly and then went to find my husband.

I found him reclining on a mattress in our lodge room reading Amma's biography. I told him what Amma had said. He responded somewhat contemptuously, "She probably says that to everyone." I was shocked at this interpretation! I did not know then that Amma doesn't say the same thing to everyone, so I could not effectively argue back. I became a little irritated with him.

Surprisingly, his attitude changed somewhat over the rest of that day. The next day when I told him that I was going to ask Amma for a mantra during Devi Bhava, to my great surprise, he said that he would also like to get a mantra from Amma. During darshan, Amma held our hands and kissed them. To me, it was like a second wedding.

After darshan, we sat on the stage beside Amma waiting for our mantras. After some time, Amma looked up and held flower petals over my head, while whispering the mantra into my ear. It was as if the angels in heaven were celebrating! I tried to understand the words but Amma murmured them so fast that I could not follow anything. I was glad to get them spoken slowly by her attendant later. I sat on stage for a few more minutes to savour the moment as my husband received his mantra. I felt lightly drunk, drunk with Amma's love.

In summer 1995, when we saw Amma again, the first thing she asked when we went for darshan was, "Where are your children?" I was completely dumbfounded and did not know what to make of this. A few weeks later a specialist confirmed that we could prob-ably not have children without artificial means.

The following year, I asked Amma if we should try artificial insemination. We did not really want to do that and in any case, we were both kind of old already. Amma supported our decision not to do anything special.

"If it happens naturally, it should be alright," she added. Sadly, I said farewell to my inner desire to become a mother.

The following year we went to Amma's ashram in India. I had been daydreaming for a while about playing with Amma as a child, romping about together in the sand, playing catch-me, swinging and having fun. When I went for darshan, tears just poured down my cheeks. Amma took me softly into her arms and wiped the tears away with the tip of my sari.

Sobbing, I whispered into Amma's ear, "Amma, I want to play with you."

Amma looked deeply into my eyes and smiled very sweetly. I bowed and left, partly fulfilled and partly upset.

Six months later, my long cherished dream was fulfilled and I became pregnant. A wonderful girl came to us in April 1998. Amma herself came to us in the form of our daughter Sharada. Now I could play with Her. I am pregnant again now for the second time.

Amma changed our lives completely on all levels. She became a part of our lives and a part of our daily family activities. Through Her, I experienced the real meaning of life and found inner peace.

Translated from German by Dania Edwards and Jake Urech

Editor's Note: The following story is written by the writer's husband.

Karin Nirmala Iser, 40, lives in a village near Zurich, Switzerland with her husband Werner and their daughter Sharada, 4. She is currently pregnant with their second child. A full-time mother, she worked earlier as a teacher in a primary school. She likes spending time with her daughter, painting, singing and working with children.

You Are OK the Way You Are

A flower doesn't need instructions on how to bloom. No music teacher taught the nightingale to sing. It is spontaneous. There is no force involved; it happens naturally. Similarly, in the presence of a Master, the closed bud of your heart opens up. If you forcefully open the petals of a bud, you won't be able to enjoy its beauty and fragrance. Only when it blossoms by following its natural course, will the beauty and fragrance of the flower unfold.
– Amma

My wife and I had both been searching for a genuine spiritual teacher for a long time. In August 1994, we made a three hour journey by train to see a woman saint on the mountaintop in Schweibenalp. We had heard about her a few months earlier. Already we had visited two holy people that year and had been disappointed. I was not very sure what this trip would bring.

When we arrived, everyone was already gathered waiting for the saint to come. I looked around. Many young and middle-aged people dressed in Indian style clothes were clapping their hands and singing something. Smiling faces and much movement. The excitement appeared exaggerated to me.

"All this restlessness! What about a meditative atmosphere?" I thought to myself. "What on earth am I doing with these hippies here?"

I looked around again. No one seemed to mind the waiting. Suddenly the singing became louder as two cars drove up. Amma got down from one of the cars and made her way through the waiting crowd, touching many hands with her outstretched hands. She glanced at me with a friendly beaming smile as she walked past me.

"Did she really look me in the eye, or did I just imagine it?" This was the first thought that crossed my mind.

She was soon gone. It felt nice having seen her.

"All this restlessness! What about a meditative atmosphere?" I thought to myself. "What on earth am I doing with these hippies here?"
— Werner Iser, Switzerland

The next day, at Amma's first program, I was plagued with doubts again. While sitting in the colourful crowd of "hippies," all kinds of thoughts passed through my mind.

"There are too many people here. Not only too many, but also all the wrong ones," I said to myself. "I am a serious seeker. What do I have in common with these lazy dreamers? With other spiritual teachers, things are more serious." I reckoned that my mood was not really at its best.

"And this strange bodyguard in orange clothes who sits right next to Amma. Who is he?"

In the meantime, my wife was behaving in a very holy manner. She did not want to listen to my concerns, which really annoyed me. I left her, put on my trekking shoes and went off by myself.

I trekked two hours to the tip of the Axalp, a mountainous area in the Alps above Schweibenalp, and then rode a bus back down. The fresh clear air in the mountains cleared my head and I felt better.

I joined my wife at the program. She wanted to go for darshan but I was not so sure. I felt afraid of physical contact with Amma. "If she really is a genuine saint then she may be omniscient and may know so many embarrassing things about me," I thought to myself. "I mean, I am no angel and my spiritual interests are still young and superficial."

I did not want to share my inner worries with my wife. Instead, I complained to her about the outer situation, the jostling of the people and the long waiting line. She was determined to get darshan and eventually I gave up and just quietly accepted the humiliation of lining up.

Something changed, however, as we came closer to Amma. I became excited. When there were only about three meters between

Amma and us, I began watching her carefully. She received every person with the same love and yet, each darshan was unique. Suddenly I noticed that my peace had returned within.

It was my turn next and I lay in Amma's arms. Everything vanished. I was not aware of anything any more. Amma whispered something into my ear, which I did not understand at all. But I felt very safe and sound. "You are ok the way you are. The way you are, it is ok," Amma seemed to be saying with her embrace.

I stood up and sat nearby. What just happened? I was not sure. The darshan was not spectacular; nor was it ordinary. "You are ok the way you are!" I wanted to yell it out loud.

I retreated to our room and began to leaf through Amma's biography in German. "Who is she anyway?" my mind wanted to know. "Could she possibly be an avatar or was she a more or less plain and simple saint?"

Quickly skimming the biography, I tended towards the second possibility. "But why on earth did she have such a curious childhood? Why did she have to throw herself into the mud and do other crazy things?" All this seemed rather weird to me.

I continued to the second part of the book "Conversations." I liked the simple language and understood the advice she gave. Some of the answers, however, stirred up a feeling of despair from within. I wanted to be free, with the responsibility for my life in my own hands. I did not want to live by any rules that were so hard to live up to anyway. "I will never be able to follow Amma's standards," I thought and put the book aside.

In the meantime, my wife had found out that she could pose questions to Amma. This did not surprise me at all. She just loved asking questions. Sometimes I would scold her for asking me many annoying questions. Not only had she already managed to ask Amma a question, she had even received an answer. She had asked Amma for advice regarding her spiritual path. Amma had told her to pray to the Divine Mother and to take Amma as her Guru. It was too much for me. I started feeling uneasy. "Just what I need now," I thought.

"Naturally she must say that to everyone," I responded to her. "What else would she say?"

"I would like to go home," I declared. "I cannot stand this circus any longer." Usually I was quite successful with such blackmails, but at the moment I was not being calculative, just struggling from a feeling of despair.

"I understand," my wife replied calmly. "I would regret leaving Amma like this, so I will remain here."

Suddenly the curtains fell from my eyes. If I continued to behave in this manner while my wife was drawn closer to Amma, our relationship would be at stake. My wife's determination to stay and the calm manner in which she communicated it to me somehow told me that I had to change my attitude to avoid bigger problems at a later date. I said that I was ready to go back to the program with her. The next day we both took a mantra from Amma.

Over the next few years, my wife's miraculous pregnancy and the beautiful birth of our daughter Sharada changed my life completely. For Sharada's birth, we decorated the hospital room so that it resembled a little temple. We played bhajans and the Thousand Names of the Divine Mother and lit candles. Sharada arrived like a gift from the heavens!

One year ago, Sharada wished for a sister. In five weeks time, our second child is due. Sharada told us that when the baby arrives, she will go with the baby and her mommy and daddy to India to visit Amma's ashram. When Sharada wants something, she usually gets it. She has very strong will power.

Today Amma is the very center of our lives. I have since learned that Amma accepts each one of us just as we are. One does not ever feel any pressure with Her. She never tries to open a bud with force, but waits until the right time comes. Then the beautiful flower opens slowly by itself. Today we cannot even imagine our day-to-day life without Her.

Translated from German by Monique Enibokum

Editor's Note: The preceding story is written by the writer's wife.

Werner Iser, 49, lives with his wife Karin and their daughter Sharada in a little village near Zurich, Switzerland. Their second child is on the way. Werner runs a small company for financial services and works as a financial consultant and portfolio manager. He enjoys astrology, reading, singing and trekking.

My All-Knowing Mother

You can read spiritual books but mere reading is not enough. Practice is also necessary. People who spend all their time gaining theoretical knowledge from scriptures without doing any sadhana are like those who try to live in the blueprint of a house.

— Amma

I was seventeen when I started reading books like the *Bhagavad Gita* and *Patanjali's Yoga Sutras*. These books nourished my soul and showed me the true meaning of life. I was fascinated by this ancient philosophy and tried, thereafter, to live in harmony with the teachings in them.

In 1999, at thirty-eight, I first heard about Amma from a yoga instructor. After reading some of her books and finding her teachings to be very clear and full of love and devotion, I felt drawn to her. In September 2000, Swami Ramakrishnananda, a senior disciple of Amma, came to visit Argentina for the first time to give some lectures. I attended all the lectures.

During one of the lectures, Swamiji said that if we needed something, we could pray to Amma with devotion and that her grace would come. At that time, I was very stressed at work and needed a change. I decided to pray to Amma to help me with this situation. Would you believe that on that same day, I was miraculously transferred to another department where things were much better? I silently thanked Amma but briefly wondered if this had been a mere coincidence.

After this incident, I felt a strong desire to meet Amma. My economic means were not such that I could travel to India or to the United States to meet her. One day I sent an email to Amma at the

> *Being with Amma was like being on a cloud. Nothing in the outside world mattered.*
> *– Berta Rebeca Petasny, Argentina*

Indian ashram imploring her to find a way for me to be in her presence.

Several months later, when I was tidying up the house, I came across an old violin my father had given me when I was a little girl. It was broken and nobody used it, so I thought that I could sell it. I placed ads in the newspaper and on the Internet with scanned photos and to my great surprise, an antique dealer in New York, U.S.A. responded with an offer to examine and buy the violin. He quoted an estimated price that would easily pay for my trip to New York.

Amma had made it possible for me to go and see her! From her web site, I found out that she would be in New York a few months later in July 2001. I made an appointment with the antique dealer for the same time and awaited the trip with great enthusiasm. When I reached New York, I was able to sell the violin for approximately the same amount of money I needed to pay for my airline ticket and to attend Amma's retreat programs. I could not believe it! Everything just fell into place, just like that, out of the blue! Or was this the miracle of Amma's grace?

I spent seven days with Amma in New York and Rhode Island and received her precious hug many times. I was the only person from Argentina at the programs and the organizers were extremely kind to me and arranged everything for my stay. Being with Amma was like being on a cloud. Nothing in the outside world mattered. I felt very happy.

In some ways, I also felt overwhelmed to realize what a great saint Amma was. She sat there, hour after hour, sweetly hugging everyone with the same love and compassion, without stopping even for a few minutes. It was the most beautiful thing I had ever seen. I understood that to really know God, one had to be able to love everyone like that and that it was not as easy as described in books. I felt a long way away from that state but I was so grateful to have the opportunity of being in the presence of a living saint.

During Devi Bhava night, I asked Amma for a mantra. Earlier, when someone was singing a bhajan to the deity of my devotion, I told Amma mentally that if she knew everything, then she knew that I wanted a mantra for that particular deity and that there was no need for me to tell her this. Later, I asked forgiveness for testing Amma in this way. I did not know that there were formal procedures for receiving a mantra. As I came to Amma's arms, first she murmured some strange words in my ear and I did not understand anything. Then she started repeating the mantra of the deity I liked. It was the same mantra I had wanted! I thought I was dreaming...

Seven months have passed since I met Amma. When I returned to Argentina, I felt very depressed for the first two months because I could not stop thinking about her and longed to be with her. It took me some time to understand that I had to start meditating and doing japa regularly to center my everyday life in spirituality.

When I think of Amma deeply, I want to cry even though I do not know why. I feel Her presence always with me. She is like a strong force inside my soul that is changing me completely. The change is often painful because it is very hard for the ego to let go. I feel grateful that Amma is guiding me patiently.

I long to see Amma again and I want my husband and children to be hugged by Her. We are all helping our small satsang group in Buenos Aires, Argentina to do everything possible to bring Amma to our country soon. Jai Ma!

Berta Rebeca Petasny, 41, lives in Buenos Aires, Argentina with her husband Miguel and their two children, Maria Belen, 15, and Francisco Matias, 10. She works as a bilingual secretary for a manufacturing company. She enjoys swimming and listening to devotional music from all over the world.

A Divine Touch

Children, love is our real nature. We are of the nature of Divine love. That love is shining in each and every one of us.

– Amma

I first became interested in spiritual matters early in 1997 when I bought and read the book *A Course in Miracles*. This book teaches in great detail where, how and why we have lost our connection with *Love*…and shows a good way back. In my opinion, this book is a masterpiece that tells step-by-step how to make changes so that we see and feel the miracles of life again. I was thirty-eight years old at this time.

In September of that year, I met a man at a spiritual workshop who told me about Amma. He asked me if I knew that she was soon coming to Netherlands. I replied that I did not, I did not even know who she was! He seemed to be a man of few words and merely told me to go and find out for myself. I decided to go. It turned out to be the best decision I ever made.

On the day Amma was arriving, I borrowed a car from a friend and drove to the address somewhere in the west of Netherlands. When I arrived, I was at first overwhelmed by the sheer size of the crowd that had already gathered. I spent some time puzzling over the ticket I received and lines on the floor that seemed to mark various waiting zones.

Tthere seemed to be chaos in the big hall. Shoes and coats were in a big pile, people were walking around everywhere and making a lot of noise chattering. I felt anger rising within me because I thought that people were definitely not paying much respect.

At that time, I was very much in love with a beautiful girl named Fraukje. The problem was that she already had a boyfriend. Their relationship was strained and I knew that she liked me so I was hoping

> *It was enough to just be in the room, or even in the parking lot for that matter, where I helped direct cars in the cold.*
> **– Hans de Beer, Netherlands**

that they would break up so that we could get together. My thoughts drifted to her as I sat down in a chair.

Suddenly I began thinking that it wasn't quite fair to hope like this and that only in completely letting go of my wish, could I hope to have her. Only in complete freedom would love be able to flow. I clearly saw that it was my very desire, no matter how sincere or spontaneous, which obstructed the free flow of love. My best option was to let love decide for itself.

About five minutes passed. My thoughts settled down and came to rest. A strange feeling of absolute quietness came over me. The one clear thought that remained was, "Love is free." I felt at ease and in peace. All this happened within the first twenty minutes after my arrival…before Amma even came into the hall!

Later as I was waiting in the darshan line, I felt a little nervous. As I went forward, however, the nervousness faded slowly to make way for joy and love. When I was only a few feet away from Amma, I felt so much love for her that I thought, for certain, that I would be giving her at least as much love as she would give me. Tears of joy started rolling down my cheeks. I felt like I was meeting a very good friend after decades.

As I reached Amma's arms, my heart seemed to grow and radiate beyond every limit I had previously known. I had been raised the Catholic way where I had learned to fear God. In Amma's arms, I knew now that nothing could be further from the Truth. How could we fear the one thing that creates and sustains everything with Love? Yet, we do. Worse, this has become our normal state of being.

The following year when I saw Amma again, this time in Belgium, the feeling of love was repeated and was even more intense.

I thought that a human being...or at least I...could not feel any more love. I felt that the entirety of my being was not large enough to contain more love. Well, I was in for a surprise!

Not only did my love continue to grow, but also I found that it wasn't necessary to take darshan or even be near the physical form of Amma to feel this love. It was enough to just be in the room, or even in the parking lot for that matter, where I helped direct cars in the cold. Amma's love radiated in such a way that it was enough to just be around.

What I learned is that the quality of pure love is such that it automatically melts away pain, fear, worry and all non-essential thoughts. All that remains after this melting is the pure essence of the stuff we are made of, the glue between the atoms of the Universe, so to speak. With all due respect, this unbounded, unlimited, divine love is something entirely different from the human kind of love.

Since that touch of pure love, my life has changed and my priorities have changed. Love decided that Fraukje and I were not to be married. Words can be twisted in many ways but a direct experience, a divine touch from inside says all that there is to say. I am grateful to Amma for setting things straight in my mind and my heart.

Hans de Beer is 43 years old and of Dutch nationality. He lives in the Netherlands and is planning a business in health products. His desire is to use his knowledge of health to benefit poor people. He has a great interest in architecture and likes to read and listen to music.

Emotional Healing

Understand that God dwells as pure con-
sciousness in all beings, including you. As this
experience becomes stronger and stronger, the
love in you also grows. This love is the best
cure for all emotional blocks.

– Amma

I love to travel, especially to Asia, as I am very interested in the philosophy of that region. As a nurse, I can save up my vacation and take a long time off at one time. In early 2001, I had two months off and decided to go on a spiritual trip to India. I had travelled to this country on my own before and had loved it, especially the people and the culture.

Although I had heard about different ashrams during my earlier visit, I had not visited any of them and was not quite sure what to think about them. Following a master or a guru felt very weird to me. Lately however, I had begun to notice that little things were making me depressed. I wanted to find inner peace and thought that perhaps in the ashrams of India, I could find it. I decided to give it a try.

I collected information from books and friends. Someone sent me a little booklet about Amma's ashram in Kerala. I felt attracted to her picture and thought that I might like to visit her. In January 2001, I arrived by plane in Chennai, open and ready for new experiences. I had decided to visit a few ashrams in Tamil Nadu first.

I visited three different ashrams during the next two and a half weeks. I met a lot of people who gave me many suggestions on how to cope with my life, but I did not find what I was looking for. To tell the truth, I got tired of hearing the same words repeated over and over again, seemingly without any inner conviction. "I have had enough of this," I thought to myself. Now, I just wanted to

> *Everyone sat around her for a brief*
> *meditation, which was followed by*
> *a question and answer session. It*
> *was like sitting around the table as*
> *a large family.*
>   – **Susanne Hill, Lithuania**

find a nice, quiet place to rest for a while.

I looked at the map to determine where I could go next. I remembered Amma's smiling face; her booklet was still in my backpack. I wasn't sure though whether I wanted to visit any more ashrams. When I looked at the map carefully, Kerala seemed close enough to Tamil Nadu, but I knew that distances in India were deceptive. It would take me several hours to make the train reservation and then the journey itself would take about fifteen hours. However, something inside told me very strongly that I had to go, so I decided to make the arduous journey to Kerala.

I left on a Sunday evening and arrived in the ashram the next day. Seeing the beautiful surroundings, I was immediately impressed. The ashram is located in between the backwaters and the ocean and has a very beautiful temple. I saw only a few people around and everything seemed quiet and pleasant. Birds were singing and I could hear an elephant trumpeting in the distance...

I settled in comfortably and explored my surroundings. The next day, I saw Amma for the first time. This day was devoted to meditation and everyone sat in the temple meditating and waiting for Amma to come. She came, after a short while, walking amongst the people and talking to some of them. I was struck by how simple and down-to-earth she seemed. Everyone sat around her for a brief meditation, which was followed by a question and answer session. It was like sitting around the table as a large family. Afterwards, Amma served lunch to everyone, and while eating, she continued talking and laughing. She seemed to be such a lovely person. Everything about her was so natural.

I waited till the following morning to receive my first hug. It was indescribable! Even though the hug itself was over too fast and I had been so very nervous, I felt Amma's warmth and a feeling of safety and security. After the hug, I sat with other devotees beside her. I looked at how she hugged people, whispered into their ears, smiled at them, accepting everybody with the same love. It touched me so deeply that I was suddenly overcome by strong emotional feelings and burst into tears. Childhood wounds came up to the surface with my tears. I had never felt worthy enough to be loved. I couldn't stop crying. After a long time, when I finally did stop, there was such a feeling of inner purification. I felt great strength and peace inside, quite unlike anything I had ever experienced before.

Earlier, I had planned to stay for only a day at the ashram, but after my darshan with Amma, I decided to stay longer. I spent the next two weeks there and would gladly have stayed even longer, had Amma not left for her North Indian tour. The time with Amma is unforgettable! Even today, I often close my eyes and remember the times we sang bhajans with her in the evenings and then watched her feed the baby elephant Ram...

After leaving the ashram, I travelled to Goa to meet some friends. I stayed for about two weeks before returning home. I did not visit any more ashrams; there was simply no need to.

I have not yet met Amma again, but I strongly feel Her in my heart. Lithuania is far away from the European countries that Amma visits, so currently I am saving up money to travel to India again.

Sometimes, I still become depressed by minor events. I have now come to realise that this is mostly related to deep hurts from my childhood. When the depression comes, I meditate and talk to Amma and try to feel Her spirit inside me. Then I can feel Amma's warmth and love and once more my inner peace returns.

Getting to know Amma is like a treasure in my heart. Through the love I receive from Her, I am slowly becoming a different person. Through Her love, I feel loved and now can pass on this love to other people.

Susanne Hill is 32 years old. She works as a volunteer for the Red Cross and the Salvation Army in Lithuania, giving medical care to homeless people. She earlier worked as a nurse in the government hospital in Mainz, Germany, before moving to Lithuania with her boyfriend. In her free time, she loves to paint, read and spend time at the ocean and the countryside.

Blossoms of the Heart

Like nectar in the fresh morning flower, let goodness fill you. The heart that unfolds all its petals spreading the fragrance of goodness is the choicest offering at the altar of God.
– Amma

How did I, a blind person, get to have such a close connection with the Divine Mother? Let me tell you the story...

July 1987: Someone who had just met Amma in Paris came home to deliver vegetables from his shop. He told me about Amma. He said that she was a woman who gave everyone a lot of love. Those were not his exact words, but that is what I understood. I asked him for a photograph of Amma. He gave me a small photograph on a cassette cover. I could not see it with my eyes of course, but I could sense Amma's greatness in my heart.

You may wonder how I instinctively knew about Amma's greatness. I can only say this; that normal people observe a lot with their eyes but their hearts may play a secondary role. When the eyes are not there, the heart takes their place. This makes one listen more to the heart and live accordingly. My first impression about Amma was very positive and very clear.

When I learned that Amma would be in Switzerland a few days later, I decided to try and meet her. For me, this was a big decision because we normally did not travel abroad from our home country Belgium. In any case, I managed to make all the arrangements for my wife and me to travel together. It was much easier than I expected. It almost seemed as if Amma took care of everything.

For instance, let me narrate a small incident to you. When we arrived in Schweibenolp, the site of the program in Switzerland, we had to hike up a small, steep hill. My wife did not have the energy to walk, so she calmly said to me, "There will be a solution." At that very moment, a car stopped and offered to take us up the hill. I was sure that Amma had sent this helping hand. Many such rich experiences made our journey smooth and trouble-free.

> *With my cane, I felt for a place to kneel and bowed all the way to the floor.*
> **– Karel Becarren, Belgium**

As we entered the hall, everything stopped for me. My heart filled with devotion. With my cane, I felt for a place to kneel and bowed all the way to the floor. I did not know, of course, that bowing to the floor was a very common Vedic tradition and one that Amma herself did often. As a child, I was a choirboy in a church where I had learned to bow. Now, many years later, the movement came instinctively.

I sat down in the hall and my heart blossomed in that heavenly garden full of devotion. Back home, I worked as a gardener and loved my job. I loved plants and flowers and everything else in nature. Even though I could not see with my eyes, I *felt* the joy as buds opened up to become flowers. In my heart I knew that it was through the surrender of the bud to the rhythm of sunlight, and the love between them, that it was able to flower. I felt the same touch of love and surrender as I now sat in the hall.

My wife had gone to the hotel room to rest for a while. When she returned, Amma was just finishing up darshan. Soon darshan ended. Instead of leaving, Amma started dancing!! A small circle of devotees danced with her. My wife went forward to have a better view.

Suddenly Amma came and took me by the hand to lead me to the middle. I was completely surprised. She also grabbed my wife with her other hand and started dancing with the two of us. It was like a present from heaven. I felt so overjoyed!

Later I wondered how she had known that we were spouses. My wife was not next to me, yet she had grabbed both of us together. With this heavenly gesture, we both felt completely included in Amma's big family! We had come home!

Next day, we went for Amma's holy darshan. Amma put her hand on my chest, creating a sensation of glowing warmth. I felt completely loved. I left the hall in order to lay on my bed in silence. The subtle connection with Amma kept vibrating for a long time. In the silence and in those vibrations, rich insights into Truth appeared. It is hard for me to express what I experienced in words.

During my next darshan, I silently asked Amma to help me in my daily life. I was so surprised when the brahmachari standing near her gave me a small piece of paper. I could not read it, of course, but he explained that it was a mantra. Amma must have somehow known that we were not staying for Devi Bhava, when mantras are normally given, and had graced me with this priceless gift right then. To this day, my mantra is my best friend. Amma answered my plea for help in the perfect way!

For the next several years, my wife and I had the blessing of serving Amma by being in charge of the flowers at Her programs in Belgium. Luckily, we both came to Amma together. Our three children and their families support our devotion to Amma and are becoming more and more interested in learning about Her.

I wish to thank everybody who has helped in making it possible for me to meet Amma. To meet Her is always heaven on earth for me.

Translated from Dutch by Hadelijn and Gabriella Strumpel

Karel Becarren, 70, lives with his wife in Belgium. He has 3 daughters and 7 grand-children. He lives a retired life now after having worked for many, many years as a gardener. When he was 10 years old, his eyesight started deteriorating gradually, until at 40 he was completely blind. He wrote the story in Braille and a family member wrote it out in Dutch for him.

2

My Mother Divine

The Inner Mother manifests visibly through this body so that her children can have a glimpse of the Mother who is deep within. This body is powerful; it has the power to express the infinite inner power. The reason the external Mother exists is to help you reach the Inner Mother. The Inner Mother has none of the external qualities. Silence is the language of this Inner Mother.

– Amma

The Earth Shook When I Met Amma

Love is the ambrosia that adds beauty and charm to life. Love gives meaning and provides fulfillment to life.

— Amma

I had always been ambitious, focussed and quite frankly, self-centered. Even as a young girl, I was driven. At six, I became a competitive gymnast. At sixteen, I moved to Australia from Canada to live with my father because it was a way to graduate from high school two years earlier. My pace was too fast for most people and I would easily grow frustrated with complacency in others. I was never very good at doing things in teams and was a bit of a loner. As for spirituality, I was brought up Christian but I had no time for reflection. I had places to go to and things to do!

In 1990, when I was twenty-three, I moved to Japan from Australia. I wanted to learn Japanese and earn my masters degree in economics from a Japanese university. I thought if I spoke Japanese and got a good degree, I would surely do well in a business career and make a lot of money. That was all I cared about. I even told my boyfriend I would get married and have children with him only if he agreed to be a house-husband. I was sure I didn't have time for cooking or raising children.

I met Amma in Japan in 1993. I was like a train speeding through life, focussed on where I was going, but never really looking around to see where I was. In addition to studying for my economics degree (in Japanese!), I had also bought a small English school with my boyfriend. Between studying, teaching English and running the school, I was very busy. So, how did Amma enter my heart? I'm still not sure, but enter it she did.

In 1992, about a year before I met Amma, I went sight-seeing on a mountain called

> *...she turned around and looked straight at me. When our eyes met my stomach did a big flip, just like when one sees their sweetheart!*
> **– Julie Cairns, Australia**

Maruyama. There were a hundred and eight Buddhist statues on the mountain. I knew nothing about Buddhism back then, but I liked one of the statues and took a picture of it. When I got home and had the picture developed, I had a strong urge to draw it, even though I had not drawn anything since my high school art class.

I spent three weeks drawing the face of the Buddha. In my ignorance, I thought the face belonged to a female because the Buddha was embracing a baby, which I thought represented a nurturing maternal icon. As I drew, I felt a strong and inexplicable feeling of unconditional love and compassion. I realised that this is what the picture represented to me, Mother Love. My heart called out to experience such love and compassion. These elements were largely missing from my driven and purposeful life.

Several months later, I met a girl who had just come from Amma's ashram in India. She was an American girl and had visited India on her way to Japan. She wanted to teach English in my school to make some more travelling money. She talked to me about Amma in glowing terms.

"She is the universal Mother. She is totally at one with the feminine energy of the universe," she said to anyone that listened. My interest was piqued, but I also thought it sounded a bit strange and freaky. I wasn't into that hippie stuff. But the girl was nice and I liked her. So part of me thought, "Hey, it can't be that bad!"

One night I went to her house for a party. During the evening, I went upstairs to her room to fetch some tapes for the tape player. As I was looking through the tape collection, I had a strange feeling as if something or someone was behind me. I turned around but there was no one, just her bed and table. On the table lay some beads and I felt strongly drawn to them. They felt so...what word can describe it...*important*. I picked them up and ran downstairs to my friend.

"What are these beads? Where did you get them?" I asked her.

"I got them in India. Amma blessed them specially for me."

"What are they for?" I continued.

"Well, this is a special kind of necklace, like a rosary" she answered. The beads were her japa mala.

Some time later my friend told me that Amma was coming to Tokyo. From Sapporo, the city where we lived on Japan's north island of Hokkaido, Tokyo was more than twelve hours by train, and the air ticket was expensive. Even so, I immediately decided to go with my friend to meet this lady. I couldn't help myself. I had to find out who this lady was and why she had such a power over my friend. And not to mention those beads!

So, we flew together to Tokyo to spend three days in Amma's presence. When we arrived, at first, everything seemed strange to me. There were probably less than a hundred people at the program. This was 1993 and Amma hadn't been visiting Japan for long. Of course, I didn't know how lucky I was to be in such an intimate gathering. To tell the truth, I don't really remember much about that first day. I do not remember my first darshan but I do remember Amma singing her heart out and laughing in bliss. I didn't quite know what to make of it but I was a little mesmerised.

I had darshan the next morning, but don't remember feeling anything remarkable. Then Amma was leaving the hall and she turned around and looked straight at me. When our eyes met my stomach did a big flip, just like when one sees their sweetheart! I felt so nervous to have her look at me like this. She smiled and let out a little chuckle. She came over to where I was standing on the side and gave me a big hug. I couldn't really think properly, which was strange because normally I was so calm, cool and collected.

The third day (I think, the chronology may be a bit of a blur), I was sitting and watching Amma give darshan. I was totally at peace. It was like everything had suddenly become a lot slower. It didn't occur to me that I didn't normally feel this way; the brain wasn't really available for such commentary. It wasn't until the plane ride back home that I realised this.

Anyway, I was sitting there and watching Amma. Suddenly, an earthquake hit. This was Tokyo! The hall was on the fifteenth floor of a tall building, which began to sway back and forth, not just a little bit, but a lot. But not only did I not panic, I actually smiled. It seemed to me that it didn't really matter. I didn't care that I might be in danger. I didn't feel any danger. Amma didn't seem to care about the earthquake either. She didn't stop hugging the person in her lap. She actually started laughing, which made me laugh too. Soon everyone was laughing and no one seemed afraid. My mind didn't question it. For some reason it just seemed funny and we all giggled and chuckled. Slowly the swaying of the building stopped and laughter was replaced by silence.

No one commented and nothing happened. Darshan just went on as before. I didn't know how long the earthquake had lasted and it did not even occur to me to find out from the news later if any major damage had occurred as a result. I had absolutely no interest in the earthquake! Again, it wasn't until I was on the plane going home that my brain kicked in enough to realise how strange it all seemed. Why had I not been afraid during the earthquake? Why had I found it so amusing instead of frightening? Why had I been so peaceful for the entire three days?

My last darshan during Devi Bhava that evening was notable. My friend had explained to me that during Devi Bhava, Amma took on the energy or mood of the Divine Mother. When I went for darshan, Amma touched my forehead with sandalwood paste and looked deeply into my eyes. In that moment in Amma's eyes, I recognised the unconditional love and compassion, the Mother Love that my heart had yearned for, while drawing the Buddha. This nearly sent me unconscious! Oh Amma! I was so grateful that she had answered my heart's call!

After I got back to Sapporo, I slowly noticed a change in my thinking. Where earlier all I used to think about was how to make other people like and respect me by looking good, being good at school, winning competitions, making money, being popular, now I started thinking about others. What happened to old people who had no money? How did the poor take care of themselves and their families? If I made a lot of money, would it really make me happy? Wow! These were totally new thoughts for me.

I realised that my constant effort to be more and better was so I could feel loved. Here, Amma had filled me up with her Love, but she hadn't asked me to knock myself out for it. She had given it freely for who I was. What a gift! And only after I felt truly loved in this manner, was I able to shift my focus a little bit away from myself.

Amma has been my beloved Guru for nearly nine years now. She has had me in Her grasp ever since that first encounter, and probably since long before. I can only pray that She will never let me go. I don't know where I used to think I was going earlier, always in such a hurry. Now I just want to be stationary, always here at Amma's Divine Feet.

Julie Cairns lives in Sydney, Australia. She grew up in Canada and spent five years teaching and studying for her post-graduate degree in Japan. She works as an economic and statistical researcher. Her interests include music, art and yoga.

Finally Safe

Bhakti and jnana, though seemingly different,
are not two. Bhakti is the means and jnana the
end. Bhakti without jnana and jnana without
bhakti are both harmful.

— Amma

I was brought up in the Soviet Union in an atheist family, so the idea of God was not natural to me. Even less natural was the idea of spiritual groups, especially those led by gurus. In my mind, gurus were some kind of parasites who brainwashed and exploited naive and weak-minded followers.

In 1993, in my early twenties, and shortly after the collapse of the Soviet Union, I had a life-transforming experience. I overdosed on LSD, a psychedelic drug and had what I would term a near-death experience. I felt divine intervention that made it clear that it was not my time to leave yet. As consciousness returned, I knew that something had changed. I became a spiritual seeker after this experience.

Soon, I was drawn to yogic philosophies. In October 1997, I moved to a spiritual community in Virginia, U.S.A. I had already moved to the U.S.A. from Russia three years previously.

In December 1997, I had an opportunity to travel to South India on a two-week tour with my new spiritual companions. My spiritual views at this time were mostly at the intellectual level. The advaita school of thought appealed to me and I considered devotional practices spiritually inferior.

After arriving in India, we rested the first two days at Kovalam beach, in the state of Kerala. On the third day, we set out on a bus to our next destination. It was a dark evening and the bus was

> *I realized that this woman must be the saint of the ashram. Something alive and indescribable was manifesting through her voice.*
> **– Igor Zhdanov, U.S.A.**

going through a rural area. Everything was totally new to me and I was experiencing mild culture shock and some anxiety about the rest of my trip.

Suddenly, our tour leader announced a stop. I understood that this was unplanned, and that we were to stop only briefly to visit a nearby ashram. We were told that this was the abode of a famous woman saint, Amma. I had never heard of her before. We got off the bus and went across a channel in small boats. We arrived on the other side where a few high buildings stood, some still under construction. We walked to the temple, which had a big courtyard in the front.

Our tour leader said that we had around forty-five minutes and that we could spend this time either by attending bhajans that were in progress or by walking around. I followed some of the other group members into the temple. It was packed! We managed to find some space and sat down.

I looked around. There were a lot of westerners, mostly wearing white. Everyone was focused on the far stage where the bhajan leader's team was seated. There were a few male monks in saffron robes and a dark-skinned woman in a white sari was in the middle of them. She would sing one line accompanied by the monks and the rest of the hall would follow. This went on for a while.

I realized that this woman must be the saint of the ashram. Something alive and indescribable was manifesting through her voice. She would cry out the divine name and raise her arms in devotion. It seemed that she was really experiencing union with something or someone, the rest of us in the hall could not see.

Soon, I noticed that our group members had started to leave. As I stepped out of the temple, I found almost everyone ready to go back. I felt sad to interrupt our visit. This is how I remember my first, very brief glimpse of Mother.

Two years went by. In January 2000, I went to India again. I found myself at Kovalam beach this time, with Uma, a lady friend with whom I had become close during my two years stay in the spiritual community. Uma had been living there for over a decade and was like a mother to me.

Suddenly one evening, my friend Liza telephoned from Russia. She and another old-time Russian friend Andrei, wanted to join us. They were interested in spiritual matters and while I was still in the U.S.A., I had told them about my earlier trip to India and had invited them to join me this time. They arrived in the next two or three days.

At this time, I still related to spirituality from the standpoint of intellectual advaita and considered devotional practices to be inferior. My friends from Russia were also like me, in that they were interested in neo-advaitic gurus and their instant enlightenment promises. So, it was surprising to me that we all decided to visit Amma's ashram, first. In our minds, Amma was not the kind of teacher we were seeking, but her ashram was nearby and so we decided to go.

One day, early in February 2000, our team of four headed to Amritapuri. In the taxi, on our way to the ashram, I read about Amma in a book we were using for our travels, *From Here to Nirvana: The Yoga Journal Guide To Spiritual India.* Some very uplifting details of Amma's life were presented in the book and I felt very inspired. The book also described how Amma individually gave darshan to everyone by hugging them. My friends from Russia did not seem to be very impressed, however. They were laughing and exchanging jokes in a very casual, tourist-like way.

We didn't know if we could have our darshan that day since it was already late afternoon. I didn't know then, that Amma always tried to receive everyone who came to her on any given day. We decided to stay overnight if we were late for darshan, and to leave if we made it.

We crossed the narrow channel and rushed into the temple. We asked the taxi driver to wait with our luggage on the other side.

Andrei and Liza were still sharing casual jokes and it didn't seem to me that they felt any sense of reverence.

As we entered, I noticed two lines on either side of the hall, one for males and the other for females. Uma and Liza joined the ladies' line and Andrei and I stood in the men's line. A lot of people were in the temple.

All at once, I felt the entire energy change. Andrei whispered something to me. I turned around and looked at him. What I witnessed before me was the most powerful transformation of a human being, I had ever known. Just moments ago, Andrei had been a young man, full of himself and joking around. Now, in front of my very eyes, he changed into a pure, innocent child with tears pouring down his face. All this happened just within a few minutes of entering the temple. The old Andrei was completely gone.

Unable to process this instant transformation of my friend, I started to feel overwhelmed. The darshan line moved forward and I looked at Amma. I recalled my first impression of her, from two years ago. Amma was greeting everyone with a hug. Soon it was my turn. When I placed my head on Amma's chest, she whispered something into my ear. I felt very comforted. Then I sat near Amma for a while, watching her meet new people. It seemed to me that love was exploding through every pore of her dark-skinned body.

Suddenly I realized that our driver was still waiting on the other side. Andrei and I went outside and met Uma and Liza. Andrei was not prepared to leave just yet. So, we all agreed to stay. In the evening, we enjoyed bhajans.

It was only over the next few months that my devotion to Amma started to grow in intensity. I met her again later that year during her annual U.S.A. summer tour. At this time, I finally realized that I had met my true master and that I was finally safe. My previous concerns about my spiritual destiny melted away. At the core of my being, I was already One with my Mother and that was all that mattered.

May Mother's love reach the lives of all beings on this planet.
May all be well.

Editor's Note: The following story is written by the writer's friend
Andrei.

---

*Igor Zhdanov was born in the Soviet Union. In 1994, he moved to
U.S.A. with his girlfriend, whom he later married. In some time,
however, the marriage fell apart. Currently he lives with his daughter
Julia, 11, in central Virginia. He shares custody of his son Timothy, 6,
with his ex-wife. He often travels to Russia and hopes to move back
there one day.*

My Way Home

Emptying the mind becomes easier in the pres-
ence of a Master. A Satguru's mere thought,
look, or touch can bring about tremendous
transformation.

— *Amma*

From childhood, I was interested in spiritual matters. I read many books, gained theoretical knowledge and learned about different schools of thought. The logical system of advaita appealed to me greatly and I understood the concepts very well.

In February 2000, at the age of thirty-three, I decided to visit India for the first time from Moscow, where I lived. My friend Igor had spent some time there and had invited me to come. I had a feeling that something would become very clear over there.

After arriving in India, I was received by my friend Igor. He suggested that we begin the tour, with a visit to Amma's ashram. I had never heard about Amma but her ashram was nearby. Just two days after I arrived, Igor and I, along with two other friends, Uma and Liza, took a taxi to go there. We crossed a narrow channel by boat, went up to the temple, took off our shoes and went in.

What happened next is almost impossible to describe. As we stepped in, I noticed a large number of people. There were two long lines, one on the left and another on the right. Straight ahead at some distance sat Amma. Suddenly, tears started flowing from my eyes in a continuous stream. My eyes were seeing and my ears were hearing, but my brain was refusing to process any signals. I tried to understand what was happening, but the brain did not switch on. Everything was like some kind of fog.

Tears continued to pour from my eyes. These were not tears of sorrow, but of ecstasy. I had never before cried like this. Somehow, we joined the line. The crying did not stop. Igor looked intently into my eyes and said something, but I did not understand a single word. I saw and heard almost nothing of what was happening around me. I was still crying when we reached Amma after some time.

> *My eyes were seeing and my ears were hearing, but my brain was refusing to process any signals…everything was like some kind of fog.*
> **– Andrei Goorrari, Russia**

I felt as though I had been wandering for very long, like I had strayed in a forest and was trying to find my way home. The situation was very difficult and I had become used to a state of tension. Something had finally led me to the right place. I felt very sure about this; I had unexpectedly come home. My nervous and muscular tension had left me and, in relief, tears had flowed.

Amma embraced me. I felt very comforted. Slowly, I returned to my usual state and my brain started functioning again, but there was a difference. My usual state now was not the same as before I entered the temple. My inner tensions had disappeared and I was calmer and quieter. It was like I had found what I was looking for.

Almost two years have passed since my first meeting with Amma. Now, I feel like I am at home wherever I go. I have not met Amma again and don't know if I ever will, but I am content to feel Her presence inside me. Amma is my guru. She is like a bright and shining image that will not allow me to get lost, even on the darkest night.

Translated from Russian by Alexandra Koulikova and Elena Andriushina

Editor's Note: The preceding story is written by the writer's friend Igor.

Andrei Goorrari lives in Moscow, Russia. He is currently studying for a degree in Psychology at the University of Moscow. He loves to travel and has visited China, Korea, United Arab Emirates, Turkey, Morocco, Germany and India. He also enjoys listening to music.

A Spiritual Journey

Children, do not harbor anger or jealousy to-
wards anyone. See good in everyone. See all
as children of the same mother and love them
as sisters and brothers. Then you will be able
to forgive them. Our attitude of forgiveness
will make our thoughts, words and actions
good and will bring us God's Grace.
                                                    – Amma

In 1994 when I first read about Amma in the *Yoga Journal* magazine,
I had already been practicing yoga and meditation for many years.
My friend Sara, who lived in our home along with my husband
and me, shared my interest in spirituality. We had the same Guru
although He was no longer in the physical plane. Sara suffered
from endometriosis and had undergone eight operations in the
abdominal and pelvic area in ten years. After the last operation
she had developed multiple chemical sensitivity and had become
severely limited by that disability.

Sara and I ordered Amma's biography and a video from the
Amma center in France to learn more about her. When I first saw
Amma on video, I started to cry without knowing why. My curiosity
was aroused but I was a little reluctant to meet her, thinking that
she was probably just another strict guru. However, Sara wanted
to investigate further and we prepared for a trip in a few months
to see Amma in Etampes, France and Koln, Germany during her
summer tour to these countries.

Sara and I began our journey with much anticipation. We
wondered whether all that we had read about Amma was really
right. We wanted to see if she was indeed a true spiritual master.
The trip, however, did not go exactly as planned and everything
was not a dance on a bed of roses.

To begin with, we landed in Luxembourg in the middle of a heat wave. I don't take the heat very well and this was the hottest summer in a hundred years! Daily temperatures averaged between

> *To my great surprise, she walked straight to Sara and embraced her dearly. She then rushed up to the front without paying any attention to anyone else.*
> *– Asa Kristin Oddsdottir, Iceland*

30-40 degrees Celsius! As the temperatures rose, so did my Viking temper and impatience.

We took a train to Paris, where we had to change stations to get to Etampes. The difference in the fare for a taxi and the underground was huge and in spite of my claustrophobia and our big and heavy suitcases, I could not justify spending that much more on a taxi. So the underground it was. What followed could have been scenes from a comedy movie.

Sara was on crutches and my physical condition was not too good either, for carrying suitcases up and down endless staircases. To my horror, I got stuck in the turnstile in the underground. People tried to help but nothing worked. I prayed to God to show me the way out of this situation. Soon a staff person with a key appeared and opened a gate that was big enough for the luggage and for me to go through. From this incident, I saw how important one's state of mind was. I had remained positive and God had sent help. If I had become irritable and negative, everything could have gone wrong.

We did not have clear directions, so we ended up somewhere in the French countryside and had to trace our way back to the right train. Again and again, up and down staircases, with big, heavy suitcases, in the scorching sun.

Tired and weary from our journey, we finally dragged ourselves to the evening meeting with Amma. We waited with about fifteen hundred people for her arrival in a large hall. People were lined up alongside the path that Amma would walk and we joined them. Soon she entered the hall. She was short, energetic and joyful. After a brief welcome ceremony, she came walking towards us. To my great surprise, she walked straight to Sara and embraced her dearly. She then rushed up to the front without paying any attention to anyone else.

Sara was too shocked and stunned to speak. We all sat down and musicians began playing and singing devotional Indian songs. Amma's presence, along with the devotional music, created such an uplifting spiritual atmosphere that it could only be described as being transported to heaven. Concentration in meditation became easy and my soul felt peaceful and at home.

After the singing, people waited in lines to be received by Amma. Parents with babies and small children were received first. Amma took each child into her lap, lovingly played with him or her, blessed the child and then received the parents. After the families had their turn, other people started going up to Amma. Grandparents with their children and grandchildren, big men with long hair and leather head bands and jackets, parents with physically and mentally handicapped kids, and so on. Amma lovingly embraced every person who knelt before her.

We watched this procession of people going up to Amma in utter amazement. Amma embraced every person as a mother embraces her child. In our understanding, rarely did a highly developed, enlightened spiritual person allow people to touch them. And here was a woman going out to hug everybody and anybody! Here was a spiritual master freely and intimately available to everyone!

After a few hours, Sara and I decided to go up to receive our hugs. We went into the priority line for the disabled and elderly. Soon I found myself kneeling nervously in front of Amma. She looked deep into my eyes and took me into her arms. I put my arms around her and rested my head on her chest. Tears of joy welled up in my eyes as I felt like a little child in her mother's arms. Streams of bliss entered my heart and I knew that I was at home with my Divine Mother.

The experience ended all too soon and I had to move on to let Amma greet the next person in line. I returned to my seat in some sort of dream-like state. We sat there, sometimes meditating, at other times gazing at Amma, until three o'clock in the morning when Amma finished receiving all who had come to see her. She looked just as fresh and energetic when she left the hall as she had when she had entered eight hours earlier.

Our knowledge of French is extremely limited; therefore, we did not understand much and often wondered what was going on. Many times, I felt that Amma was watching me. Sometimes, she would get a bit distracted while hugging someone, perhaps when someone else was asking her a question, and the person in her arms would get a much longer hug. I kept wishing that this would happen to me. As if in answer to my longing, Amma granted this wish during my next darshan. I felt so happy.

One evening, I was looking at Amma when I saw an amazing vision. All around her were beautiful shining colours and her tongue was hanging out of her mouth. I later realised that this was similar to Kali's image. I continued looking at this sight for a while with wonder.

The days in France passed way too quickly. The atmosphere was sweet and everyone was nice and helpful. We then took a train to Koln, Germany and attended the program there. Amma gave a lot of attention to Sara but not to me. My negative feelings of jealousy and anger and feeling sorry for myself came to the surface. The heat was even more unbearable in Germany and my irritation rose. Somehow I just did not sense the same sweetness I had felt in France.

When the program ended, we stayed to help clean the hall. I saw Amma on the stage looking lovingly at Sara. Annoyed, I went down on my knees to clean the floor. After a while, I noticed Sara signaling to me to move to one side. I was irritated with her and was not about to let her boss me around so I just continued working where I was, fixing my gaze on the floor. When I finally looked to the side, I saw Amma on her knees cleaning the floor next to me. She just laughed.

Amma left Koln in a van. She stood for a long time in the door of the van as we looked at her. I felt awful. I suddenly wanted so badly to make everything all right between Amma and myself but I did nothing.

We went back home to our daily routines. My relationship with Sara remained a bit strained for a while. It was very difficult for both of us. I also wanted to be loyal to my first guru, but my thoughts kept wandering to Amma all the time. I struggled within for a whole year.

The next summer we returned to see Amma again. This time, I accepted her as my Guru. Amma continued to pay attention to Sara, but also made things better inside me. I felt that I was loved and that all was forgiven in my Divine Mother's arms.

Since then, we have returned every year to see Amma. Each time has brought new experiences, both wonderful and difficult. Hard times followed for Sara. In 1996, Sara's physical condition worsened considerably when her multiple chemical sensitivity became more severe. She could no longer attend Amma's indoor programs and had to wait outside the hall the entire time doing japa or some seva in the cold. She saw Amma either when Amma came into or left the hall.

In looking back now, it is easier for me to understand our compassionate Amma's actions. She had perhaps seen what was coming to Sara in the future. Hence, She had showered so much love on her. Around Amma, the smallest happenings have significance, even though the learning may not dawn until much later.

The greatest miracle of Amma is the power of Her love, which has a transforming effect. To me, Amma really is the Divine Mother who has come to love, console and help me in my life. I am eternally grateful to Her for holding my hand and not giving up on me, in spite of all my shortcomings and mistakes.

Asa Kristin Oddsdottir is a housewife. She lives in Seltjarnarnes, a small suburban town in Iceland, near the capital Reykjavik, with her husband Thorkell and their friend Sara. She has two children and three grandchildren. Her interests include painting, playing the piano and gardening.

Gentle Awakening

Though the sun is thousands of miles away,
still the lotus blooms. Distance is no barrier.
Amma is with you always.

— *Amma*

I met Amma in August 1998 when she came to Finland for the first time. I was nineteen years old and in the early stages of my spiritual journey, at least in this lifetime. I had begun to try to change my life for the better. Earlier, I used to smoke pot and drink alcohol, and had gone from bad to worse.

One day a friend asked me, "Have you heard about the Holy Mother, Amma? She is said to be an incarnation of God!"

I had not heard about Amma. I did not believe that it was possible for a human being to be an incarnation of God. Still, my curiosity was aroused and I wanted to meet Amma to find out for myself. I learned that she would be visiting Helsinki in a few weeks.

On the day of the program, I reached the hall after Amma was already there. She looked very serene seated in the front, hugging people one after another. I watched her for some time. At times, I felt that she was looking at me. She was forever smiling and happy.

I received a darshan token and was told that I would have to wait a few hours for my hug. "The hug is worth the wait," the lady handing out tokens said to me. "Amma will hug you like no earthly mother ever can." I had the time and was happy to wait. I did want to experience the hug for myself.

At first, I tried to meditate at the back of the hall while waiting. Many kids were running around and playing and there seemed to be a lot of chaos. After some time, I gave up. It was impossible to

> *I watched as Amma took a drunken old man full of bruises and smelling like a sewer into her arms as if he were her precious baby.*
> *– Sami Vaha-Herttua, Finland*

meditate. I returned to the front of the hall to continue watching Amma give hugs to people.

She seemed so full of sweetness. She was really giving her best to every person. I watched as Amma took a drunken old man full of bruises and smelling like a sewer into her arms as if he were her precious baby. Next she whispered some wisdom into the ear of an ancient granny in a wheel chair, who started crying and laughing at the same time. She played with little kids as if she knew them from birth.

I could feel the strong vibrations coming from Amma. I tried to let go but my stupid mind would not completely allow it. I felt like crying but there were no tears in my dry heart. After some time, I joined the darshan queue and moved closer to Amma. As I came closer and closer, I was able to see Amma's cute little face very well.

My turn was next. Amma put my head on her lap and held me for quite some time. She started repeating into my ear, "My darling son, my darling son."

"What is this?" I immediately thought. "She speaks perfect English!"

I guess I had expected some strange mantras in her native language. I looked up as Amma let go of me gently. Smiling ever so sweetly, she reached out to take me into her arms again.

The world crumbled at my feet. I almost burst into tears. I am not the crying type but this felt very nice.

The next day I met Amma again and experienced the same feelings of my heart opening. Intuitively, I understood that Amma was my real Mother, who wished only my very best. I was like a three-year-old and I felt that she loved me more than anybody else.

After two days, Amma was gone, but I remained really, really happy for some time. Then right back to earth! Over the following year, I tried very hard to put effort into staying close to Amma by meditating every day, reading Her books and trying to follow Her teachings.

Since then, I have met Amma every year. I have noticed increasing signs of true happiness with each passing year. I love Amma and myself and the people around me more and more. I wish I could be with Her longer. Seeing Amma once a year is just not enough!

Sami Vaha-Herttua (Rajan), 23, lives in Helsinki, Finland. He is single and of Finnish nationality. An artist by training and profession, he wishes to become a yoga teacher in the future.

Mother of All Faiths

Selfless service, even-mindedness, seeing good
even in the mistakes of others, these are things
which Mother likes.

— *Amma*

From the very first moment that I set eyes on Amma, I loved Her without any hesitation. She gave me the Love that no one else could ever give.

I first met Amma eight years ago. A friend from my yoga class had told me about her. When he said the name Amma something moved within me and I felt that I just *had* to meet her. I somehow felt that she was the one I had been waiting for, for a very long time. She was coming to Paris soon. What luck!

My friend gave me Amma's biography to read. I was very moved by her difficult childhood. It reminded me of my own mother's life. We were a Muslim family from Algeria and I was one of thirteen siblings. Even though we were poor, and my father often ill-treated my mother, she always smiled and gave her all to her children. She was our strength while we were growing up. She was always there for us and never let us down. Now while living in France, I missed my mother very much. Amma's likeness to my mother attracted me greatly to her.

I counted the days to Amma's program in Paris. I was extremely nervous but happy. I talked about Amma and my upcoming meeting with her to everyone around.

On the day of Amma's program, I arrived at the hall, already feeling very happy. When I went in, I immediately felt as if I had come home. The atmosphere, the fragrance of the incense, the music, I related to them easily. They reminded me of my home country Algeria. The colours and the dresses took me back to my childhood.

Quickly, quickly, who is Amma? Where is Amma? I wanted to see her. I was very excited.

> *Amma reminded me of my oriental origin, the welcome and warmth of Arabic mothers, the mother who gives, loves, consoles and shares.*
> *– Sahara Raith, France*

Far away an Indian woman in white was cuddling people just as a mother cuddles her little ones. I broke into tears seeing this scene.

I felt so full of love as I watched Amma. Time stopped and all thoughts ceased. I closely looked at each person taking Amma's darshan. There was a difference in them before and after darshan. Amma's touch was giving them something special and each one's face was radiant as they were leaving her arms. I was fascinated. How does she do it? Every person seemed so happy. There was such a joyous atmosphere around her. I was certain that I knew her.

I wanted to be in Amma's arms. I was ready to wait the entire night if needed. I joined the line and the closer I got, the more my longing to be with her grew. I felt like a little girl, even though I was thirty-seven years old. When my turn came, I rushed into Amma's arms. It seemed to me as if I were falling into a wide open space, but I was not scared. Far from it!

I could have stayed for an eternity in Amma' arms. I looked up into her deep eyes and at her smile. It was delicious, beautiful, pure magic! For the first time in my life, I felt totally accepted and understood. I have no words to explain it. When I got up, I had the feeling that I was returning from a very long journey. I felt different and happy.

The day of my first darshan was the most beautiful day of my life. Amma reminded me of my oriental origin, the welcome and warmth of Arabic mothers, the mother who gives, loves, consoles and shares. Amma connected me again with all these aspects of my childhood. I told my other family members about her.

In November of 2000, one of my sisters came to see Amma in Paris. She was very touched. After Amma's darshan she said,

"I can't say what, but something happened for sure!" In October 2001, eight of my siblings came to see Amma with their families. Eight families! I was surprised! They came from different towns: Lyon, Lille, Chalons, and some Paris suburbs. By Amma's Grace, we had some very deep and introspective times together as a family.

Our elder brother had left his body four months earlier and we were still grieving his loss. Amma cheered us all up so much! My brothers and sisters remembered all that I had done for them when they were young; washing, cooking, and helping with their studies. The family felt united. Nothing like that had ever happened before. I was deeply moved by their happiness at meeting Amma and felt very grateful to her for bringing us together.

Amma gave me the name Sushama, which means the very patient one. Last year, I visited Amma's ashram in India. I have looked to Her to face many difficult times in my life like my father's death, the loss of my job, and my heart attack. With Amma's Grace, I want to give, forgive, and live without expectations always seeing Amma in others. Amma gives Herself to others all the time. I want to follow Her example. I am so excited for the possibility of Amma's ashram in France. I feel that it could be the home that I have been waiting for, for a long, long time.

Translated from French by Danielle Cherel

Sahara Raith lives in Paris. She has studied psychology and personal development. She works as a healer, taking after her grandmother who was a very well-known healer in Algeria.

I Could Do That Too if I Wanted

Remember that all those who are associated
with Mother in this lifetime were also with her
in their previous births. There is a predestined
time for each one to come to Mother. Some
come earlier, some come later. You can see only
this lifetime and therefore you think that you
did not know Mother before. But you have
all been with Mother before.

– Amma

I will never forget the phone call I received on July 26, 1990, the day before my wedding. Everyone who has married knows that this day is very special. The whole world seems to revolve around just this one event. Well, a close friend was calling me to tell me that he would not be able to attend my wedding because he wanted to see Mata Amritanandamayi Devi, whose program was taking place the same day in downtown Munich.

At first, I felt upset. But somewhere in the corner of my heart, I wanted to see Amma too. I had read her biography a few months back and it had created such a deep impact on me that I had decided to visit Amma's Kerala ashram the next time I was in India. For four years, I had been travelling to India regularly not only because of my spiritual interest but also because I was engaged to an Indian man, Shekar.

Shekar's sister lived in Germany where we had met in 1984 when he came to visit her. It was love at first sight but we were getting married only after five years, during which time, we had to do a lot of convincing of both families. Shekar came from a traditional Brahmin family and I belonged to a very conservative German family. For some time, I had tried to live in India but life was very hard

> *As we got closer to Amma, however, my sarcasm started crumbling down.*
> *– Susanne Wecker-Shivshankar,*
> *Germany*

for me there. So Shekar had moved to Germany a few months before our marriage.

All this was forgotten, however, and the marriage was ahead of us. I brushed aside the desire to see Amma and resumed worrying about the many things that still had to be done at that point.

Until two days later, when everything was over. Suddenly, I had a strong desire to go downtown to see whether Amma's program was still on and whether we could get a glimpse of her. My husband, mother-in-law and I headed downtown not even knowing the proper address. As we were cruising along, we heard bhajans from a distance and found a parking spot right in front of the entrance to the hall. What a miracle for Munich!

We entered and sat down. The excitement of the past few days settled a bit as I tried to concentrate on the music and relax. Seeing Amma sing with so much devotion made a deep impact on me and I felt refreshed, as if my soul had bathed in a pond of love and energy.

After bhajans, we lined up for Amma's darshan. It took us about one and a half hours to get close to her; during that time I watched her intensely. After the first few minutes, my mind started saying, "What is the big thing that she is doing here? Hugging people? I could do that too, if I wanted!"

As we got closer to Amma, however, my sarcasm started crumbling down. Seeing her receive people, one by one, without a spark of hesitation and with so much love, as if they were her very own children, my heart started aching. My mother had passed away when I was eight years old and I had always longed for a mother's love, a love that was unconditional and that accepted me the way I was, no matter how many mistakes I made.

By the time we reached Amma, my heart was beating strongly and my emotions were boiling. There was no crowd, no bhajans, no husband, no mother-in-law, just Amma and I. I "woke up" when my mother-in-law, who was just ahead of us and in Amma's arms already, started crying and talking to Amma in Tamil. Later, my husband told me that she was complaining to Amma that her only son had married a Christian. I did not understand the exact words but could follow the gist of the conversation.

Amma said something to her with a smile and then lovingly turned to us. She spoke in Tamil and Shekar translated. "Finally, you have come!" she said. I couldn't really understand what this meant but somehow I felt that we were in the right place at the right time. On the way back home, my mother-in-law told us what Amma had said to her.

"Can you not see that these two are made for each other? Don't worry, they are Amma's children and Amma will take care of everything."

What a promise! What an encouragement for us! Shekar and I felt so grateful to have received Amma's blessings for our marriage in this manner.

One year later, we saw Amma again at the Munich program. She recognised us immediately and asked Shekar whether his mother was still unhappy. We were so amazed that Amma remembered us and our story even after one full year. That year we were involved with the organisation of the program and had the great pleasure of driving Amma to and from the hall. Amma chatted and joked with us during these drives and we felt very comfortable in her presence, as if we had known her for a long time. Shekar invited Amma to stay in our house the following year and she readily agreed! Since 1992, we have had the blessing of hosting Amma and all the Swamis during the Munich program.

During the next few years, Amma came through on Her promise to take care of everything. Slowly my mother-in-law accepted me as a part of the family and even started feeling happy to have a daughter-in-law who was interested in Hindu philosophy and religion. Today she often tells people that anyone who tries to realise God is a Brahmin. Shekar became successful in his career in Germany and won not only my family's hearts but also their respect.

Today, both my husband and I feel that Amma is our loving mother, whom we can turn to anytime for advice and blessings. She guides us gracefully through everything we experience in life, whether good or bad. I often think back to my first arrogant thought when I saw Her giving darshan…*I could do that too if I wanted!* Now having known Her for a period of time and having seen how available She is to Her children almost every minute of Her life…Her divinity unfolding right in front of our very eyes…I feel ashamed for having thought in that manner. I pray that Amma's love touches the hearts of many, many more people around the world. May we all be worthy…

Susanne Wecker-Shivshankar currently lives in Munich, Germany, with her husband Chandrashekar. Since obtaining a degree in art therapy in 1996, she has been working with children and elderly people. Earlier, she worked in the fashion field for a few years. Susanne considers India her second home and enjoys learning to cook Indian dishes.

3

The Gift of Healing

*When Mother sees suffering in the world,
she feels it as her own and wants to respond
to it immediately.*

— Amma

Healed by Pure Love

Experiences indeed, are the guru for each person. Sorrow, my children, is the guru that brings you closer to God.

– Amma

One day in 1993, when I was living in my home country Italy, I learned about an introductory seminar in Ayurvedic medicine. Out of curiosity, I decided to attend. I was already on the path of spiritual learning, meditation and natural therapies and was searching for the right way.

I was so impressed by what I learned at this seminar that soon after I made the decision to quit my secretarial job and go to India to learn more. So in February 1994, I travelled to Poona, India. I was thirty-eight years old at this time.

I first studied *Pancha Karma* with Dr. Joshi whose seminar I had attended back in Italy. After three months, I decided to go to Trivandrum in Kerala, South India to study Ayurvedic massage. After completing this course, there was still a month left before my return to Italy. I decided to spend this time as a holiday in India.

One morning I woke up with a severe backache.

In a few days the pain had become so intense that I could no longer walk. Even a small movement caused me an unbearable amount of pain. The doctors were not able to diagnose my condition or ease my pain. I wondered if I should return to Italy earlier than planned. The doctors advised me not to embark on such a long trip in my condition.

I was in such a bad state that my Indian friend Sivaprasannan had to bring me food every day. I used to eat often at his vegetarian restaurant while learning massage therapy and we had become good

friends. He was like my guard-
ian angel during these days.

Totally exhausted one
night, I went to bed crying.
That night I dreamt of an Indian woman. She was sitting in
a chair in what seemed to be a

*She had the sweetest face and her
smile made it glow. Her eyes were
so full of love, they inspired trust...
she kept waving at me.*
– Marilena Garbo, Italy

courtyard. She was wearing a green silk sari and a silver crown and
was waving her hand asking me to come closer.

She had the sweetest face and her smile made it glow. Her eyes
were so full of love, they inspired trust. I responded however, by
saying, "I don't want to come close to you. I don't know who you
are and what you want from me."

She kept waving at me. Suddenly she burst into laughter. I woke
up in that instant, feeling very strange. The woman's face was still
in my eyes and her laughter in my ears. I was feeling a little scared
but at the same time it was as if I had always known that face.

Soon my friend arrived with breakfast. Finding me upset, he
asked what had happened. I told him about the dream, thinking
surely he was going to think I was mad. At first I didn't notice, but
soon I saw tears in his eyes. He remained silent but his eyes were
filled with wonder.

"You dreamed of Mother!" he said shortly.

"I know your mother very well. She was not the woman in my
dream," I replied with a smile.

"No, you dreamed of Amma, the Holy Mother. If she has called
you in a dream, it is because you must go to her. She will be able
to help you."

I had never heard of any Amma or Holy Mother before this.
I reacted with anger. "I don't want to hear about no holy people.
I have a serious problem to solve and that woman in my dream
could have been anyone. With all the pain I am in, I am not going
anywhere for no reason."

But my friend wasn't listening to me anymore. He had left to
fetch Maria, my Italian friend who lived nearby. Together they tried

to convince me. They would not take no for an answer. I barely had time to eat and get washed when they fetched a car. My friends carried me to the car and we all left together.

Along the way I began to accept what was happening even though I was still in pain. It seemed like an adventure. Something had moved me deeply; it was the woman's eyes. "If it is the same woman, then even if she cannot do anything for my pain, I will go to her just to see those eyes," I thought to myself.

Soon we arrived at Vallikavu. Here I faced another difficult test. We had to take a boat to get to the temple. I am terrified by water. When I was a little child, floods had damaged my village in Italy. Since then I have always been afraid of big expanses of water. I would have run away if I could have!

My friends put me on the boat. I was petrified. The boat started gliding on the water. My friends tried to distract me by pointing to the fishermen's nets, the palm trees, and the tip of the temple now becoming visible in the distance. Suddenly a strange feeling of peace pervaded my entire being. It is impossible to describe. My body was still in pain but it was not important anymore.

As the boat neared the shore, my friends helped me out. I didn't know where they were going to take me, but I let them carry me. I blessed them for being so kind. My heart was filled with a beautiful feeling. Everything was peaceful and tranquil. Even the water seemed like a friend.

Slowly we approached the temple. It was like being in a dream. I had let go of my resistance and anger. My heart was open and ready to receive anything. I was now sure that whatever happened could only be good. We entered the temple but were disappointed to find it empty.

"If you want to see Amma, she is behind the temple." We turned around to see a young man pointing towards where Amma was.

My heart started pounding with excitement. I was eager to know if Amma really was the woman in my dream. I saw her and almost fainted. She was sitting in a courtyard wearing a white sari. But it was her, the same smile and the same eyes!

She was talking to a small family. A little boy had handed her a toy and she was playing with it to figure out how it worked. There were very few people. I wanted to go near her. I just wanted to look into her eyes. That would be enough.

Soon the family left. Amma turned around and looked at me. And just like in the dream, she waved at me. My heart started pounding faster. My head spun and my entire past life passed in front of my eyes in that moment. I stood still, almost paralysed. I was filled with wonder. Amma kept waving and smiling.

My friends helped me come closer to Amma and kneel down in front of her. For what seemed like an eternity, we looked into each other's eyes. Then she hugged me. She stroked her hand on my back many times. I felt as if my whole being was sailing in an ocean of pure love. I wanted to remain in her arms forever. In that moment I knew which way I had to follow.

Gently she let go. Then Amma helped me stand up. She tweaked my cheek and once again smiled at me.

"Let us go pray," she said in Malayalam. My friend Sivaprasannan translated.

We followed Amma to the temple. As we entered, I saw a small crowd of people waiting for her. Amma sang some bhajans while I continued to feel an infinite love and peace. Suddenly I realised I was not in pain any longer.

Evening came and with infinite sadness we had to leave. Back in Trivandrum, the pain slowly returned but my heart remained full of joy and love. Amma seemed present every moment. Soon the pain began to ease and within a week I was able to walk. My return to Italy, originally planned for October 1994, was delayed. This was a blessing because I could visit Amma many more times.

After returning to Italy I found out that my back pain was the consequence of a bad operation ten years earlier for a herniated disc. The new disc was compressing my spinal cord and the nerve endings in my legs. Amma's love healed me. I believe my illness was a means for me to know Amma.

From Amma I learned how important it is to be compassionate and to love everyone. Today I try to practice this teaching in my life and work.

Marilena Garbo is 46 years old. She is single and lives in Turin, Italy. After working as a secretary for 18 years, in 1994 she quit her job and travelled to India to study Ayurvedic medicine. Today she works as an Ayurvedic massage therapist. She teaches massage techniques to mothers of newborn babies and caretakers of the elderly and debilitated for free. She loves to bike and stroll along the riverbank close to her home.

The Sun in Our Lives

Light the lamp of love within you and move forward. When we take each step with good thoughts and a smiling face, all the goodness will come to us and fill our being. There won't be a moment in our life without peace and happiness.

– Amma

I live in Araruama, Rio de Janeiro, Brasil with my husband and our daughter, Michele. My husband is of Portuguese descent, and in one of our trips to Portugal, we visited the holy city of Fatima. I was very devoted to Our Lady of Fatima even before this visit but since then I had felt a very strong connection to Mother.

One day in 1996, I received a picture of an Indian saint named Amma from my brother who lives in California, U.S.A. A friend had invited him and his wife to see this saint who was visiting California at that time. My brother had gone alone to see her because my sister-in-law was working that afternoon. The saint was embracing everybody and greeting them. When it was my brother's turn, she embraced him and he felt very moved. She gave him two chocolate kisses and immediately he knew that one was for his wife. The next day both he and my sister-in-law went to see Amma.

When my brother narrated this incident to me, I wondered how this saint Amma knew that he had someone to share the chocolate with. Then I thought that she must know everything about everyone, including us.

In June 1996, when Amma was visiting California, my husband and I decided to go to meet her personally. Our daughter couldn't come with us because she had final exams and couldn't miss school. We flew from Brasil to San Francisco and went to my brother's

> *...Amma was so sweet, intimate and caring, it felt as if she already knew us....when I left her arms, I felt like I was drunk, drunk with love.*
> **– Leonor Maria de Souza, Brasil**

house. The next day was Amma's first program in San Ramon, which is about an hour away.

We went very early and found the ashram to be a beautiful place in the mountains. Many people were already there when we arrived. Someone told me that I should stand right by the doorway and wait for Amma to come. They explained the pada puja ceremony and said it was very auspicious to watch. I did not know anything about this but wanted to experience it, so I waited near the doorway with anticipation.

Soon Amma arrived. As she got out of the car and started to come into the temple, my heart started beating so hard that it felt like I was the one who would be doing the pada puja. I was fascinated by her smile and the way she looked. She seemed so loving. I could not pull my eyes away from her.

After the pada puja, Amma went to the front of the hall. After a brief meditation, my husband and I joined the line for darshan. When it was our turn to get an embrace, Amma was so sweet, intimate and caring, it felt as if she already knew us. When she embraced me, I had a sensation like I was diving into an endless something and losing myself. I can't remember exactly what I thought at that moment, but when I left her arms, I felt like I was drunk, drunk with love.

Throughout the rest of the day, I did not leave the hall. The whole time, I kept watching other people get darshan from Amma. Everything around was full of love. Even though it was all new to me, nothing seemed strange. Some people were very emotional after darshan, so I thought to myself that what I felt was natural. My husband felt very moved also.

We stayed for about a week in California. Every day we went to the ashram to meet Amma. On our last day I thought to myself, "My God, thank you for this opportunity. One doesn't meet beings like this on the street corner every day. We came from so far, thank you." I knew that my life from now on would not be the same. In Amma, I had felt the same connection with Mother that I had felt when visiting the holy city of Fatima. I knew I had seen the Divine Mother face to face.

"Why not dedicate my life to Her?" I thought.

After returning home to Brasil, we told our daughter about Amma. She became very intrigued and wanted to meet her. At that time she was fourteen and suffering from a congenital eye disease. The doctors had predicted that she would be totally blind by the age of eighteen. Our lives revolved around her as we had tried for many years to come to terms with her condition.

continued on page 81.

A New Life

First, I want to thank Amma for the opportunity to relate an experience that made such a mark on my life, indeed gave me a new life.

I was nine years old when I developed some trouble in my eyes. The doctors found out that I was suffering from *Starguard Syndrome*, a congenital disease that would probably make me blind by the age of eighteen.

After the doctors told this to my family, our lives changed completely. I did not know what my life was going to be like from then on. We moved to another city because my mother said that with my problem, it was better to stay in a place without pollution. We went to live in Araruama, on a piece of land that was forty-three thousand square meters or about ten acres. When Amma's Swami came to visit later, we learned that this land is very similar to Kerala, Amma's home land in India. Rich vegetation all around, coconut palms, mango trees, jackfruit trees and many other fruit trees. We slowly changed our life-styles and became vegetarian.

My parents visited California in 1996 to meet Amma. At that time, I was fourteen years old and my eye condition was bad. My parents called me every day to tell me what was happening. The more I heard their stories, the greater became my curiosity. When they returned, I felt that they had somehow changed. Something very important seemed to have happened in California.

"Who is she?" I asked. "What power is this, that transforms people so much?"

> *Surrender will come if you develop love and faith. If we lead our lives with this attitude of surrender, we will be free from sorrow. God will always guard and protect us.*
>
> *– Amma*

The next year I travelled with my parents to see Amma in California. My biggest desire in meeting her was that she should help me understand and live with my eye condition.

My first encounter with Amma was full of love and tears. I couldn't stop crying as Amma looked at me with a love and compassion that I had never before experienced. I couldn't say a word. Amma told me not to cry and guess what? She said that in Portuguese!!!!

"*Nao chora, nao chora, nao chora,*" she repeated over and over again. This means, "don't cry, don't cry, don't cry".

In that moment, I understood that when we are in Amma's arms, she knows everything about us. Where we are from, what we do, how we live, essentially everything. I understood why my parents had been so attracted to her.

Since that first darshan, I went to California whenever I could, for one more encounter with my beloved Amma. I never asked her about my eyes because I knew that she already knew and I had faith that she would help me. My parents would pray for me and in their meditations would ask Amma to help me, but never asked her directly. My condition was improving slowly.

When I turned eighteen, I was watching T.V. one day when I saw a woman running in the Olympics who was blind. The reporter said that she was born with the same defect that I had.

I began to cry and told my mother that I was afraid, I did not want to become blind. My mother replied that I should talk to Amma the next time I saw her.

In 2001, I asked Amma about the possibility of going blind. Amma looked at me and said, "Don't worry about this. Forget it!" That response ended all my fear. Today I am twenty years old and can still see. In fact, I can see better than I could five years ago. Although there are a few limitations like driving, by Amma's Grace, I live a normal life. It is by Her Grace that I am here.

Amma gave me the spiritual name Durga, which I like a lot. Durga is a form of the Divine Mother. Amma gave me direction in my life. No, She gave me a new life! This year I am going to the U.S.A. to study English and I am excited because this means that I can also spend much more time with my Amma.

Michele de Souza Morais is 20 years old. She lives with her parents in Araruama in Rio de Janeiro. She has completed her college education and is currently studying English. She loves nature and plans to continue her studies in oceanography.

The following year all three of us travelled to California to see Amma. Michele fell in love with Amma instantly. Slowly, Amma cured her eye defect and today she leads a normal life.

Amma gave me and my family so much love. I wanted to share this love with other people. I prayed to Amma to help me find some volunteer work. Soon an opportunity appeared. A yoga teacher in my city invited me to help with some community projects for the care of elderly and sick people.

I started this work in 1997. We were four volunteers and we started teaching classes in yoga, meditation, water aerobics, arts and natural cooking. My role was that of a nutritionist and I taught about the importance of a good diet. As a result of our work, overall, the elders and the sick people in the community now have a much better quality of life.

Six years have passed since my first darshan. Amma helped my family and me rediscover the best parts of ourselves. She is like the sun in our lives that makes everything shine with Her light. Today, our family is building the first temple dedicated to Amma in South America. About thirty people attend weekly satsangs. Many of them have never met Amma personally because it is too expensive to travel to California, but they feel attracted to Her sweet smile and compassionate looks. We are trying hard to make it possible for Amma to come to Brasil soon, so that the Brasilian people can experience the same blessings that millions of Amma's children all around the world have already experienced. Jai Ma!!!

Translated from Portuguese by Meenamba Hass and N. Cruz

Leonor Maria de Souza lives with her husband and their daughter in Araruama, a city that is 100 kms from Rio de Janeiro, Brasil. She is a nutritionist and gives talks and workshops, counselling people who want to improve their dietary habits. Her husband Sanatan has a furniture export business.

Mother of Compassion

No matter what difficulties we have to face,
we should always have the awareness that we
are resting in God's lap, and that we are safe
in God's hands. This attitude will help us to
overcome any adverse situation.

– Amma

In 1994, I developed hepatitis that became chronic. I relapsed many times, each time losing more liver cells in my body. In April 1996, my liver failed. As a result, I developed jaundice, ascites and oedema.

At that time we lived in Findhorn, Scotland and my daughter Sonera was just two years old. My skin had turned yellow from the jaundice and I had painful diarrhea. Because of the ascities, my belly was full of fluid and I looked about six or seven months pregnant. I was so weak that I could hardly make it to the bathroom. I talked with my husband about death, cremation and our concerns about our daughter.

My husband and I had been on a spiritual path for many years. Our Guru was no longer in the body but I had a strong connection with Him. We chanted beautiful prayers to the Divine Mother that He had taught. I knew about Amma from a friend who had visited her a few years ago. She had told me that Amma was considered a *Mahavatar*, that is a great incarnation, of the Divine Mother. I knew that Amma lived in Kerala, India but not much more about her.

In my meditation one day, I felt my Guru directing me to go to Amma's ashram in Kerala. I was surprised. Given my serious condition, I was not fit to travel in any way. I immediately phoned my friend who had told me about Amma. She gave me information about *Friends of Amma*, Amma's organisation in England. When I contacted them, they sent me her photo and biography.

> *I cried seeing the ashram and Amma giving darshan there. It was as if Amma came to my living room on the very day I was to fly to her.*
> **– Helen Angel, U.K.**

After the photo arrived, I was amazed and delighted to find that Amma looked just like I had imagined. I read the biography and the healing miracles it described. This gave me hope and I prayed for help.

"If it can happen to others, it can happen to me," I thought. I wanted to live.

I started to feel Amma's healing and loving presence within me. I booked my flight to Kerala to visit Amma's ashram. Lori Sunshine, a close friend, offered to come with me to take care of me.

My husband thought I was crazy. Here I was bed-ridden and could not walk very much and yet I was booked to travel to India! I prayed to Amma, "If my health improves, it will be easier to travel. What ever is your wish, may that be done."

Slowly the diarrhea stopped and the ascities reduced. Blood tests showed that I was out of immediate danger, even though I was still very sick and weak. My husband remained very concerned and we decided to phone the ashram to ask Amma if I could travel. We were put in touch with an English devotee living at the ashram who agreed to ask Amma on our behalf. We phoned again and received this message.

"Amma says to postpone your visit and come to see her in London."

I was terribly disappointed! It was only May and Amma's London visit was not until July. Three more months to go! I cancelled the flight tickets with regret. On the day I would have left for Kerala, I was very sad. A friend phoned to say that Amma would be on TV that night on a travel channel. I watched the program with great anticipation but saw no sign of Amma. Then at the very end, there was Amma's ashram! I cried seeing the ashram and Amma giving darshan there. It was as if Amma came to my living room on the very day I was to fly to her. This was a miracle for me!!

My health improved steadily over the next few months. I felt Amma's presence very deeply. Looking back, I understood why I felt I had to travel to Amma when I was so sick. That had given me a goal, something to hope for, something to live for. That may have been what got me through that first month, when I could have so easily slipped away.

When July came, my husband, daughter and I all went to London to see Amma. We travelled by car and stayed with relatives for two nights during the journey. By this time, I was much stronger. Still the journey was very tiring for me.

When we finally arrived, a devotee took us to the front of the hall where the sick and elderly could sit on chairs but still be close to Amma. As we waited in the hall for Amma to come, I was filled with great anticipation and excitement. Our little daughter Sonera kept asking, "When is Amma coming? When is Amma coming?" Every one was chanting mantras.

Suddenly then there was complete silence. I saw her! She looked so beautiful! Sonera pointed to her and cried out delightedly into the silence, "Oh Amma, we have been waiting for you for so long." She seemed to express the longing that I felt.

Amma smiled beautifully at her as she passed us and went up to the stage. Sonera wanted to run to her. "I want to go to Amma," she cried. I regret now that we didn't know the rules and didn't let her run into Amma's loving lap.

We listened to inspiring talks and many uplifting bhajans. When Amma started giving darshan, I felt awed to be in the presence of a living *Mahavatar*. The volunteers were very kindly looking after me. They allowed us to be one of the first ones in line for darshan.

Amma first hugged Sonera, then my husband and then me. As she gently pulled me into her embrace, my face in her sari, I felt engulfed by her love. Words can't quite express the feeling…it was as if I was totally loved and cared for. Amma murmured, "Ma, Ma, Ma" into my ear and smiled at me. She gave us all prasad and asked me to sit down near her. I felt I was in heaven!

I could not sit for very long and lay down with some children who were sleeping near Amma. On the second day, however, I felt stronger and sat near Amma for some more time. On the third day, Amma asked me to sit beside her again. I sat for four hours holding the back of her chair, drinking in her healing energy. At the end, I could stand up and walk around easily! For Devi Bhava, I stayed up the entire night and did not feel tired at all!

Every minute of those three days was beautiful! Full of love and wisdom and healing! When Amma left on the last night, I could not stop crying. It felt so painful to be separated from her. Sonera kept giving me wonderful hugs whispering, "Ma, Ma, Ma," into my ears just like Amma. My husband who had been skeptical before was totally won over.

We went back home to Scotland where I continued to get stronger. The doctors were surprised and pleased with my improvement. In November, my husband, daughter and I went to the ashram in India and stayed for three months. It was such an amazing experience!

Today, my husband says that Amma postponed my visit so that he could also come to the ashram with me. He is totally surrendered to Amma and feels very close to Her in his day-to-day life. Sonera says Amma is Love and prays to Her when she needs help with anything.

As for me, I live a fairly normal life. Not only did Amma give me my life back but She also changed the way that I live it. She gave me a core of love and bliss that nothing can touch. Words can't express…only the experience of Amma can say…

Helen Angel (Pavana) currently lives in Derbyshire, U.K. with her husband, Arun, and their daughter, Sonera (Amrita Varshini). A doctor by profession, she has worked for many years in developing countries. Arun and Helen moved to Findhorn, Scotland for the birth of their daughter in 1993. The family moved to U.K. in 1999.

Amma's Little Seed

Amma's hugs and kisses should not be considered ordinary. When Amma embraces or kisses someone, it is a process of purification and inner healing. Amma is transmitting a part of her pure vital energy into her children. It allows them to experience true unconditional love and awakens the dormant spiritual energy within.

— Amma

I first learned about Amma on November 1, 2000. This was only a few days before her visit to Italy that year. My sister Silvana, who was in India had sent me an email describing her visit to an ashram where she had heard about Amma. She had not written much but something made me search on the Internet for more information. I found Amma's Italian website easily. There she was, smiling radiantly, beside the following announcement.

Amma will be in Italy on November 9-11 at Collegno's Palasport, Torino.

Torino was less than two hours away from my house and the 11th was a Saturday. Perfect! I decided to go.

I still remember the trip. The day was unusually warm and sunny for the month of November. When I arrived, the Palasport was already crowded. It wasn't immediately clear to me who Amma was. Somebody approached me and said that if I wanted to have darshan, I needed to get a number. I was puzzled; I didn't know what darshan was and didn't think to ask. I looked around but still wasn't able to identify Amma. I decided to visit the stalls nearby.

> *There was no red carpet or throne or special lights. This was something very different from what I had expected.*
> — *Manuela Ceresola, Italy*

At the stalls, I learned about Amma's orphanages, hospitals, schools, colleges and many other charitable works. I gradually became more aware of whom I had come to visit. I had planned the journey impulsively and had not given it much thought. Now suddenly, I started to feel inadequate and overwhelmed.

I gazed around again. At last, I was able to identify Amma. There she was, a smiling little woman in a simple, white sari hugging people, one by one. There was no red carpet or throne or special lights. This was something very different from what I had expected. I had thought that I would perhaps see her from a distance. I really hadn't expected to receive an individual blessing in the form of a hug. This seemed too much!

I joined the queue, glad that there were many people before me which would give me enough time to study Amma carefully. I looked at Amma, her gracious smile, her sweet features and the softness of her body. Suddenly, she lifted her head and looked straight at me! I felt my look reflected in Amma's gaze.

"How weird!" I thought. I shyly lowered my eyes.

After a while, I looked at Amma again and once more she looked back at me over the heads of other people. This time, I felt too fascinated to move my eyes away. Amma smiled and I got lost in the depth of her gaze. When I finally approached her for darshan, Amma gave me a vigorous hug.

There was only one thought in my mind, "Amma, I love you too!"

Back home, I regretted that I had underestimated the importance of Amma's darshan. Had I known more about her before going to see her, I might have prepared myself better. I might have prayed and asked her to guide me along the path of life. I might have asked her to help me deal with the severe asthma I was suffering from, for the last eight years. But I did nothing.

Over the next year, I read Amma's books and learned more about her. I learned that one could pray to Amma even if one was not physically near her and that she would surely hear the prayer. I understood that when we receive Amma's darshan, we actually receive a little seed inside us that stays hidden until the time is right for the seed to sprout. One year later, I met Amma again.

I have now taken Amma's darshan two times. My asthma has slowly healed but that is not the major transformation that Amma has brought about in me. I am grateful for Amma's hug of love that returned my breath, the very symbol of life, but Amma has given me much, much more than just that. I am slowly learning many lessons in love and life. Perhaps the little seed that She planted inside me has begun to sprout. I know that a long road lies ahead before the petals of the heart can fully open in love but I trust that Amma's guidance and protection will show the way.

Manuela Ceresola lives near Milan, in the north of Italy, with her two children. She teaches English and Italian and works as a translator. She likes to bicycle and considers it as a form of meditation where the wind makes for the feeling of oneness with nature.

The Divine Mother's Grace is Always with Me

When we are in Mother's presence and look into her eyes, we are given a glimpse of our real Self. Mother's eyes reflect infinity. In Mother we behold our own purity, the purity of taintless love, the purity of the Self.

– Amma

My search for an authentic master started when I was eighteen years of age. I met a Hindu yogi in Colombia, who taught me hatha yoga and the essence of yoga. The teachings touched me in the most profound way and laid the foundation for my first meeting with Amma twenty years later. Over the years, I met many great masters in Colombia and later in Spain, where I lived for a while. I felt inspired by them but none left any real imprints on my soul.

I got married in Palma de Mallorca, Spain, where my two children were born. My husband and I divorced when the children were still toddlers and I struggled financially and otherwise to bring them up in a foreign country. After a while, we returned to Colombia and I began working for an advertising agency.

I first heard about Amma in February 1996. Sonia, a dear friend, had just met her in California, U.S.A. and told me about her. She said that Amma was a wonderful saint who spent many hours every day embracing thousands of people, with unconditional love. She did this without eating or taking any breaks.

"No human being could ever do such a thing," Sonia said. She was completely captured by Amma's divine love.

Sonia's wonderful experiences awakened in me a profound need to meet Amma. Unexpectedly, I started to feel Amma's presence in my day-to-day life. My salary was just enough to cover the expenses of my small family. A trip to California seemed like an impossible dream. Still, I prayed to Amma with all my heart asking her to give me the means for a trip to meet her.

Within a few weeks, I was miraculously offered a job in a multinational company. Within a few days of joining, I received orders to present a series of seminars in California during the same dates as Amma was visiting! I just could not believe it!

> *Amma smiled at me with great sweetness and showed me her wrist saying, "No time" while she moved her head from side to side...*
> **– Maria Isabel Harker, Colombia**

In June 1996, Sonia and I arrived at Amma's ashram in San Ramon. Amma was already in the hall. She looked so beautiful and radiant in a simple, white sari. Hundreds of people were there...

My heart started beating very fast. Many questions came to mind. Would Amma really touch my soul? Would she really fill my heart with love? Would she be that divine abode that I had been searching for so long?

When I approached Amma to receive darshan, I felt her look penetrate my entire being. As if I could not hide any feelings or thoughts from her. Amma embraced me and I felt so deeply loved.

The next day Amma's program was in the outskirts of San Ramon. There were many more people and Amma was giving darshan a little faster than the previous day. When I went for darshan I was thinking to myself, "Amma, why so quickly? I would like to be in your divine embrace forever." Amma smiled at me with great sweetness and showed me her wrist saying, "No time" while she moved her head from side to side...

During the retreat, I prayed to Amma to help me with the osteoporosis I suffered from. Over the previous year, I had had severe pains in my back which greatly limited my normal day-to-day activities. That night, while I was asleep, Amma appeared to me in a dream. She rubbed and massaged my back with her loving hands. Her presence was so strong that I woke up immediately.

After that day, the pains started easing and slowly went away. By Amma's grace, I was also able to complete my work seminars successfully and returned to Colombia. My doctor was very surprised when I told him that the pains had vanished. He ordered new x-ray exams and found, to his great surprise, that the bones had gained density and had healed. There was no sign of the osteoporosis!

"This is unbelievable," he said...

This was how my search for an authentic master ended and I came to Amma's divine feet. Amma fulfilled all my expectations and I received far more than I could have imagined.

Three years later, I saw Amma again. My sister who lives in Virginia, U.S.A. invited me to work in her restaurant for a few months. She sent me a salary advance which enabled me to see Amma first in California. This encounter with Amma was also very beautiful and transcendent. On the day of Devi Bhava, I saw such loving tenderness in Amma's eyes that I felt paralyzed! I felt I should not touch Amma any more, so divine was Her beauty! She was a Goddess, the Divinity itself!

Today, even though the possibility of seeing Amma again may be remote, it does not really matter because I know, in the depths of my heart, that Her Grace is always with me. How fortunate I am to receive such Grace!

Maria Isabel Harker was born in Bogota, Colombia in South America where she studied journalism. She lived in Palma de Mallorca, Spain for 10 years where both her children, David, 22 and Carolina, 21 were born. Currently she lives in Bogota and works as a hatha yoga instructor.

4

My Guru Finds Me

*It is awakening of the disciple within you
that brings the master to you. Your intense
thirst to know the Truth gives birth to the
disciple within. When the lover within you
awakens, the beloved appears. Without the
lover, there is no beloved. Similarly without
the disciple, there is no master. The master
still exists, but not in your life.*

— Amma

Captivated by Love

When one really loves, one's intellect becomes
empty and one stops thinking. No thoughts,
no mind, nothing, only love remains. This
forgetting-all-else kind of love culminates in
innocence.

— Amma

"There is a young Indian girl near Kollam. They say she is special. If you are going to Kerala, you should visit her."

This was in 1978. I was in Madurai at the time visiting the famous Meenakshi Temple. I had already spent the last four months in the Indian subcontinent, wandering and searching. From Delhi to Nepal and Benares to Sri Lanka, from mountains to holy cities and spiritual masters to temples, I had been everywhere. Twenty-two years old, I had completed my university degree back in England, and had set out with a friend on a spiritual quest in India.

Over those four months I had many rich experiences. I became full with all that India had offered. It was thus that I was unable to take proper note of these words of a pilgrim I met in Madurai. I did go to Kollam and actually spent Christmas there but did not travel to see Amma, the young Indian girl the pilgrim spoke about. I have to maintain that when I actually met sweet Amma nearly eight years later, that was the right time.

In the meantime I returned to India many times. During my second trip in 1981, I met my first Guru. I was able to spend much time with Him in the foothills of the Himalayas and receive His direct guidance. I also met my future husband, Mike.

My Guru passed away in 1984. The next three years were extremely difficult as I reassessed my understanding of just about everything. On July 16, 1987, I met Amma for the first time. We were living in England and had been invited to a friend's house in a nearby city to watch the video *A Day With Amma.* After seeing the video, my only question was, "When can I meet her?" Mike felt the same way.

> *She reached to take Kim into her arms. I was instantly flooded with a deep sense of relief. "She accepts me" I thought, "She is taking it all away...."*
>
> **– Ray Sofroniou, U.K.**

We were told that Amma would be in Paris in about a week.

Our newborn daughter Kim was three months old at that time. Mike and I were slightly wary of flying with such a young baby. We nevertheless booked our tickets to Paris in a dream-like sequence. We did not really know where we were going or how we were going to get there. We had the address of a family that lived somewhere south of Paris. The flight was only the first step. Several train journeys followed. It was late at night when we finally reached our destination, hungry and exhausted and very anxious about our daughter.

Our hostess was very friendly. Kim was offered a doll's bed for the night. I briefly wondered what on earth we were doing there.

The next morning at about 10:00 a.m. we made our way to a larger house. As we entered the sitting room, I noticed sunshine streaming in through the windows. Most of the furniture had been cleared. About thirty people, mostly European, were seated on the carpet.

My eyes immediately fell on Amma. She was sitting on a chair surrounded by flowers. She looked up and smiled broadly at us, beckoning us forward. In no time at all, I was kneeling in front of her, noticing her white sari and her exquisite feet. She reached to take Kim into her arms. I was instantly flooded with a deep sense of relief. "She accepts me" I thought, "She is taking it *all* away...." The *all* was the fear, pain, and sorrow I had felt the three years following the death of my first Guru.

As Amma took Kim into her arms, she caught my hands and placed them gently under her feet with a movement that was exactly similar to something I had experienced with my first Guru. This single movement of Amma meant so much to me that the three-year gap seemed to be wiped away immediately. My feeling of being back on course was almost overwhelming.

Tears started streaming down my face. Amma lifted me into her lap.

"What is this?" she enquired as she released me.

She was pointing to the eczema on my face with great concern. She was speaking in Malayalam and someone was translating.

"How long have you had it? What are you doing about it?"

I was surprised by the detail and intimacy of her questions and answered as best as I could. She showed unusual concern and understanding. It was not what I expected from a spiritual master. She continued asking questions.

Pointing to Kim she said, "Are you feeding her? She looks very small. She needs to put on weight."

Kim was tiny. She had weighed just under five pounds at birth and was very slow to gain weight. Amma started unwrapping a large chocolate and as if it were quite normal to feed a three-month-old thus, fed it to Kim. Kim had never had any solid food prior to this. For three months I had concentrated so hard on giving this little scrap my all, in that utterly determined way new Mums have. Now I felt myself surrender to this quietly powerful and irresistible person known as Amma. Kim began to cry.

"You can feed her now" Amma said.

I proceeded to do that. I was in a total daze. I have no recollection of anyone else around me. Presumably Amma continued to give darshan in that way I have watched so many times since then.

Suddenly Amma stood up and glided out of the room and up the stairs. I was still dazed. My husband and I were told that we could come back again around 3:00 p.m. to meet Amma in her room. It was already past noon.

We wandered for a while searching for food. We did not quite know where we were. We scoured the small Parisian suburb but did not find anything suitable to eat. The day's events were on our minds.

By 3:00 p.m. we returned to Amma's house and were ushered into her room. Amma was sitting on a bed. She invited us to sit close to her. We were all smiling widely including baby Kim. Everything was very calm and still. I just couldn't take my eyes off Amma.

I had the 'no mind' feeling. This is something I have often felt when I am close to Amma and never more so than this first day. Kim started crying. Amma looked at her laughingly.

"Siva is the name of your soul," she said.

After some time she took some pieces of paper and after touching them one by one to her forehead, she handed them to us. On these pieces of paper, was a mantra for each of us. I felt most honored by this unsolicited action of hers. She had shown so much interest in us and now she seemed to be entrusting us with something valuable. But the day was not yet finished. We were told that we could come to town in the evening, Mother would be singing in a hall there.

We searched for the hall and arrived there around 6:00 p.m. I remember even today the electric effect of Amma singing alone during the early tours. The bhajans were thrilling, and if I had any doubts about the experiences of that morning or afternoon, they were stripped away. Anyone who could call on the Divine in this powerful way and could stir my soul thus, had to be taken notice of. I remember Amma sang *Sri Krishna Saranam Mama* followed by *Om Namah Shivaya*.

All too soon the singing stopped and it was time to return. I was elated, inspired and captivated. A day with Amma was over, and it was different from the video we had seen a week earlier. But it had nevertheless been so wonderful. This day became a marker in my life. Before Amma and after.

When we returned home to England, Kim started to improve in a very satisfactory way. She gained weight rapidly. Amma had suggested that I use turmeric paste on my eczema. By the time we obtained the powder from India a few months later, my condition had improved so much that I hardly needed to use it.

Today fifteen years later, Mike and I have three children. Each one of them has been brought to Amma in the same way. I remember

Amma teasing me as I stood before Her holding two children, with one beside me, "Wait a little before the fourth one…," She said.

My first meeting with Amma was not until eight years after I first heard about Her. This was not by accident. Amma called me to Her at the right time and when I was ready. In Her own extraordinary way, She came and found me. Today I don't honestly know how I live without Her for so much of the time. We travel whenever possible to see Her. My constant prayer to Amma is that I experience Her more and more wherever I am and whatever the physical distance between us. And that I am able to live according to Her teachings and follow Her example more closely. Then I believe Her love for me will not be wasted.

Editor's Note: The following story is written by the writer's husband.

Ray Sofroniou lives in Warwickshire, a small village in middle England with her husband Mike and their three children Kim, 15, Miranda, 13, and Adam, 11. She is a primary school teacher who loves life. She enjoys walking in the countryside, reading the classics, going to the theatre and spending time with her family.

A Day in Eternity

Eternal beauty and divine fragrance are potent within you. Through spiritual practices, the flower bud of your heart will eventually open up its petals.

— Amma

I first met Amma in 1987 when she came to Paris. Three years earlier, my previous spiritual master had left His body and I had not expected to find a guru again.

My wife Ray and I had gone to a friend's house one Saturday in July of that year to see a video of Amma. Looking at the video, I felt a deep desire to see her. I was struck by Amma's deep impassive calm and her joyfulness as devotees poured water as a ritual *abhishekam* during Amma's birthday celebrations. *Abhishekam* is normally offered to images in a temple when substances such as milk, honey and rose water are poured over them. Nothing, however, could prepare me for meeting Amma in person.

We were told that she would be in Paris the following weekend. Ray and I decided to travel from England where we lived, to Paris to meet her. On Friday evening, July 17, I left work to pick up Ray and our three-month-old daughter Kim to drive straight to the airport. When we arrived in Paris, we had a great deal of trouble finding the right station to take a train to Dourdan, in the south of Paris, where we would stay. We spent a lot of time walking the streets and a journey that should have taken an hour and half took us three to four hours. Kim had spent a lot of time strapped in a sling to either one of us during this time.

By the time we got to Dourdan, it was the middle of the night and we were exhausted. It was a blessing to be met in this strange place by friendly faces of people whom we didn't know. The next

> *There was no hurry, everything was perfectly relaxed and each darshan was a very intimate meeting between Amma and the person in her arms.*
> **Michael Sofroniou, U.K.**

morning our hosts took a leisurely breakfast, after which we drove to the house where Amma was staying.

As we approached the house, I remember walking up the drive feeling a little apprehensive, but with no clear thoughts in my mind as to what might lie ahead. We climbed the steps and I noticed a pile of shoes at the door. We added our shoes to the pile and went in.

About forty people were gathered together in a medium-sized living room of a modern house, in this Parisian suburb. Amma sat in the front on a chair surrounded by vases of flowers. She seemed like a small, shining figure in her beautiful white sari. Within minutes, the overpowering intensity of the atmosphere reached me. I felt as though I were engulfed in an ocean of incredible softness and sweetness...and that it emanated from Amma. We found a place to sit in the middle of the room.

Amma was slowly taking people in her arms and holding them. She radiated a tangible joy, freshness and energy. To my surprise, tears started rolling down my cheeks. This was not the sort of thing I normally did and I could not understand why I was crying. Later, I realised that it was because I was witnessing something beautiful... almost too beautiful to bear.

Tears continued to pour from my eyes. I blew my nose and watched Amma as she very slowly and gently embraced each person. There was no queue, only people sitting and watching Amma. As one person left her arms, she would beckon to someone else and that person would come forward. There was no hurry, everything was perfectly relaxed and each darshan was a very intimate meeting between Amma and the person in her arms.

As I watched, I was surprised by how this seemed like the most natural way for one human being to behave towards another. It struck me that Amma was totally extraordinary and totally ordinary at the same time. She was the most human of human beings I had ever seen and at the same time, she was divine. Simple and open, with a divine beauty which I can't quite put into words.

Time no longer existed in its ordinary sense. We were transported into eternity. At some point, Amma beckoned to Ray who went up to the front. Amma took Kim in her arms as Ray pranammed at her feet. She hoisted Kim with her left hand as Ray went into her lap. At some point I became aware of Amma saying, "Is your baby sick?" Kim was still very small as she had not been feeding well. Afterwards, Amma unwrapped a chocolate and put it into Kim's mouth while asking Ray to feed her. Ray sat at Amma's feet feeding Kim, while others went for darshan.

At some point, I became aware that my turn would also come soon. To have people watch such an intimate experience made me nervous and I began to feel self-conscious. "What will I do or say when I go up there?" I thought to myself.

Amma turned to me and smiling sweetly, she beckoned to me. I went up and knelt before her. Tears came again to my eyes. With whole-hearted concern, she took a paper tissue and wiped them. Through a translator she asked, "Do you have anything to say to Mother?"

I didn't really have anything to say to Amma, I was simply over-awed by her presence. Suddenly however, I blurted out, "I offer everything to God." Immediately realising my presumption, I altered my statement to, "I would *like* to offer everything to God." Amma took me in her arms and in that sweet softness, all my anxiety melted away. I was at peace. Amma motioned me to sit with Ray at her feet.

After a few minutes, she looked over towards us and said, "Sing!" I knew some bhajans that I had learnt with my previous spiritual master and I started singing one of those. Amma joined in, even while she continued to give darshan. It was very humbling to see the way in which she readily joined in the singing. Suddenly, nothing in my life seemed to have any importance, except to become like her. Of course this was an impossible aim...yet what else was there? To become an instrument of such love, there could be no higher purpose in life.

That first morning with Amma seemed to last a lifetime, although it could not have been more than two or three hours. We were told that if we would like to have a private interview with Amma, we could come back in the afternoon. We stumbled from the house and wandered down the street, not knowing where we were. We arrived at a market place where all the shops were shut but one. We went in hoping to find something to eat.

No food…this was a bar and there were many locals smoking *Galloise* and sipping beer, while chattering away at the top of their voices. This seemed very surreal after just having been in another world that resembled paradise, a world of significant silence and intense care. In the bar, life with all its smoky noisiness was going on, regardless of that divine presence up the road.

When we returned to the house, I tried to think of meaningful questions to ask Amma. "When would we have this chance again?" I thought. As it happened, never! But nothing came to mind; it was as if my mind had gone completely blank.

We were ushered up the stairs to the attic room where Amma was staying. She welcomed us and sat on the bed, while we sat at her feet. Almost as soon as we sat down, Amma began to talk. "If you bring up a parrot in a liquor shop, it will only learn to swear and curse. If you bring it up in a church, it will learn to pray," she said. She emphasised the importance of having a goal to live for. She gave us the example of the past being like a cancelled cheque, delighting in saying it in English, in a child-like way, "cancelled cheque!" She gave us some advice on bringing up children. As she talked, she showered us with overwhelming love, stroking our arms in turn, as though she could not get close enough to us.

The whole of that day I was aware of the way in which Amma embodied opposites simultaneously and naturally. She had a gentleness that was incredibly powerful, and at the same time, an uncompromising adherence to the ancient teachings of Vedanta. Alongside, there was an open, non-judgmental and non-reproachful love for us. She seemed to be contradiction in action. It struck me forcibly that although Amma seemed so soft, as soft as the softest down, at the same time, she was as hard as a diamond and as uncompromising.

As we were about to leave, Amma gave us each a mantra on a slip of paper. She held it up to her forehead as she gave it to us. We found out that Amma was giving a program in the centre of Paris that evening and somehow we found ourselves in a devotee's car being transported up the motorway. I remember seeing the incredibly grand clouds, great piled-up peaks moving majestically across the sky, as glorious sunshine and showers interspersed. My heightened sensitivity made it seem as if the whole of nature was engaged in our meeting with Amma and was reflecting her beauty and divinity.

Somehow in Paris we managed to buy some food, the first food we had had all day. We sat in the crowded foyer of the hall where the bhajan program was to take place. Suddenly, I noticed a small white figure deftly shoot through the crowd, followed by the swamis. It was Amma. We dropped everything and hurried in to the hall.

Amma sat throughout the bhajans with her eyes closed, rocking gently backwards and forwards. She began singing "Sri Krishna Sharanam Mama." Never had I seen such intense devotion in anyone and such wholehearted concentration. Amma seemed to throw herself completely into the singing and I was deeply moved. This was another aspect of herself that she was showing us and I wished it could go on forever. When she sang "Durge Durge," an intensity built up which was exciting and at the same time, totally sincere. I felt swept into another world where only focussing on the divine existed and the rest of the world was forgotten.

When bhajans finished, Amma came and sat in front of the low stage and smiled broadly, beckoning for people to come up for darshan. I thought to myself, "Surely she can't be doing it again?" But she was! We all went up again, one by one. Amma sat until every person had come up to her. Many people had left at the end of bhajans, as though they had simply been at a concert and missed the opportunity of experiencing Amma's divine love. Finally Amma finished hugging the last person and left. For us, it was the end of a momentous day. We went back to Dourdan.

Sitting in a cafe, drinking coffee in the shadow of the great cathedral of *Notre Dame* on the banks of the Seine, I wondered how on earth I would now reconcile what I had just experienced with Amma, with the rest of the world and my life. Everything in me was crying out to be with her, but we had to return to our lives. How were we going to survive? We returned to London the next day.

Around Amma, I have never regretted what I have done, however crazy it may have seemed or whatever risks it may have entailed, I have regretted only what I have not done. Fifteen years after that first meeting, I only regret the fact that we did not immediately follow Amma to Switzerland, where her next program was or get on a plane and go straight to India. However, it was not to be. Seven years passed before we finally got to Amritapuri.

We did not see Amma again until she came to London in 1988. The intervening year was filled with intense dreams of her. We tried to keep in contact as much as we could through listening to tapes of her bhajans, reading books we had bought and looking at Amma's pictures. We also attended satsangs with her swami who came once a month to London from Paris.

Today, day-by-day, the immense project of trying to follow Amma's teachings and absorb Her love remains. The task has not become any easier. If anything, it has become harder. As time passes by quickly, I am always painfully aware of how much I waste. However engaging the affairs of my life might be, nothing in the world is as important as this. My only prayer is that I am able to follow the supreme example that Amma sets in Her every action and moment.

Editor's Note: The preceding story is written by the writer's wife.

Michael Sofroniou is an English literature and fine arts graduate. He has worked as an artist for the last fifteen years, painting and selling pictures. He also teaches part-time in secondary education. He lives with Ray, his wife and three children in a small village, population about 1000, not far from Stratford upon Avon and about an hour and half north-west of London. He loves the countryside, walking, reading and the theatre.

I Once Was Lost but Now I'm Found

You are God's own child. God would never close all the doors around you. They may look as if they are closed, but they have in fact, been left slightly ajar. Just a mild knock and they'll give way. My child, never lose courage, never lose your faith in God.

— Amma

I had a great childhood filled with innocence. We lived in Sweden near the sea and I loved it. I was free to run around in nature with my friends. In the summer we would pack a picnic and row our boat to a small island, pick wild berries and have the greatest time ever. I was like a child in the Garden of Eden.

Then, when I was fourteen, my family moved to England. Culture shock! After a year, I still had not made any friends in school. About four years later, my father became ill. He developed tinnitus, which meant he had a constant noise in his ears and would have blackouts and collapse. Three years later, he was diagnosed with a terminal motor neuron illness called ALS and given six to eighteen months to live. The months were to turn into years, however, as he fought a long and bitter battle with death.

This was a very nerve-wracking period for the whole family. I was in my early twenties and my world turned into one of fear and disillusionment. Many questions bothered me about human behaviour and our existence. What was death? I could not really identify with anyone or anything going on around me and felt like an alien on this planet. My lack of understanding turned into despair and I went into a state of depression, which lasted over two years. Total hell was raging in my mind.

> *Even before I reached the hall, I experienced a very strong feeling that reached deep into my being.*
> *– Ann Louise Feron, Sweden*

One day I was in greater despair than ever and I felt that my head was going to explode and my heart was going to break. I deeply cried out for help from within. Suddenly, an extremely bright light came and totally engulfed me. All my worries and pain disappeared in that instant and I was floating in serenity, peace and bliss. After this experience, my condition improved somewhat but things were still difficult. After a short time, a dear friend told me about Amma.

"…a woman who travels around the world to give everyone a blessing and a hug," he said.

Straight away I knew that I had to see her. A tremendously strong feeling grabbed hold of me and impatiently I awaited her visit to London. Nine months later, in July 1994, I made my way to the hall where Amma would be giving out her blessings and hugs.

Even before I reached the hall, I experienced a very strong feeling that reached deep into my being. As I walked on the sidewalk in the center of this big and busy capital city, I suddenly knew that this meeting would somehow change my life forever. I reached the venue both relieved and a little afraid to meet this stranger for the first time.

The large hall was crowded and at first, it was hard to make out exactly what was happening. I felt a greater awareness and a heightened sensitivity of being present. I noticed that there were many Indian people among the Europeans. The music was loud and not to my taste. I struggled to see Amma but there were too many people surrounding her, so I made my way closer to the front. Finally I saw her.

My mind went fuzzy and I experienced many contradictory feelings. I found a place to sit down and watched Amma for a while. I observed people going up to her. As they left after their hugs, I saw that some had great smiles on their faces and others were crying, some staggered away and others left without any expression at all, some were respectful and others laid back. Everybody was different, it was like a miniature world gathered in one place.

I started to find the music very loud and annoying and wished that they would turn it down. I could feel something happening to me and my mind was bewildered. After about an hour or so, I joined the darshan line. Inching my way forward, I started feeling very heavy. At times, I felt as if my mind was out of control. A few meters away from Amma, I felt as if my body and mind were no longer with me. I was somewhere else, not in control of myself, still managing to move forward when asked to. All those people helping me, telling me what to do, guiding me towards Amma. Finally my turn came and unable to control myself, I fell straight into Amma's bosom.

"I can see only darkness, please show me the light," I was praying.

Amma whispered something into my ear. Unable to move or breathe, I thought I was going to suffocate. This was exactly how I felt in life also. Amma moved me away from her slightly to put something on my forehead and then continued her whispering. After some time, which seemed forever, she gave me a chocolate kiss and I moved away from her. I staggered away, hardly able to walk and sat down as soon as I could.

I could feel something heavy on my forehead. Slowly I started to wake up to a feeling of peace and happiness that I had not known in years. I knew that Amma knew what I was searching for. I also knew that she could guide me there. I had never been so sure in my entire life of anything like this Truth. At that moment she became my guru, even though I did not realise it or even know what a guru was.

When it was time for Amma to leave the hall, she stood up. I was near the exit and as she came closer to me, I felt the greatest desire to throw myself at her feet. I had no clue why I felt like this and had to force myself to keep standing. My knees were trembling and my palms were folded together. I could feel Amma's energy radiating several meters away from her and as she passed me, I felt one in her divine love.

The first time I met Amma, my life really started. Before meeting Her, my life was in a state of confusion. I was searching in the darkness for something, not knowing what it was or how I would get it. Only when I met Amma, did I begin to see light. Slowly, She helped me to know myself and to have a greater understanding of everything in the universe. She changed my life! It is Her amazing Grace that I once was lost but now I'm found.

Ann Louise Ferón was born in Sweden in 1968. In 1982, she moved to the U.K. with her family and lived there for 17 years. Her sister and mother still reside there. In 1999, she moved back to work as a marketing assistant in Taiwan's Trade Council in Sweden. She has a Masters degree in Environmental Management and is currently studying part-time to become an Ayurvedic health advisor. She also practices yoga regularly.

Meditation and Compassion

*To show compassion towards suffering human-
ity is our obligation to God. Our spiritual
quest should begin with selfless service to the
world. We cannot close our eyes to the world
in the name of spirituality and expect to evolve.
A smiling face, words of comfort, compassionate looks, all these are also meditation.*

– Amma

I first met Amma when she came to Estella, Spain in August 1997.
Estella is a town fifty kilometres away from my house in Pamplona
and I went with a friend to see Amma. Both of us already had a
Hindu Master who had initiated us in a meditation technique that
we practised daily.

I remember that when I approached Amma for my first hug, I
felt a current of peace. Afterwards, sitting on the carpet next to
her with my eyes closed, I smelled her wonderful perfume. It was
so strange because the current of peace, mixed with Amma's sweet
scent, persisted for a long time that day.

My friend burst into tears as Amma whispered the words, "hijo
mio, hijo mio" ("my dear child, my dear child," in Spanish) into his
ear. He immediately decided to receive a mantra from Amma. I
tried hard to dissuade him because his decision to take a new master
seemed very premature to me. I could not however convince him.

The news of Amma's visit to Estella was shown on television and
soon the hall was packed with people. I saw a young woman who
had come on a stretcher assisted by nurses. I saw her face just for a
moment, but when meditation started I felt such a deep compassion
for her that I forgot about myself and prayed for her for hours. I
did not know who she was and did not see her again, but I realised

For the first time in my life, I felt as if I came out of my ego.
– Patricio Hernandez Perez, Spain

that the miracle I was asking for her was actually taking place in me. For the first time in my life, I felt as if I came out of my ego. I was overwhelmed with a great feeling of compassion towards everyone.

Someone asked me if I could help to look after the sick and handicapped people who were coming to see Amma. There were very few volunteers and before I knew it, I was carrying out other tasks as well. I was asked to coordinate transportation for Amma's group to and from the program. This forced me to be the last one to go home at night on the first day. The next morning, I was back again after only a few hours of sleep to transport people back to the program. For three days, I carried on like this and got only a few hours of sleep every night. To my surprise however, I felt neither sleepy nor tired. I would just sit for a few minutes near Amma and meditate or listen to bhajans and feel as if I had rested for hours. It was strange for me to have so much energy.

On the last day, after my friend got his mantra, I hesitated for many hours before I finally also decided to receive one. At the very last minute I got up on the stage, still plagued with doubts. Just then, Amma interrupted the initiations and invited the people travelling with her on the tour to come for an embrace. This gave me an opportunity to watch the devotion of those who were closest to Amma. In astonishment and with an open heart, I watched their faces that were bathed in love as they went up to receive Amma's darshan. Seeing this, my doubts slowly washed away. When the initiations resumed, I happily received Amma's mantra.

When Amma left Estella, I felt empty. At first, I thought I would sleep for many hours but it turned out to be impossible. I decided to go to her next program in Ardene, north of Bordeaux in France. I was blessed once again to feel the joy of her presence there.

When Amma returned to Estella the next year, I asked from the bottom of my heart for my wife to experience the joy of Her presence. That same evening, my wife unexpectedly came to Amma's program. I thought she would look around, see what was going on and then quickly leave, but to my surprise, she not only spent the entire evening at the program but also started helping actively.

Today both she and I are very active members of Amma's family in Spain. Since meeting Amma, our lives are changing day by day. We work in Her mission with gratitude. I have learned from Amma through Her teachings and from Her own example that it is not enough to sit in a particular posture and meditate in order to grow spiritually. Of course, meditation is necessary to find peace of mind, but we cannot stay isolated, forgetting others. We need to also serve. Our seva gives us an opportunity to do that and share Amma's love and compassion with others.

Patricio Hernandez Perez lives with his wife Mercedes in Pampola, Spain and works as a professor of Spanish literature at the Public University of Navarra. He has written several poems and articles about mysticism. The couple has two children, Aurelia, 24, and Enrique, 22.

Transformed by Love

It is impossible to change life's circumstances completely. Instead of changing our external circumstances, we need to change our "mental-stances", that is our mental attitudes. Only then can we truly become happy. The way to do this is through spirituality.

– Amma

In the summer of 1991, a friend who had just returned to Sweden after a spiritual pilgrimage in India, invited my husband Per and me to his home. He had visited a lady guru named Amma in India and he told us about her. Per and I were both interested in eastern spirituality. I had been meditating for twenty-two years. I liked the Bengali saint, Anandamayi Ma, and felt sad that she was no longer in the body. In fact, it seemed to me that all genuine gurus were already dead. I was not really interested in hearing about yet another one of those so-called gurus and today, thinking back, I cannot remember a single word of what our friend said about Amma.

When we were about to leave, he gave us a photo of Amma. I did not like it very much but accepted it, just to be nice to him. He told us that Amma would be in Stockholm in August.

Summer went by. Even though I was not interested in meeting Amma at first, the closer the time for her arrival in Stockholm came, the more I felt a longing to meet her. I think this may have been because she was a woman like Anandamayi Ma. Eventually, both my husband and I decided to take some days off from work to meet her. In any case, we both really needed a break. I worked at an art gallery and had been suffering from a pain in my chest for the previous few weeks. I also had difficulty breathing and often had to stand still to concentrate on my breath in order to get enough air. I was sure that these symptoms were related to my stress at work.

> *After darshan, she sang Ram Ram Ram Sita Ram Ram Ram, played cymbals and danced in a circle with us. It was just lovely!*
> *– Karin Sandberg, Sweden*

August 14, 1991, the day of Amma's arrival in Stockholm came. I woke up that morning feeling very happy for some reason. I had told my two sisters and their husbands about Amma. They were also interested in spirituality and had decided to join us. Per and I, together with my sisters and their families, made our way to the National Museum of Ethnography to see Amma. When we arrived, the hall was already quite crowded. It was a small but beautiful hall and we found some seats at the back to sit down.

Suddenly, I heard some singing. Amma had come! She seemed so small and simple in a white sari. She had a garland of red roses around her neck. Someone was waving a light in front of her. She looked so lovely!

Then Amma went up on the stage and greeted everybody. She started talking and explained to us the importance of leading a spiritual life. She sang some bhajans, which I thought were absolutely wonderful! Soon it was time to stand in line for a hug and I queued up with my husband and elder sister. I felt a little shy and nervous about getting a hug in front of so many people but when I was in Amma's lap, I forgot about everything. I felt so happy just looking into her eyes!

We stayed until the program ended. As we drove home that night, I realised that my chest pains and breathing difficulties were much better. Per and my sisters had also liked Amma and there was a happy atmosphere in the car.

The next day, Per and I returned to the hall very early in the morning because we did not want to miss anything. During the morning program, I found out that we could ask Amma questions. I immediately decided to ask her about my work situation. My boss was a very evil woman, in my opinion, and I felt very dissatisfied working for her.

I got in line for darshan and when it was my turn, I asked Amma to help me.

"...Amma, it is very difficult for me to work there...my boss is not at all good," I told her.

Amma replied, "My daughter, we should always try to have the correct attitude. We should not be aggressive or jealous, but we should be patient. If we change ourselves, other people will also change. Thank God for *everything*, good and bad. Dear daughter, Amma will pray for you."

Saying this, Amma blessed the silver bracelet I had bought and slipped it on my arm.

After darshan, she sang *Ram Ram Ram Sita Ram Ram Ram*, played cymbals and danced in a circle with us. It was just lovely! In the evening, when I went for Amma's darshan again and lay in her lap, I suddenly knew that Amma was my guru. Just like that! I knew for sure and it felt completely natural! It was amazing, but I had come to love and trust her so much in just those two days!

After darshan, I sat on the floor near Amma, so that I could see her clearly. I did not want to miss even a single second of seeing her. She might do or say something very important in that moment. I almost did not even dare to twinkle my eyes for fear of missing something. So I just sat...and stared...and stared. Suddenly, Amma looked straight into my eyes! It felt like she threw a flash of lightning from her eyes into mine!! Every cell in my body filled with her light and love!!

Slowly as I sat there, I became aware of my inner chaos and negativity. It wasn't that my boss was an evil woman but that my own expectations were completely wrong. Until now, I had thought that I had led a spiritual life but I now realised that meditation alone was not enough. I also needed Amma's love and guidance to transform and purify myself.

When we left to go home that day, I suddenly realised that all my chest pains and breathing difficulties were completely gone. I felt a deep inner peace and my whole being was filled with Amma's love.

On the third and final day of Amma's visit, we again returned to the hall early. Amma danced with us and it seemed to me that we were dancing with God! It was so easy to meditate in Amma's presence! I spent a lot of time in deep meditation.

When Amma left the hall that evening, I rushed after her like a mad person. "How will I ever live without her now?" I was thinking to myself. Amma was already in the car. She rolled the window down and held her hand out. Then with a loving glance and a slight brush of her hand, she was gone.

I did not want to forget what had happened during those three days, so I immediately bought a notebook and wrote down my experiences. This was new to me, as I had never kept a diary before.

The next year was very difficult and I missed Amma greatly. I had bought some books and tapes at the program and these were my only sources of comfort and solace. I would read a few pages from one of the books every day, careful not to read too much because I had to make them last the entire year. I also listened to Amma's tapes again and again all the time.

Per missed Amma too, but not nearly as intensely as I did. My sisters and their husbands had liked Amma but their devotion was relatively slow to grow. It was only a few years later that they realised that Amma was their guru and teacher as well. Today, they never miss an opportunity to see Her.

Amma has helped me become more aware of what is going on in my mind and as a result, I am more careful with my thoughts and actions. Per and I have travelled to India four times now to see Amma. To be with Amma is to be at home because She is our real home. Both of us hope that some day soon it will be possible to live with Her forever!

Karin Sandberg is 49 years old. She has been married for 21 years and resides with her husband Per in the Swedish countryside. She worked as a teacher for several years and today is an adviser to many schools, helping them increase their cultural activities. She and her husband love to spend time outdoors.

So Much Simply with a Hug

*Where love exists, there cannot be conflict of
any kind. Peace alone will reign. May the
light of love and peace shine within our hearts.
Let us all become messengers of this love and
peace and illuminate the hearts of everyone,
dispelling the darkness of hatred and conflict
that overshadows the world today.*

— Amma

Even as an adolescent, I was attracted to spirituality. I loved to talk
with my cousin's husband, Victor, who was a yoga professor, about
yoga and spirituality. I felt attracted to his spiritual practices despite
our family's discomfort with his way of life and vegetarian eating
habits. When I finished my secondary studies, I joined law college
but immediately realized that I did not want to become a lawyer.
Next, I took a course in computers but still felt that something was
missing. In 1992, Victor had just returned from a trip to India when
I went to him for advice.

Based on his suggestions, I started learning hatha yoga and
practicing meditation. Within a few months, I noticed that I felt
a great deal happier, even though nothing had changed externally.
I began to understand the importance of leading a spiritual life.
In three years, I became a yoga teacher and started teaching yoga
classes. In 1995, Victor returned from another trip to India, where
he had met Amma. He had been greatly impressed by her and told
me about her.

"...Amma is a saint who hugs everybody. Being in her arms is
just like being in the arms of the Divine Mother," he said.

I thought Amma must be a special person but did not feel very moved. I asked many questions which were to be answered only after I met Amma myself.

> *In that moment, I understood everything I had read over the years in different books on self-help and spirituality.*
> **– Gabriel Lombardi, Argentina**

In early February 1997, I was able to travel to India along with a small group of people including Victor. We planned to visit Amma's ashram first and then travel to other parts of India. We arrived in Mumbai and flew to Trivandrum the next day. From Trivandrum, we took a taxi to Amritapuri and crossed a small canal in a boat. We finally reached the ashram by 5:00 p.m.

I will never forget that Sunday, Devi Bhava day. Victor had explained to us that during Devi Bhava Amma assumed the form and mood of the Divine Mother. He was the only one in our group who had met her before. There were already many people at the ashram. I started to photograph the grounds and was immediately informed that this was not allowed. We registered in the office and settled into our rooms.

In about an hour, we entered the temple and I saw Amma for the first time. She was dressed in blue and wore a crown. She was embracing all the people, one by one. Two lines had formed on either side of the temple, one of Indian men and the other of Indian women. The hall was packed with people waiting for a hug. The sound of swamis and swaminis singing bhajans gave a beautiful feeling.

The atmosphere felt very peaceful and deeply moving at the same time. A member of our group started crying. I looked at Amma and thought how lovely it would be to get a hug from her. I began to feel different somehow.

Meanwhile, Victor received permission for our group to join a shorter line for visiting westerners like us. After standing in this line for half an hour, we found ourselves very near Amma. At this point I was already very emotional, and at approximately five meters from her, I broke down and started sobbing openly like a small boy.

I continued crying until I arrived in Amma's lap. She embraced me and said something in my ear that I did not understand.

After the hug, I sat down near Amma. I do not remember ever crying like this since childhood. Slowly my crying stopped. I felt a great love towards everyone and there were no feelings of any conflict. In that moment, I understood everything I had read over the years in different books on self-help and spirituality. Concepts like, "love is the best cure for all wounds and problems" and "conflicts, no matter how strong they seem, do not really exist, they are real only in our minds."

Earlier, my understanding of these things had been purely intellectual. I do not believe that the understanding was genuine; perhaps I would just echo words from books. Now after receiving Amma's hug, I understood with my heart, without anybody having to explain anything to me. I had read that nothing was impossible for a person established in the Self. I now saw that. Amma had given me so much simply with her hug. I remained seated near her for a while longer, meditating in the love, peace, and harmony I felt.

We stayed at the ashram for four more days. I received many more darshans from Amma and experienced the same feelings of love and harmony each time. For every hug, I arrived in Amma's arms feeling peaceful and serene and left with even greater inner peace and serenity. My last darshan was at Devi Bhava where I had the grace of receiving a mantra from Amma. The days I spent at the ashram were unimaginable!

We continued our journey through India, but nothing could make me forget the saint in Amritapuri who had hugged me and made me feel so much love. We traveled to many sacred places: Rishikesh, Haridwar, Allahabad, Vrindavan, Benares, Calcutta, Dakshineshwar, Tiruvanamalai, and Puttaparti. We had the good fortune of meeting many great saints. After staying in India for a total of thirty-five days, we returned to Argentina.

I spent the first few weeks after our return, talking about Amma to anyone who would listen. A year later, in June 1998, Amma's grace touched me again when I unexpectedly went to Los Angeles,

U.S.A. to attend a spiritual retreat with her. This encounter was different in that I already knew what to expect. Amma showered more of her energy and love on me; it was just marvelous. I returned to Argentina full of joy, rejuvenated and ready to continue with my activities.

Currently, I teach classes in hatha yoga and tell my students about Amma, Her splendor and greatness. About twenty of us gather regularly for satsang. Though many among us have not yet met Amma in person, we all feel attracted by the stories of those of us who have met Her. Twice, we have hosted Swamiji Ramakrishnanda Puri who filled us with Amma's love. We are doing everything possible so that Amma will visit us. Through Her Grace and our small efforts, I trust that She will bless us with Her physical presence in Argentina very soon.

Translated from Spanish by Virginia Cook and Elsie Silva

Gabriel Lombardi, 35, lives in Capital Federal, Buenos Aires, Argentina in a neighborhood called Barracas, with his parents and an uncle. He is a hatha yoga instructor and a Reiki healer. In the future, he plans to study Ayurvedic massage.

No Longer Stones in My Heart

There is a child within everyone. The desire to search for this child is felt by all living beings. Children, when you go deeper and deeper into your spiritual practices, you will discover the child within you. You will experience the innocence, the joy and the wonder inside of you. You will realize that they were always there but you had merely forgotten for some time. This childlike innocence deep within you is God.

– Amma

The morning was still fresh when we arrived at Ardenne, France. Five of us had travelled together from Spain; two women who had known Amma for several years and three others, including myself, who were to meet her for the first time.

During the previous few weeks, my mind had thought non-stop about Amma. I had learned about her earlier that year, 1993, when I bought a Spanish book, "Mujeres de Luz" (Women of Light). The book described Amma as an Indian saint who travelled around the world, hugging people and awakening their "inner child".

I had passed half of my life trying, without much success, to dig out my inner child from beneath the tons of fears and other debris that had been piled on top of it. I was searching for that place within myself that was infinitely compassionate and wise, but was hidden inside a hard shell of ignorance and fears. How then could someone with the characteristics the book described not appeal to me? My desire to meet Amma was very intense but natural at the same time. Soon I had been able to contact a woman who met Amma every summer in France. She had agreed to take me along a few weeks later to meet Amma.

I still remember the trip with a lot of affection. We travelled along a beautiful road

I joined the queue and waited patiently as it moved forward. I was struck by how similar this wait was to life itself.
– Cristina Rodriguez, Spain

through fields of sunflowers and gently rolling hills. Everyone in the car was silent. Perhaps everyone was contemplating the landscape and the upcoming encounter with Amma. I had imagined a thousand and one reactions. Now that the moment had finally arrived, my mind was surprisingly quiet.

As we reached the program, I heard music coming from a large tent on the lawn. A lot of people were hurrying along with blankets or cushions under their arms.

"You have to leave your shoes outside," the two experienced companions said.

Obediently, I left my white slippers on the floor amidst a sea of sandals, boots and moccasins of all shapes and sizes. We entered the tent.

My eyes adjusted slowly to the dim light inside. Hundreds of people, many dressed in white, were seated on the floor on cushions, blankets and mats of all different colours. At the back of the tent was a wooden stage lovingly decorated with large sunflowers. The vision of a radiant woman with a dark complexion, sitting on the stage hugging people somehow seemed familiar.

"She is the same as *That*," was the single thought in my mind.

Thirteen years earlier my husband and I had met our first spiritual teacher who had also been Indian. That encounter had made a great impact on our lives. Through Him, I had a glimpse of what the Infinite was like. That wonderful intuition of fullness and bliss was what I called *That*. On seeing Amma now, I felt the same experience of *That* again.

Nine years ago, our teacher had left His physical body. Nine years, during which I cried and laughed as I felt His presence in every corner of my house. Nine years, during which I often sat down before his photograph to meditate and contemplate. Nine years, during which gradually and without any apparent reason, I started calling Him "Mother".

Many people have a sense of guilt when they feel drawn to a spiritual master after having been with another teacher. Not so with me. I knew that my first teacher had led me to Amma to leave me in her hands. I knew that those nine years were my preparation to finally find *That* again. I felt as if a new phase of my spiritual life was about to begin.

At that time, there were no darshan tokens, only a queue to reach Amma's arms. I joined the queue and waited patiently as it moved forward. I was struck by how similar this wait was to life itself. At times, my mind was totally extroverted and I chatted away about a thousand things, totally oblivious to the divine presence only a few meters away, tirelessly embracing one person after another. At other times, the mind was directed inwards and I adopted a meditative attitude.

At last, after about four hours in the queue, I was with Amma. The sound of bhajans vibrated around me as I smelled her marvelous perfume. It was as if I was in a dream. Amma took me into her arms, pressed sandalwood paste between my eyebrows and whispered into my ear like a grandmother, "Ma, Ma, Ma, Ma ..." Nothing fantastic happened. I didn't see any lights or hear any trumpets or heavenly music. But my heart burst open!

I can't express in words what happened. Amma touched something in me, something very deep. Something that, in spite of my not being able to define or even fully understand, gave me a feeling of absolute confidence in her wisdom and her capacity to guide me.

Outside, the July morning had grown brighter and the leaves on the trees danced in bliss.

During our next day with Amma, I felt dead inside. I expected to be immersed in a marvelous state of happiness. On the contrary, I felt awful. Where was the sweet sensation of belonging and security that had surrounded me the previous day?

I felt like I was behind an enormous wall that I could not cross over. I felt like a prisoner behind this wall. When I reached Amma's arms, I prayed as intensely and as sincerely as I could for her to help me. Later, during satsang, Amma showed me a way.

"My children, give Amma all your pain," she said. "Don't continue carrying it on your shoulders."

After satsang, I joined the question line and wrote out my feelings in my poor English. Although tremendously subtle, these feelings were more real to me than the floor beneath my feet.

"Amma, I feel that I belong to Mother, but I also feel that there is a part of me that is closed. What can I do?"

Amma answered through a translator. "My daughter, try to cry for Love," she said. "The path of *Prema Yoga* is best for you."

I came out of the tent into the night's darkness. The stars appeared to be shining in the heavens as never before. Sobs arose from the deepest parts of my being and I welcomed them. All the pain I had hidden in my heart for who knows how many past lives started flowing away in the river of tears. Slowly I felt my being fill with Light and Love. Amma had blessed me with being able to cry and was showing me the way to reach my inner child.

When the program at Ardenne ended, I accompanied my companions to Paris for three more days with Amma. My horrible feelings had disappeared and I was again totally immersed in the bliss of her presence.

After returning home, I tried to explain my meeting with Amma to my family. I wanted to share with my husband the great joy that I had felt. The truth, however, is that I could not quite do this. Words failed me even as I tried to describe my feelings.

Two of my children met Amma in Ardenne during the following years. When Amma visited Spain for the first time in 1997, my husband and our youngest daughter also met Her. Today, my entire family is devoted to Amma. I experience an immense joy in knowing that they too have found their true Mother.

Meeting Amma changed my life immensely. Over time, I understood that it is the small, small stones...of rage, guilt, longing, pain, nostalgia…that form the great wall in our hearts that imprison the inner child. We trip over these stones every day in our ignorance. The greatest blessing we receive from Amma is that She offers to take these stones from us. I gradually discovered that when I place the stones at Her feet, not only do they disappear but also they change into flowers of love!

Translated from Spanish by Virginia Cook

Editor's Note: The following story is written by a friend who was introduced to Amma by this writer.

_____

Cristina Rodriguez, 53, is a housewife and mother of three children. She lives with her husband Fernando and their children, Alvaro, 30, Eva, 28, and Radha, 15, in the countryside, about sixty kilometers from Barcelona, Spain.

Sailing with Divine Guidance

The parents are the two Gurus that the chil-
dren see from birth until they come into contact
with the world. If the seed of love is not sown
at home, how can it sprout or blossom?
                                        – Amma

I first learned about Amma in 1992. I was forty-seven years old at that time and was exhausted physically and emotionally. My first marriage had ended years ago. After a long and painful divorce trial, my children had come to live with me. But life with my second husband was also difficult. I felt alone without knowing whom to turn to.

It was in this state of mind that I talked to my friend Cristina one day. She had met a woman saint named Amma the previous summer in France and had been greatly impressed by her. She planned to return to see her again in July. Without understanding much of what she told me about Amma, I said that I would go with her. To this day, I have no idea what made me say with such certainty that I would accompany her. Then without thinking about it much more, I returned to my daily life.

This is how I found myself travelling with Cristina and two other women that July towards Bordeaux to meet Amma at the airport. I felt some trepidation; like going to see someone very important and not really knowing how to act in front of them.

We arrived at the airport and sat down to wait. Other people had also come to receive Amma and I watched everyone anxiously. Suddenly there was a great excitement in the air! The plane had just landed and Amma was about to appear! I ran forward and pressed my face against the window looking intently towards the spot she would emerge from.

> *I remembered reading in a brochure that we should leave all our suffering and sorrows at Amma's feet and that she would take care of them.*
>
> *– Carmen de la Vega, Spain*

Suddenly I saw her! How little and how chubby she was!! Amma looked through the glass at that same instant and our gazes locked for a few seconds. I broke out into a cold sweat. After a few moments, she came through the door and everyone crowded around her. Someone put a garland of roses on her.

Everything happened very quickly after that. Amma embraced all the people, but I don't really remember my hug. We returned to the car and continued our trip to the hotel. When we arrived, I retreated to my corner in the room not wanting to speak to anyone. I felt so dirty inside…I wanted to be left alone…

On a piece of paper I wrote out a small prayer. "O Lord, like a powerful, clear, fresh waterfall, let Amma wash away all the filth that I feel has hardened inside me!" After praying and feeling aware of my impurities as never before, I tried to go to sleep.

The following day we arrived at the program site. What a pretty place it was! A tent in the middle of a field surrounded by a forest! When we entered the tent, many people were already waiting. We joined the queue. I remembered reading in a brochure that we should leave all our suffering and sorrows at Amma's feet and that she would take care of them. That is exactly what I needed, I told myself. It would be wonderful to let go of my heavy burdens.

The tent continued to fill with more people. Suddenly everybody started whispering, "Amma is coming, Amma is coming." From my spot, I could look outside. She came down the road, walking with the children, as if one among them. As she entered the tent, the mood suddenly changed. Amma stood at the entrance, motionless and majestic, while someone did a welcoming ritual. She looked so beautiful!

Darshan began and I watched from the queue. "Aha! She knows that person, of course!" I told myself. From her demeanor, it seemed that she was embracing her best friend whom she had not seen for a very long time.

"But wait…she knows this one too…and this one… and the next one."

As I watched, her hugs did not seem to vary, no matter who it was that she took into her arms. The hug was always wholehearted, complete and total. "But how could she know everyone?"

I was touched. A faint sparkle of love arose in my own heart. "This is true love," I thought. "I don't know love, I have never loved, I don't know how to love."

What I was experiencing was new to me. "I will have to learn how to really love."

The queue advanced very slowly. I saw someone showing some photographs to Amma. Can you show her photos? If I had only known! I searched my purse…and what luck…two small photos of my son and daughter appeared! The photos were very old…my teenager children were little kids in these photos. "What should I do? Should I show them to her or not?"

"Yes! I will show them to her," I decided. I turned the photos over and over again in my sweaty hands until my turn arrived. Finally in front of Amma, I just thrust them into her hands and dissolved in tears. I could not see anything…I just sobbed and sobbed. I threw myself at Amma's feet…I wanted to worship and kiss them. Someone raised me by the arm as Amma hugged me. Still sobbing uncontrollably after the hug, I dragged myself away.

The next thing I remember is lying outside the tent on the grass. I was crying out loud, "Amma, everything I have is for you. I give you everything. I put everything into your hands." I have no idea how long I kept sobbing like that.

I felt someone's hand on my back. I turned around to look up into the love-filled eyes of a young boy.

"Do you need anything?" that angel asked. I shook my head.

Slowly, I returned to myself. Many things came to my mind with absolute clarity, like great truths that I had just discovered.

I had had a very difficult childhood. My parents were never there to give me love. Because of that, I had a hard time giving love to anyone myself. I clearly saw that my husband had many good qualities. He was loving, patient and generous but I had made him suffer. I understood in that moment that I had to love him and dedicate myself to him. I also understood that my children were not really my children but that they were from God. I needed to love them just for who they were.

With these realisations, came a tremendous relief from the burden of my sorrows. After spending two more days with Amma in France, I returned to Spain and to my routine life. But something had changed. I felt much lighter and freed from the weight of my sufferings. By Amma's Grace, the relationship with my husband began to improve and slowly it became very sweet and beautiful. To my children, I tried to show as much affection as possible. It was not too late to begin.

Under the guidance of a divine wind I am now able to navigate my way through life in a tranquil manner. Once in a while a gust of wind catches me unprepared but then I pray to Amma and She shows me the way. Sometimes I feel that there is no breeze at all and I stop. Just then a breeze comes to caress me and I know that that is Amma. My path is laid out and a safe haven awaits me ahead!

Translated from Spanish by Virginia Cook and Faith Fennessey

Editor's Note: The preceding story is written by the friend who introduced this writer to Amma.

Carmen de la Vega lives in Barcelona, Spain. Since the death of her husband in October 2000, she lives by herself. She has two children Jose Maria, 31, and Carmen, 29. She works as a professor of physical education at the Institute of Secondary Teaching. She likes spending time with her family.

5

What Young Ones Say

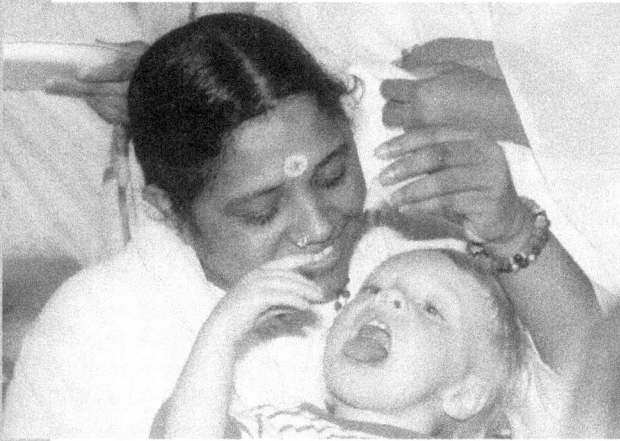

God has the nature of a small child. God won't even look at those who do tapas with ego but God will shower grace on the innocent-hearted ones who do not do anything. This may be due to God's childlike nature.
– Amma

Forever in My Heart

The innocence of a child, which is pure and spontaneous, has a beauty and charm of its own.

– Amma

This is Devi Bhava night. As I sit in the darshan line with my mala to be blessed and a peach rose clenched tightly in my hand, I wait patiently wondering whether or not to ask Amma. I edge down the darshan line behind my Mum with a slight feeling of apprehension. The atmosphere is magical, musicians lighting up the mood with fervent devotional songs to the Divine Mother. Amma is adorned in a sparkling silver crown and a dazzling deep blue sari.

Now, I am on the stage beside Amma. Hesitantly, I hand the mala and the rose to Her. Everything else seems like a blurry dream. Amma accepts the rose, blesses my mala and puts Her arms around me in an all-accepting motherly embrace. Her overwhelming love and motherhood make me realise, yet again, how blessed I am to have Her as my Mother. I burst into tears. Burying my head in the soft folds of Her sari, I let myself go.

Amma gently lifts my head. She smiles and sighs as if to say *finally*, drawing me close again in a tight hug. My heart pours out and tears stream endlessly down my cheeks. In my heart, I ask Amma to accept me and give me a mantra. I feel so small and vulnerable. I can't be pulled away from Her now and She knows it. She holds me for as long as I truly need to be held. I feel so safe.

Amma gazes into my tear-filled eyes and with a compassionate smile and gestures for me to join the mantra line. I am so filled with awe that She has understood my heart without my saying anything out loud. In a tiny voice I manage to choke out "Amma, mantra?" To my utmost relief, Amma responds with the biggest and happiest yes I have ever received.

Leaving Amma's lap and the darshan line, I am not I

> *Every moment from the time I first met Amma has become a part of me, not just a memory. I was six years old when I first saw Amma.*
> *– Srimayi Lee, Australia*

anymore, I am Amma's very own child in every way. Everything within me continues to burst out in buckets of tears. Even after knowing Amma for the past eight years, it is not until now that I truly feel that I am Amma's own child and have always been. Although Amma has so many children and their needs to fulfill, She still remembers little me.

The moment I first saw Her, I immediately fell in love. It was like reconnecting with someone very dear, someone that I had always known. Every moment from the time I first met Amma has become a part of me, not just a memory. I was six years old when I first saw Amma. My thoughts travel back to my first meeting with Her...

It was the month of November in the year 1993. I was living in Melbourne, Australia with my Mum. We were going to see this new lady saint that day. I hardly knew anything about her, except that she wasn't an ordinary person. Yet somehow I was ever so excited, like I was about to meet a relative that I barely ever saw.

When my Mum and I arrived at the program hall, I remember that I had noticed a lot of people. I had felt something in the air, like waiting with excitement at Christmas and nervousness too, all mixed together. Then, all at once, the people in the hall had started chanting. I was too small to see or know what was happening.

Then, as if she had just appeared from thin air, a little lady dressed in white had emerged from the midst of the crowd and had stepped onto the stage. She had bowed all the way to the floor, greeting the people in the hall with a boundless smile, like she knew each one of us. Lovingly gazing at everyone, she had circled her hand near her heart. It was as if she was holding everyone inside her.

Not long after, people had sat down on the floor in a long line. I had never seen anything quite like it and yet, it had felt so comfortable. There she sat, hugging everyone, young and old, with the same motherly affection. It had seemed a little strange that she was hugging all the people like they were family. And yet, I had truly felt at home in her presence, as if she were a relative of mine too.

As we entered the line, I had suddenly started feeling very scared and nervous. I was afraid of how Amma might be with me. I was not sure whether I wanted to be hugged by someone I didn't really know. I had not noticed much of anything else, as I got closer to her, I had been ever so wrapped in my own child's world of uncertainty.

Then Amma had opened her arms with a smile and had given my Mum and me a warm welcoming hug. The world around me had gone away like no one was there but Amma and me. My previous fears had melted away in Amma's love. Deep down I had sensed that Amma was really like my own Mum and more.

As my thoughts slowly come back to the present time, I realise that when one meets Amma it is like a meeting of both the physical body and the heart, and it is this that makes it impossible to forget Her. Amma has become an important part of my life and has given it such a good flip. Unlike most other teenagers, I have no interest in guys, loud music or parties. Instead my interests are focused on satsang, bhajan and seva. I still have bad habits. Ok, lots of bad habits! But Amma is always there to say *no*, and ever so gently, bring me back to the correct path. Amma is everything, She is my Mother, Guru, God, Best Friend, everything!!!!!

Srimayi Lee is 14 years old. She is of Chinese-Indian origin and was born in Melbourne, Australia where she currently lives with her mother. She studies in the ninth grade at the Melbourne Rudolf Steiner School. When she grows up she wants to be able to help other people. She enjoys playing the violin and piano and participating in Indian classical dance recitals.

My Guiding Light

One who has faith and devotion to God, which
stems from their innate innocence, can behold
God in everything, in every tree and animal
and every aspect of nature.

– Amma

I met Amma for the first time on May 28, 1996, in Yokahama, Japan.
I was nine years old and studying in the third grade, which is called
3-nensei in Japan.

A friend of my mother had told her about Amma. She said
that Amma was a very unusual Indian saint who travelled around
the world hugging people. She advised my mother to meet Amma
when she came to Japan. The next time Amma visited Japan, my
mother took my two younger brothers, Hirotaka and Hiromasa,
who were six and three years old at that time, her mother, that is
my *obaachan* (grandmother) and me to see Amma. All five of us
traveled by train from Tokyo and it took us almost two hours to get
to Yokahama.

As we entered the hall, I heard some nice music playing. I told
my mother that it sounded kind of familiar. She asked me if I had
heard the music in school and I said no. I did not really know where
I had heard it before. It was a mystery to me.

Soon all five of us got into the darshan line. Actually, I did not
really understand what was going on or the meaning of darshan.
Amma hugged us all, one by one and then together. It got over
very quickly. I remember that Amma smelled very good and I felt
nice. After the darshan, my *obaachan* said that Amma was very
sweet. My mother felt happy. My two brothers were too young to
feel anything much, I suppose.

> *I remember that Amma smelled very good and I felt nice.*
> *– Hiroaki Suzuki, Japan*

When we returned to Tokyo, we started attending Amma's satsang. One day I went hiking in the mountains with my family. Suddenly I was all alone, deep in the woods and there was nothing but nature all around me. I remembered Amma and strongly felt her presence and longed to see her again. After this, I waited for May to come as quickly as possible.

When we returned to see Amma, I felt very nice after darshan. There was a warm feeling of lightness and I felt like I was in a trance.

Amma slowly started becoming more and more a part of our lives and we grew attached to her. In May 2000, my brothers and I received spiritual names from Amma. I was given the name *Sandeep*, which means "holy light." Hirotaka received the name *Vishal*, which means "expansive heart" and Hiromasa was given the name *Haran*, which means "the one who removes evil."

We have a pet, a marmot, in our house. It doesn't look anything like Amma, but it reminds me of Her. Today I realise that Amma is a great soul. Whenever I am in trouble, I pray for Her guidance and She gives me the strength to go forward. My family also feels the same way and I am very grateful that we all met Amma.

Translated from Japanese by Keiko O. Bailey

Hiroaki Suzuki is 14 years old. He lives in Tokyo with his family. He likes to study social studies, physical education, art and drawing. When he was little, he liked to draw cartoons. He loves travelling to the mountains and the sea during his school vacations.

Divine Guidance

Parents should try to inculcate the value of leading a spiritual life in their children's minds. This is the most valuable wealth that parents can give to their children. Material wealth will perish, but spiritual wealth is imperishable.

– Amma

I was eight years old when we first met Amma in August 1996 in Tournai, Belgium. Our family had been invited to someone's house earlier that year where we saw Amma's picture for the first time. My parents brought some bhajan cassettes and a video of Amma home. Upon watching the video, I thought that Amma was a lovely woman. My parents decided that we would all visit her during her next trip to Belgium, which is not far from where we live.

When we arrived in Tournai, I was astonished to see how large the hall was and the number of people gathered. Some unfamiliar music was playing and then an announcement was made that Amma was coming. Everyone rushed to the entrance where there were two roped off lines. I stood up from my seat and looked around. I didn't really know where to go. My sister noticed me and asked me to come closer to where she was standing. It did not help much because a lot of tall people were standing in front of me. My father asked me if I wanted to come on his shoulders so that I could have a better view. I said, "Yes," and he hoisted me up. Now I could see very well. I became very excited and eager to find out what the Indian saint would be like.

Suddenly Amma came. The music was switched off and I heard deep voices chanting. Amma came down the rope-line, quick as a weasel, slipping through the crowd, laughing happily and touching people with her out-stretched hands. I held my hand out but

> *Amma took me in her arms first, smiled at me and gave me a little kiss and a sweet. Then she hugged my sisters followed by my parents and then everybody together.*
> *— Sarada Scholer, Luxembourg*

perhaps I was too high for her and she did not touch it. I felt a little sad.

continued on page 140

Eternally Blessed

My first meeting with Amma was in August 1996 in Tournai, Belgium. At that time, I was twelve years old and leading a spiritual life with my family. My father was a meditation teacher for Maharishi Mahesh Yogi and when I was six years old, he had initiated me with a T.M. mantra. I had never seen Maharishi in person, just some photos and videos. It was not very easy for me to meditate properly and get concentration. I just followed my parents' wishes but I did not really feel a connection with Maharishi.

Before meeting Amma, I wanted to be like the others in my school and had started smoking and being disobedient to my parents. I was not so good in studies and brought all the negativities from others home.

Summer came and we went to Tournai for Amma's program. There weren't many people and there were no darshan tokens at that time. While waiting for Amma to come, everybody started chanting *Om Amriteshwaryai Namah*. I didn't know the mantra and felt a little strange because I did not want to appear as though I was there for the first time. I wanted to appear like the others who had already known Amma and the Indian mantras for a while.

Soon, Amma entered the hall. A woman next to me asked me to move forward so that I could see her better. This kind gesture from a stranger made me feel good. Some swamis started chanting for the pada puja and I listened to the Indian voices. I already knew a lot of things about India, gurus and pujas from our family's connection with Maharishi.

Amma passed by very quickly, holding her arms out to touch people's hands as she walked to the front. I did not feel anything special on seeing her.

> *The happiness that we gain from the outer world is fleeting; it never stays for long. It is there for one moment and the next moment it is gone. But spiritual bliss is not like that. Spiritual bliss is infinite and lasts forever.*
>
> *– Amma*

After meditation, darshan started. I think it was in the early evening that we went for darshan. I remember that my parents had some trouble in their legs from sitting in the line. As we came close to Amma, I prepared myself by remembering the instructions I had read about how to behave during darshan.

I have to apologise, however, because I really can not remember the darshan itself. I know it sounds strange, but I have lost my memory about that most important moment in my life. I don't know if Amma smiled at me or how I felt at that moment. I think she just whispered "Ma, Ma, Ma, Ma," into my ear. I know I didn't cry. We got the family darshan and returned to our seats. I ate my prasad sweet and watched darshan continue.

From that day on, my life has changed so much in all regards. I no longer want to be like the others in my school and have slowly given up my bad habits. Before it was difficult for me to meditate properly and concentrate but now I really like to meditate and do archana every day. Because of Amma, I have changed inside and become happier. I now try to view bad situations as a gift to help me grow spiritually.

Today I know what God's Love is. I can't imagine life without my loving Mother, Amma. She is both my Mother and Guru and I offer pranams to Her Lotus Feet.

Satya Scholer is 18 years old and lives in Luxembourg. She obtained a diploma in commerce and is now studying for a secretary's degree, which she will obtain in 2003. She enjoys singing and listening to devotional music.

A Mystery

I was thirteen when I heard that my parents wanted to visit the young Indian saint, Amma. I was not at all enthusiastic. I had seen a small part of a video with bhajans and I felt very strange about this woman who moved her arms up in the air during the songs. This indicated some signs of craziness to me.

My parents decided to go and I had no choice but to accompany them. I decided to read Amma's biography in order to be "informed". After reading the book, I developed a feeling of respect for someone who had suffered so much but still the thought of meeting her was frightening. I was afraid that all my youthful dreams of having fun with friends, a nice job, a nice relationship and a life where I could decide what to do would be lost. My impression about following a master was that I would have to do whatever the master, that is Amma, told me to do.

I had started meditating when I was six years old but I had no real connection to any divine source or master. I had never met a realised master and had no idea what such a person was like.

I still remember a lot of details of my first meeting with Amma. There were so many people and the hall was so big. My parents were very impressed. During the puja, everyone sang such strange songs while closing their eyes. I remember the hotel we stayed at...the food and even the toilets! But what about the darshan itself? Nothing!! I don't know why I can't remember Amma, my feelings or my thoughts.

When we returned home, we found out that there was an Amma Centre in France, *Maison Amrita*. We started going there for satsang every weekend. We would arrive around 11:00 p.m. on Friday night after a four-hour drive. Even so, we were the first ones to wake up for archana the next morning. My parents slowly started learning the thousand names of the Divine Mother and later we sisters also learned them.

Slowly, we simplified our lives and started doing sadhana regularly. We bought Amma's books, photos, malas and an Amma doll. The doll helped a lot. We named her *Amlala*, which means "Little Amma". We strongly felt that the doll wasn't simply a doll, but that Amma herself was always present. We sold our beds and started sleeping on the floor.

> *Sadhana is essential. Even though the seed contains the plant, it will bear fruit only when it is properly cultivated and given fertilizer. In the same way, even though the Truth resides in all living beings, it will shine only through sadhana.*
>
> *– Amma*

The next summer we visited Amma in Bonn, Germany. This is the first darshan that I remember. Amma was very sweet to me. She gave me long, deep darshans and I felt so happy. We stayed for the entire three days of the program and I only got a few hours of sleep during this time. The ending of Devi Bhava was so much fun. Amma stood on the stage and we all sat down looking up at her and singing *Amma Amma Taye*. I was singing very loudly because I felt very happy and could not understand why people around me were looking at me strangely. Later on, I realised that instead of *Amma Amma Taye*, I had been singing *Amma Amma Kali*. I did not really know the words but had simply wanted to participate.

After this darshan, I started to feel that Amma was all right. My ideas about life, such as why we are here, what we should do, were slowly changing. Over the last six years, my feelings have become clearer and deeper. There is no doubt in my mind that Amma planted a seed in my heart during our first meeting, which has now become a little tree spreading its roots and growing. That first darshan is still a mystery for me, however, and only Amma knows about it!

Sita Scholer is 19 years old. She is in her last year of art studies and wants to continue her education in Brussels, a nearby metropolitan city which has a lot of good schools. She enjoys reading, painting and listening to devotional songs.

The next thing I remember is watching darshan and wanting to be in Amma's arms. As my family got closer to Amma, I became more eager to receive her hug. Amma took me in her arms first, smiled at me and gave me a little kiss and a sweet. Then she hugged my sisters followed by my parents and then everybody together. She was smiling sweetly the whole time.

I cannot remember anything else about this first meeting. I cannot remember what I said or how I felt. To tell the truth, I did not have any positive or negative feelings, I was rather neutral.

Six years have passed since that first meeting with Amma. My family's relationship with Amma has become very strong over these years. In 1999, with Amma's blessings, my parents started Amma's Centre in our home. Devotees come three times a week to sing bhajans. We try to fly to Amma's ashram in India every year to see Her.

Amma has changed my life in so many ways. Spiritual discipline has become a part of my everyday life. The day starts at 6:00 a.m. with archana and ends with bhajans and meditation. When I have important questions I know I can always ask Amma for help and answers. I feel blessed to receive Her divine guidance always.

Sarada Scholer is 14 years old and lives with her family in Luxembourg. She is in her first year of college and does not yet know what she wants to become when she grows up. She enjoys going to college and singing devotional songs.

With Mother at Last

*It is Mother's wish that all of her children
completely dedicate their lives to spreading
love and peace throughout the world. If you
children love Mother, you should love and
serve all living beings. Then only it can be
said that you truly love Mother.*

— *Amma*

I live in a small village in the south of France. When I was ten, I
became a vegetarian. A few minutes from our house two French
devotees of Amma, known to everyone as Vandana and Krishna,
lived in a house in the hills called the *Col*. My parents knew them
and we would sometimes go to their house and have a meal. I loved
going there as the atmosphere was very peaceful.

In May 1997, when I was twelve, I heard about a three-day
retreat with a swami at the *Col*. I really wanted to attend but I was
in school in Toulouse, an hour's drive away. On the last day of the
retreat, when I returned home from school, a neighbour telephoned
to say that the swami was still at the *Col* and that if I wanted to go,
she could take me. I was delighted.

When we arrived, Vandana welcomed me and took me by the
hand to the little meadow where an Indian man dressed in red sat
on the grass, surrounded by a few people in white. I saw an altar
with Amma's picture. I am English, so I could communicate with
the swami directly without an interpreter. He asked me many questions about my school and my family. During satsang and bhajans,
I was moved by his devotion to Amma and by the way he sang. I
was very inspired and thought of Amma as a loving mother. In a
way, singing and praying with the swami felt familiar and I think
that my desire to see Amma started then.

> *I felt I had arrived, no use running about any longer. Here was my Mother. Here was where I needed to be.*
>
> *– Vani, France*

After that retreat, I started going to the *Col* regularly to sing bhajans. Amma became more and more present in my life. I loved hearing devotees talk about their experiences with her. One day I went into Toulouse, where I go to school, and got completely lost. I started to panic and was nearly in tears when I thought of Amma and pulled myself together. I started singing a bhajan and silently asked her to help me. I just kept walking without really thinking about where I was going. The road led me to the right bus stop to take a bus home. Many little incidents like this one followed.

I made a little altar to Amma in my bedroom. One day, I dreamed of her. I was on a big boat, surrounded by men who wanted to kill me. Amma was with me and her very presence gave me protection. The men were unable to approach me and I felt very safe. Amma was wearing some of my clothes, which told me that she was within me. A few months later I had another dream. This time I was in school and my friends and I were doing a treasure hunt. At one point, we had to go into a room to get clues from someone. To my delight, when I entered the room, I saw that Amma was going to give us clues to help us reach the goal.

My longing to see Amma grew stronger and stronger. At last, in the summer of 1998, I went to meet Amma in Paris. I had saved up for the plane fare. Krishna and Vandana had agreed to pick me up at the airport in Paris and look after me. My parents knew them well and trusted them and hence allowed me to travel alone.

Finally, the day arrived. Full of excitement and a little anxiety as well, I said goodbye to my parents and got on the plane. In my mind were a thousand questions. Was Amma really going to be as extraordinary as I was expecting? Did she really love me? The flight lasted an hour, and as I looked out of the window at a magnificent sunset, I was filled with joy at the idea of meeting my Mother at last.

Krishna and Vandana met me at the airport and while we were driving to where they were staying, they pointed to the Eiffel Tower. I had never been to Paris before, but I could barely look at it. I was just so excited thinking of meeting Amma that I could think of nothing else.

The next day, my excitement grew as Krishna and Vandana told me that we would meet Amma at the airport. I barely had time to realise what was going on before we were there with a small group of devotees. We waited for quite some time and I could feel the excitement. Many questions were still bubbling within me. Would she really know me? Would she recognise me? Would I be disappointed? I kept trying to imagine what Amma was going to be like.

Suddenly, someone said that Amma had arrived but we didn't know where. We all started running round the outside of the airport. All the time I was saying "Amma, Amma," I really couldn't help it! Suddenly, there she was! I was ahead of most of the others and ran to her.

Amma looked at me and laughed, shaking her hands and putting an expression on her face as if to imitate my excitement, before taking me into her arms. As soon as I touched her shoulder, tears started streaming down my cheeks. The tears were a mix of all the angst pouring out, love for Mother, the feeling of being loved and understood, the joy of being with her at last. I felt I had arrived, no use running about any longer. Here was my Mother. Here was where I needed to be.

As I was in her arms, my face in the folds of her soft sari, Amma talked to someone. When I heard her sweet voice against my ear, I knew that this was my Mother's voice. After a while, she gently lifted up my head, and with much love in her eyes, put a sweet into my mouth. Tears kept running down my cheeks and I felt a great happiness and peace within me as I watched her give darshan to others.

I spent the next two days with Amma. I can't remember precisely what those days were like. All I know is that my emotions were very strong. I couldn't go to darshan without crying. I couldn't sing bhajans without crying. I loved bhajans with Amma; I cried and cried thinking, "Here is God singing before us!" It was as if all the little worries and accumulated tensions were just pouring out and Amma was untying the knots within me.

The last morning, I took a darshan ticket and waited for my turn. I had to take the train back to my parents before Devi Bhava. As the end came near, my tears became tears of grief. When I realised that the queue was too long, and that I probably wouldn't have time to go for darshan, my sadness grew unbearable. At that point, Vandana noticed me and took me to the front of the darshan queue, just near Amma. Because of the state I was in, I was allowed to go through.

Amma gave me a very beautiful darshan. I looked up through my tears into her sweet eyes and said, "Mother, I am leaving, please come with me!" Amma had a sad and concerned look on her face as she asked, "Today?" She took me into her arms, and lovingly stroked my back. She then gave me an apple and put two sweets into my hand. Tears were still streaming down my face as I sat in the train, clutching my apple.

By the time I got home, however, I wasn't sad any more. I felt as if Amma was with me. I gave a piece of the blessed apple to each member of my family and to my grandparents who were visiting, and then went off to eat my piece on my own. I went to a beautiful little meadow glistening with the morning dew. With sunlight stroking my face, I started crying again thinking of my beautiful Amma. Suddenly, a seed from the apple fell into my hands. I was surprised to see that it had germinated! I took it back home and carefully planted it in a pot. A little plant grew from it and even my parents were amazed at this little miracle. We had never heard of a seed germinating in the apple itself. I was sure that it was because of Amma and that Amma had given me a little spark of herself. She was still with me.

When I heard that Amma was coming to Paris again in November of that year, I was delighted. Although I had school, so many classes were cancelled that it was as if "all the teachers conspired to somehow find a way for me to attend Amma's program," in my mother's words. So I stayed for the whole program, including Devi Bhava, without missing much school at all! I have been to see Amma every year since then, and in 2001, I was even able to spend a month in her ashram in India!

As I have grown older, I have started to realise what an incredible blessing it is to have a guru, especially a Satguru like Amma. Her very presence gives life a meaning. Amma shows us how to live in the world with the right attitude. Whenever we stumble, She is there to wipe our tears and shower us with motherly love. What then is left for us to do, but to try and follow Amma's example of boundless love and service to all of creation!

Vani, also known as Daisy Rockliffe, is 16 years old. She currently lives in a small village, Ariege, in the south of France (in the Pyrenees), with her parents and brother. She was born in England, but moved to France with her family when she was 5. She is studying in the final year of her secondary school.

The Incarnation of Love Amma

Turn children's attention to positive activities
when they are very young.

– Amma

I was fourteen when I first met Amma. She was visiting the
M.A. Math in New Delhi as part of her North Indian tour in
March 1997. I remember the day very well. My parents told
my elder sister Latika, my younger brother Ishan and me that
we would all go to the Math for Amma's darshan that day.
They had met Amma a year earlier when a friend had told
them about her and had felt very happy with their experience.
Otherwise, we did not usually go to such places. We did not
have much understanding of spirituality and our concept of
God was limited to prayer only.

At first my sister, brother and I were reluctant to go. Like
other kids of our age, whenever elders talked about satsang or
God, we rejected these ideas thinking that they were boring top-
ics and not meant for people of our age. This time, however, our
parents really insisted that we come along and we had no choice
but to obey them.

In the car, on our way to the Math, our mother told us that what
she liked most about Amma was that she was personally accessible
to everyone, unlike other saints. She advised us to meet Amma
with an open heart and without any preconceived ideas. I listened
to her carefully. I liked what I heard about Amma and decided to
meet her with a pure heart.

There was already a very big crowd when we arrived at the Math
and people were being seated for *Sani Puja*. Someone explained to
us that during *Sani Puja* Amma leads the chanting and everyone

participates. This sort of com-
munal worship is very powerful
not just for the devotees but
also for the environment. My
mother, sister and I were asked

> *...there was a feeling in me so vast and deep, a feeling that is really impossible to put into words.*
> **– Benu Verma, India**

to sit in one of the rows on the ladies' side. My father and brother
went to the gents' side. We were very far away from the stage and
I could not see it very well.

When Amma came, my first glimpse of her was from the large
T.V. screen set up in front of me. Before this glimpse, I only knew
of Amma as a saint who met people differently. But now suddenly,
there was a feeling in me so vast and deep, a feeling that is really
impossible to put into words. Today, five years after, tears come to
my eyes while I write this...

I felt a deep longing in my heart as if I wanted love and a *lot* of
it...and that only Amma could give it to me. All the vulnerability
of this world came to me and I felt like a child desperately in need
of its mother's love, Amma's love. I knew her touch could give me
that love but first I had to wait for several hours.

When it was finally time for darshan many hours later, I don't
remember exactly what I was thinking but I do remember that I was
feeling a great high. Amma embraced me and I felt so loved and
happy. Afterwards, I found my brother and sister who were also
beaming after their hugs. Our parents were happy that we had all
liked Amma. We kept talking about her as we returned home that
evening.

Since that day, all five of us regularly visit the Math every
year and participate in all the pujas when Amma is in New Delhi.
Amma has become an important part of our lives. Today, we know
for sure that nobody loves us like Amma does. She is love in its
purest form, a love one can feel and touch and see. Amma is the
very incarnation of Love.

Really I have never felt as if Amma was away from me. Whenever I need Her, I just close my eyes and call Her and She comes!

I know She is there to guide me through anything I do, She is my very best friend!!!

Benu Verma is 19 years old. She lives in New Delhi, India with her parents and siblings. She is currently studying for her English (honours) degree, first year at Indraprastha College. She is a classical dancer and also enjoys singing and writing poems.

6

Not Right for Me

Whoever comes into the river of Love will be bathed in it, whether the person is healthy or diseased, man or woman, wealthy or poor. Anyone can take any number of dips in the river of Love. Whether someone bathes in it or not, the river of Love does not care. If somebody criticises or abuses the river of Love, it takes no notice. It simply flows.
– Amma

From My Head to My Heart

*The mind has two powers, the veiling power
and the power of projection. First, the mind
veils the true nature of a phenomenon. Then
it misinterprets. It covers the Truth and makes
us mistake the Truth for something else. To
befriend the mind, is to befriend a fool.*

— Amma

I had already been searching for approximately fifteen years before I
heard of Amma. What exactly was I looking for? I was convinced
that there had to be a higher power; my job and my son could not
be everything. God was present for me since childhood, not as a
bearded man in the sky, but as energy and love. But I did not know
where I could find Him.

In 1995, my life had become very turbulent. I was a single
mother fighting against prejudices and condemnation from family,
neighbours and friends. At work, I was the only woman in the management team, and many people reacted to this with envy. I had to
spend a lot of time at work, frequently from five in the morning until
ten at night. My son was ill with asthma and I badly wanted to be
a good mother. With all these pressures, I was repeatedly pushed
to my physical and psychological limits.

I started reading books about great eastern saints to find comfort.
I read books about Ramana Maharishi, Milarepa, and other saints.
Daughter of Fire by Irina Tweedie made a great impact on me. This
is a thousand-page diary of a middle-aged Russian woman who lived
in the twentieth century. She travelled to India and was spiritually
trained by a Sufi master. Irina seemed similar to me in many ways.
Reading this book awakened in me a longing to find my own master.

Soon after this, Amma's biography came into my hands. While

reading it, my longing kindled again to find my guru. "If this book is really correct, then this girl has to be the living Jesus Christ of this time. Isn't this a

> At that moment, it became rather clear to me. This was no guru. This was a charlatan.
> – **Ruth Herzig, Switzerland**

unique chance to meet the highest incarnation, to ask her questions, to get advice from her and to be led by her?" I thought to myself. Oh, how gladly I would have lived in Amma's ashram in the early days as described in the book.

I did not have any trouble believing the miracles the book described, for was everything not energy? Nothing then, was impossible. I did find the somewhat blooming language a little unusual. My mind was quick to point out though, that anything could be put on paper. Maybe, much was only a fabrication. However, when I read in the appendix that Amma travelled around the world once a year, I enquired with the publishing house about Amma's next attendance in Switzerland.

"Oh, she comes in a few weeks," I was told. They sent me a brochure of her program.

A short time later, in July or August, I drove with my sister from Weinfelden where we lived to Schweibenalp where Amma was coming. I carried with me big hopes and expectations. On the way, in Brienz, we met a large Swiss man, who was also going to see Amma. He was literally overflowing with exuberance.

"This Amma must have given him something really unusual; he is so radiant and smiling," I thought. "Is he experiencing the same states of bliss that Irina describes?"

We soon arrived in Schweibenalp. There was a tent, and curiously and very carefully, we approached the side entrance.

"Oh no! I cannot bear this smell of joss sticks…I will get sick," my sister announced, immediately. The loud, unusual music too, did not find favour with her.

"Oh, what a great start!" I thought. We stayed by the entrance because it was not so loud and fresh air could fight the eastern influence.

I saw a small Indian woman sitting in front, embracing everyone. People approached her submissively.

"Oh, what is this? Realised souls are humility personified. Jesus, Ramana Maharshi are examples. But here seems to be someone who wants to be celebrated," my mind warned.

With thoughts of false gurus and black magic in my head, I inspected everything closely. In the back of the tent were many stands where books, cassettes, clothes, joss sticks and other such things were being sold. My hopes for a genuine master sank further. "How is this different then, from someone just making money?" I asked myself.

Next, I looked at the followers. They sat in long queues and when finally a few meters away, they would approach the woman on their knees. At that moment, it became rather clear to me. This was no guru. This was a charlatan. "Why would a normal human being degrade themself before another in such a manner?" I wondered.

I continued to watch the followers closely. It repelled me to see their 'bliss' after darshan. Some even seemed to be hysterical. This fit exactly with my image of cults that made their followers puppets and eventually ruined their lives. Pictures of American sects that drove their followers to suicide flashed before my eyes.

"Why are humans so uncritical in the spiritual scene? They cannot master their everyday lives but they believe these speech artists when they say that they can give them a place in the sky. What an illusion! We must ourselves gain what is to be gained in spirituality. Nothing can be bought or obtained by trickery." Totally disgusted now, I watched with contempt.

We continued standing at the side entrance and observing. We were alone and undisturbed because everyone pushed forward to be as near as possible to Amma. Suddenly Amma looked across the room at us.

"Uff, now she is reaching her invisible arms towards us also?" I thought.

Fortunately, the few meters separating us from her gave me a certain sense of security. I also mentally tried to make a protective armour of thoughts around myself to resist any possible hypnosis or manipulation.

"Oh no, this is not my thing! Me, this white-dressed woman catches not, even if all the others fall into her trap!" I triumphed internally.

I thought that this would leave Amma in the cold. No, instead she once again smilingly beckoned us for darshan. She repeated this gesture twice.

"Oh no, us you don't catch, you catcher of souls! That will be your mesh to bait us. First we will struggle, then you will never release us."

So we remained standing as if we had not noticed anything. Once again, Amma looked at us while she gave darshan to someone else and smiled cheerily. The whole scene was becoming extremely embarrassing and unpleasant for me. I felt pressed and somehow threatened by her. But there was also something that was pushing me to experience darshan myself and judge. I could see this so-called holy one receiving everyone very kindly, even now after many hours. But fear of manipulation and losing face in front of my sister held me back.

Finally, we had seen enough. We fled to the catering stand for a belated lunch. We decided to take a walk in the area before our journey home. Suddenly, my sister asked me if my crown chakra was also hot like hers. Curiously I touched her and then myself on the head. Oh, the chakra seemed to be literally glowing for both of us! This made me somewhat thoughtful.

"Can a false guru cause the activation of the thousand-petalled lotus? That too, from a distance? Can it be that Amma is genuine?" I wondered.

Many thoughts whirled around in my head, while we walked. Our walk in this untouched nature was wonderful, even with our smoking heads. Lake Brienz in the valley below was lovely, as were the gurgling mountain streams and the misty waterfalls.

One year later, I again received a brochure for Amma's next visit to Switzerland from the publishing house. This time she would be near Zurich. Strangely enough, something pushed me to go again. For weeks prior to her visit, I was in a very elevated mood. My whole body was inexplicably hot, as if I had fever or was anxiously planning to participate in a competitive sport. I drove to the meeting on the first morning of the program. This time, I went alone. I planned to scrutinise Amma in peace and mingle with the crowd. My doubts still persisted.

After I arrived, I watched the activities for some time. Then I courageously placed myself in the darshan line. I was like an animal on the way to battle. With a pounding heart and ready to protect myself from manipulation, I slowly slid near Amma in the line. Oddly, the line seemed to not move forward at all. People were constantly smuggled into the front through a priority line where the sick, elderly and children could go quickly to Amma. This meant, a still longer wait for me. I was in the line for over three hours sitting on my bottom. It hurt!

"Does Amma feel I must suffer now?" I asked myself. After all, I had not listened to her, when I had her invitation one year ago to come for darshan without waiting in the line.

Finally I was kneeling in front of her. She took my head and pressed it firmly into her lap, while signing a book on my back that someone handed her just at that moment.

"Does she want to signal to me that I carry my head too high? That I should work on my humility?"

She pulled my head to her shoulder and murmured "Ma, Ma, Ma" several times into my ear. Then she pressed a sweet wrapped in a rose petal into my hand. I looked up at her face. She was twisting her mouth, as if she had just bitten into a lemon.

"Am I real or not? What do you believe?" she seemed to be asking me.

Since my intellect was on defense and my heart was closed from fear of black magic, I felt nothing during this first darshan. I was disappointed. Irina had described so many blessed states but I had felt nothing. No bliss, peace, or harmony.

"Is this not the only yardstick I have by which to judge Amma's authenticity?" I asked myself.

After the embrace, I squatted down in the hall. I was a bit lost and helplessly continued to watch the whole fuss.

I looked at the followers of Amma and her companions somewhat more closely. Watching the Indian men who were dressed in orange and yellow, a strange feeling of familiarity arose in me that I could not explain. One man especially seemed to radiate sincere cordiality and warmth. His dark brown eyes radiated so much love, they reminded me of Ramana Maharshi. Irina had described the eyes of her guru as dark, brown, deep seas, in which golden lights sometimes sparkled, calling and enchanting her. Somehow the swami's eyes also seemed to call me, but where? I enjoyed the feeling, bathing in those wonderful stars. My heart became warm and my mind switched off for some time.

"What is this, Ruth? Are you flipping slowly?" My mind was back. I must confess that I was confused. I could neither understand what was happening, nor could integrate it anywhere. And of course, I had no control over it. At the same time, I was in an elevated mood and feeling very happy.

My gaze wandered to Amma. "If she is really genuine, should she not have charisma and irresistible attraction?" my perplexed mind asked. But I found nothing there. Finally, I got a headache and left. I would have liked to have stayed for the evening and listened to the Indian songs but my headache became worse. I decided that this was enough for the day. I was somehow frustrated, but also very thoughtful and confused. The caring eyes of the swami accompanied me as I drove home.

I needed some time before I could finally open up to Amma. After my first and second meetings, something magically drew me to her programs every year, although my mind raised objections and warned again and again. With each year, I also stayed longer, until in 1999 when I finally belonged to the helper team. That year I helped with kitchen co-ordination, which hardly left any time to see Amma at all. The following year I was allowed to coach the question line and was able to spend much time near her.

For a long time Amma dismissed me after each darshan with the same distorted, questioning grimace as she had on my first darshan. At least, this was the way I felt. I believed that I was the only one on whom she was not showering love. This sometimes hurt me. Slowly my heart opened and banished the prefabricated pictures out of my head. Then the real Amma came into my consciousness quietly. Finally, I could experience the same states of bliss, peace and harmony that Irina had described.

So I truly cannot claim that it was love at first sight between Amma and me but I can finally say this, that Amma was not false, but my expectations and attitude were wrong. I have since learned that everyone has their own relationship with Amma that is completely different from anyone else's and so our experiences also differ. It was no small consolation to me when I heard years later, that even some of the swamis were at first sceptical and were not enchanted or convinced even after their first darshan.

A picture emerges before me while writing this story. A beautiful, blooming, red rose with a lovely smell is being caressed by the sun's rays. One can approach the rose or rush by it with a thousand thoughts in the head or even stay away from fear of the thorns. The rose is there, whether we notice it or not. Exactly the same it is with realised souls such as Amma. Do they not live among us to disseminate so much love, ready always to give? Is it not up to us then, to stop and open up to them and imbibe their blessings deeply? Be that as it may, shortly I am flying to the ashram at Amritapuri for half a year. Yes, this seems like magic...magic of the heart!

Ruth Herzig is a single parent who lives with her 20-year-old son in Switzerland. She recently worked as the director of controlling, financial, personnel, administration and purchase in a major company in her country. Her experience has been varied and she has served in the upper management in many companies. For some time, she has been interested in natural healing methods and helps friends and family with massages and therapeutic touches.

By Her Grace

Human effort is limited and can take you only
so far. God's Grace is unlimited and divine.
The sincerity of our effort, however, is what
draws God's Grace. So do your sadhana
sincerely with an attitude of self-surrender and
love, then the Grace will surely come.

— Amma

I first saw Amma in November of 2000. I had heard about her the
month before from two different friends. The first was a friend of
my husband's who had met Amma shortly beforehand. He told us
how he had changed totally after meeting her. I casually mentioned
his story to a fellow musician, who also turned out to be Amma's
devotee! I was quite surprised! As she narrated her story to me,
I decided to find out for myself if indeed I could also experience
something as dramatic and life-changing as these two friends had
described. And for free!

If it is good enough for me, it is good enough for my family. So
I rounded up my son and daughter, then eleven and eight years old,
and my husband, who is always supportive of my activities, to go to
the program. When we arrived, I noticed many Americans dressed
in white saris. I could handle that though. "Each one to his or her
own," I told myself. I am open-minded to other cultures and proud
about the fact. We sat on the floor waiting for Amma to come.

Amma came shortly thereafter. As she stood at the entrance,
the foot washing ritual, the chanting, and the praying took me back
to my childhood religion which is so against this sort of a thing. I
was raised in the Seventh-Day Adventist Church and had learned
that there was only one way to worship God and that idol worship
was for the heathens, who need to be converted. As I watched
Amma being worshipped, I was turned off, even while I was trying

> *As we got closer to Amma and the "life-changing hug", I kept thinking about where I would put my hands.*
> **– Patricia Tanner, U.S.A.**

so hard to like her. How could anyone be so naive as to worship another human being? In my mind, God was the only one worthy of worship.

The activity began with an *Om* chant followed by meditation. I could relate to that. I had a mantra from the Transcendental Meditation organization and had meditated for many years.

When Amma started hugging people, the worship atmosphere quickly changed into some kind of bazaar, with announcements about sales and charities. I had thought that the atmosphere would be more spiritual. This, however, seemed just like going to a K-Mart; only the announcements were louder and more obnoxious.

As we moved down the line, I could not really see Amma hugging people very well so I knelt to have a better view. I felt transfixed by something, but was not exactly sure what. I felt a little overwhelmed by all the rules about how to go for darshan. I understood their need, but still found it a little nerve-racking. I was afraid that I might hug Amma incorrectly and get yelled at or be embarrassed in front of everyone for making a mistake. Many people were watching, some sitting around Amma on the floor and some looking on from the balcony. As we got closer to Amma and the "life-changing hug," I kept thinking about where I would put my hands.

I don't remember the actual hug. It did seem like a hug anyone else could give. It lasted only a few moments. My husband put his hand on Amma's back by mistake and the attendants politely took it off. No one yelled at him though, or at any of us.

I appreciated getting the hug early because I wanted to leave quickly and saw no point in waiting around for a long time. Both friends had mentioned that they had watched Amma hug two thousand people or more throughout a single night and I really did not want to sit for that long. I felt it would be a waste of my time, not to mention boring.

continued on page 160

A Goddess After All

In November 2000, I had my first darshan with Amma. Someone told me that she is like a goddess. That scared me because I felt that Amma could read my mind. I thought she might come to me at night, hurt me, and put a curse on our town.

I remember now that I kept looking at her. She seemed really popular and many people were bowing down to her. If someone is really popular then they must have a big house to live in and a lot of power. I felt scared of her and did not feel like hugging her.

> *Parents should start explaining spiritual ideas to children at an early age. Wealth will come today and will be gone tomorrow but good character will last the whole life.*
> *– Amma*

We sat in a long line to get darshan. Amma hugged my sister and me first and then Bruce, my stepfather, and my mom. Then she hugged us all. She rubbed my cheek with her hand. It was a cold hand, too.

In June 2001, when Amma came to San Ramon, I did not want to see her. My mom went to meet her with Bruce. Not long after, she started taking my sister and me to satsangs at the M.A. Center. At first, I did not like it because it was so boring but soon I made many friends and it became fun.

In the satsangs, we got ready for Amma to come in November. I had darshan with her on November 18, which is my birthday. After Amma hugged me, she gave me a flower and an apple, and hugged me again. I felt very blessed and happy. I really liked Amma this time.

During Devi Bhava later in the week, I could not find my mom in the crowd. I felt mad and upset. Then I thought of Amma and felt better. After some time, my mom found me. We stayed almost all night and I helped with carpooling and later in the snack shop.

Now I am looking forward to Amma coming again this summer. I am no longer scared of Her. I want to get a spiritual name from Her.

Elliot Kane, 13, lives with his mother, stepfather, and sister in California, U.S.A. He attended school until the fifth grade and is now being homeschooled. His main interests are computer and video games.

As we drove home, I asked my kids if they had liked the hugs. They had not. Amma had scared my daughter and my son was noncommittal. I told them that they did not have to return. My husband said that he felt good and could sense that Amma was not just an ordinary person. I admitted to feeling good also but overall the entire experience had been very uneventful and short. Certainly nothing life-changing had happened.

During the next six months, I mentally asked Amma for help a few times. I thought I would test her and see if she would help me when I read someone's Tarot cards. Or perhaps she would give me a good meditation. Amma always came through with flying colors. I experienced her influence many times but I still thought that I could never follow a guru. I would not be taking responsibility for my own life if I gave my soul over to someone else, was how I felt. I could only follow God, not a human being. It never occurred to me that a being like Amma could be one with God.

One day I saw Amma in one of my meditations. I saw her very clearly and after a year I can still see her. She was sitting in a lotus posture on a brown grassy hill. I was some distance away when she turned towards me and smiled. I saw her face with the nose ring and the white sari covering the bun at the back of her head. The vision seemed so commonplace and insignificant. Only now I realize that it was very special. I have not seen her like that since. What I do
continued on page 162 .

Growing Devotion

One day my mom told us that we were going to get a hug from a saint. I did not know what a saint was. I thought that a saint was a person from India; not like a god but like a person from India. We went to the program and before we went inside, we took off our shoes.

I was scared of Amma at first and did not want to get darshan from her. I kept asking my mother what I was supposed to do when she hugged me. I felt nervous.

We waited in a long line. It was hard sitting on the floor and I wished I had brought a pillow. I wanted to get up and run around but when I looked, nobody was running around.

> *Satsang is the best thing for spiritual advancement. By going there, one can attain peace and concentration.*
>
> – *Amma*

To me, everyone looked like they were from another country.

When it was our turn for a hug, I felt like walking away from Amma because I was still scared. When she hugged me, I just wanted to go home. She whispered something in my ear, which also scared me. She then hugged my brother, mom, and stepdad, and then she hugged us all together. Afterwards she gave us kisses, I mean chocolate kisses. Then we left.

I started to like Amma when we began going to satsang over a year later. Amma came again in November 2001 and I had my second darshan from her. This time was different because I was not scared of her and also liked her more. I still did not understand what she whispered into my ear but I don't know if that makes any difference.

In December, I attended the kids' retreat at the M.A. Center with my brother. I learned to say *Om Amriteshwaryai Namah* after each of the hundred and eight names of Amma. I also learned a little about meditation.

My mom chants the hundred and eight names every morning. Occasionally I sit with her and repeat *Om Amriteshwaryai Namah* after each name. Sometimes I fall asleep before the chanting is over. At night, we put Amma's picture on a chair, and sing the arati to Amma before going to bed. I like singing the arati and moving the lit camphor around Amma's picture.

During the November visit, I got my beanie baby blessed by Amma. I also have a picture of Amma that is decorated with a dried garland. Whenever I feel bad, I light a candle, sit in front of the picture and talk to Amma. I know She can hear me.

I am looking forward to Amma coming in June 2002. I want to ask Her for a spiritual name this time.

Laura Kane, 10, lives with her family in California, U.S.A. She finished her second grade in school and started homeschool in the third grade. She has three hamsters. Her main interests are drawing, life science, rocks, and miner

see of her now during meditation takes considerable concentration and effort, and in fact I have trouble seeing her most of the time.

When Amma came again in June 2001, I thought I would go for one more hug. My husband accompanied me. My kids were very clear about not wanting to see Amma again so I did not push them to come.

I am not exactly sure how it happened, but somehow as I was watching Amma hug people, I suddenly started to see how selfless she was. Here I was, antsy just a few minutes after sitting in the hall. Amma, on the other hand, was there most of the day and would be there most of the night too, hugging people. It began to sink in that she did this almost every day of her life.

All of a sudden I felt so unclean inside; so selfish and unaccept-able and yet she was going to hug me as if I were OK. The whole realization was more than I could bear. I have a revulsion about crying in front of anyone, let alone in a public place. However, as I watched Amma and those she hugged, I began sobbing uncontrol-lably. I would get myself under control somehow and then look at her only to start crying all over again. I carried on in this way for at least half an hour and it seemed like I would never stop.

It was with a mixture of embarrassment and shame that I got into the line with my husband, sobbing as silently as possible. I cried all the way down the aisle and into Amma's lap. She held me like a long, lost child. It was only for a few moments. Again I don't remember the actual hug, but it was enough for me to feel truly loved and accepted.

I did not have money for the retreat, but I signed up anyway. It was too expensive for both my husband and me to attend and since he was not that keen about it anyway, I signed up alone. During the retreat, I received darshan every day and basked in a peacefulness and tranquility that I had never before felt. I felt loved and did not think about anything else except Amma and God. No family, no work, no conflicts, no school, no ex-husband! Nothing existed outside the ashram grounds for me. I was truly in heaven on earth! I just wanted to be with Amma, nowhere else!

I walked away from the retreat feeling close to Amma and to my God. I sensed that I had somehow changed. I was much calmer around my children and they reacted favorably in turn. I did not have as many knee-jerk reactions when talking with my ex-husband. My overall relationship with the people around me improved.

I started reading the *Awaken, Children!* books and more and more problems and bad habits started to resolve themselves. After reading about how emotions, especially anger, limit one's spiritual capacity and create karma, I tried to see Amma talking to me whenever someone said something irritating or hurtful. If this were God testing me, how would I respond? With anger? No! I would swallow my pride and really try to listen. It was not easy but with Amma's Grace, I was slowly able to change in this way.

For a few months, I still had trouble understanding how Divinity could be in a human being. But I finally accepted it as it had changed me. Amma removed some of my bad habits and increased my capacity to turn my attention towards God. How could someone do that if they were not immersed in the Divine?

So was it a dramatic experience for free? No, the hug was for free but I had to work hard for the changes, although Amma gave a lot by Her Grace. Was it life-changing? Yes, definitely. I am very different now than I was nine months ago. I am constantly learning, growing, and developing new abilities. These changes have come about rapidly in comparison to very few changes over the last forty-five years of my life. I also believe that I will be able to say every year for the rest of my life, that I am a completely different person than I was the year before. My husband does not feel very devoted to Amma yet but I am confident that that will change! As for my two children, I will let them speak about their experiences in their own words.

Patricia Tanner, 45, lives with her husband Bruce and her two children, Elliot, 13, and Laura, 10, in California, U.S.A. She worked as a music director at a Unity Center until 2001 when she quit her job to start homeschooling her two children. She likes spending time on the beach.

Only the Driver

It is the deeper understanding of the Truth of the oneness of all creation, which teaches humans to love nature and to develop a sense of reverence and devotion to all.

— Amma

Back in the early spring of 1995, a co-worker gave me a magazine called *Yoga Journal*. I brought the magazine home. It had an article about Amma that mentioned that she was going to be giving a retreat at the Fort Flagler State Park on the northwest coast of Seattle. We live in southwestern Canada in a province called British Columbia, and Seattle is not too far from our home.

My wife Stefania took one look at Amma's picture in the magazine and immediately said, "I want to go see her!"

We planned our trip to see Amma in the summer of that year. My wife became the main driving force behind the trip. We decided to rent a motor home and drive down. I love to drive and was going only as the driver, not for any spiritual reasons. I did not really believe in all these eastern gurus. Everything I had read and experienced so far in my life told me that divinity lay within us and that real teachers were very few and far between. In fact, there was probably just one...Jesus the Christ. But Stefania wanted to go see Amma and that was that.

Two friends, Hans and Axel also joined us. Hans was interested in eastern spirituality and he wanted to meet Amma. Axel was curious and liked the idea of going on a trip in a rented motor home to an interesting-sounding experience. He also wanted a girlfriend and thought he could meet new people there.

We arrived at the retreat site on June 2, 1995, a Friday afternoon. It was a drop-dead beautiful spot by the ocean. We underwent a

> *...I was looking into a beaming face that murmured strange things into my ear while embracing and hugging me fiercely..."Weird!" said my mind.*
> — *Klaus Kollmann, Canada*

procedure not unlike checking into a hospital, and settled in. We were told to get to the hall early if we wanted good spots. We went and sat in anticipation. The place was decorated with an Indian flavor. There were many people, mostly dressed in white. Soon a chanting began.

"Strange!" said my mind.

The chanting rose in volume and suddenly a murmur ran through the hall. I heard conch shells sounding and saw a diminutive, dark woman standing by the door in a prayerful position. Someone was pouring things over her feet and waving smoky lights in front of her.

"Stranger!" said my mind.

This small person started coming to the front. She was waving and smiling and was stopping here and there to say a few words to someone or the other. I looked over to Stefania on the other side. We were separated because males and females were seated on either sides of the hall. She stood there, with tears streaming down her face.

"Odd!" said my mind.

Then came some interesting stories narrated by Amma, followed by music. Soon I found I was in something called a darshan line edging up to this person on my hands and knees. There was an incredible cross-section of people...young, old, male, female, children. Finally, it was my turn. After mopping my brow with Kleenex, I was looking into a beaming face that murmured strange things into my ear while embracing and hugging me fiercely. Something was pressed into my hand and a whitely dressed person quickly moved me to one side.

"Weird!" said my mind.

I met up with Stefania. When she said that Amma seemed very familiar to her and she felt as if she had come home, my mind warned that she was being drawn to something very unconventional from a western standpoint.

Saturday dawned. First, there was meditation and then a talk by a swami. The talk was extremely funny and I was glad that the day had started on a more normal note. Later, while in the darshan line, I closed my eyes momentarily when I suddenly had a vision of my ninety-five year old grandmother, Oma. My grandmother was a very spiritual person and a devotee of Mary, the Mother of Christ. I had heard stories about her younger years in Germany, when many people in the neighborhood would come to her with problems and were helped, miraculously. I was very close to my grandmother.

Now in my mind's eye, I could see Oma beaming at me. Her features dissolved slowly and became those of Amma! I spontaneously burst into tears. I cried all the way up to Amma's arms. She consoled me, as I sobbed and sobbed. I became aware of a wondrous scent of roses, emanating from her. I breathed deeply over and over again and slowly became peaceful in her arms. I then wandered away in a daze.

Outside in the bright, sunlit field behind the hall, laughter began bubbling from my throat. It became wilder and wilder until tears burst forth from my eyes. I suddenly saw a deer, almost within arm's reach, quizzically looking at me. This was a tame deer and many wandered all over the park.

I fell to my hands and knees, and sobbed and sobbed uncontrollably. As the sobbing slowly stopped, I saw an ant making its way through the grass. With perfect clarity, my eyes watched as it went here and there. In that instant, I knew I was one with that tiny creature, indeed with the entire creation itself. Words fail me as I try to explain the feeling...

The moment seemed to stretch into eternity. Suddenly my rational mind returned, with a snap. I looked around and saw with relief that I was alone and that no one had seen me making a fool of myself. I got up and wandered over to our motor home. A feeling of bliss remained all that day and the next. It subsided only over the next few days after we returned home.

Over the next year, I studied Hinduism and read about the qualities of a perfect teacher. Even though my Christian upbringing screamed "cult," "anti-Christ," and "false messiah," I had to admit that Amma seemed to fit all the criteria of a genuine teacher. When June rolled around again, I found myself going to see her again along with my wife, and our two children, Katrina and Josef, as well.

That year Amma gave me the spiritual name, Arun. In Hindu mythology, Arun is the charioteer of the Sun God, Surya. Yes, I had gone to see Amma only as the driver, but She had caught me in the snare of her unconditional love. Hans and Axel also became devotees. Axel even found a girlfriend.

Today, through Amma's grace my entire family loves Her. We have been able to see Her every year since our first meeting. However, our wish is that we could live closer to Her and see Her more often. Here, in our small town of eight thousand, we seem to be the only ones attracted to Her and there are no other devotees that we know of. Please Amma, next life, let us be reincarnated closer to you, if only as flies buzzing around your head!

Klaus Kollmann lives with his wife and two children in Revelstoke, British Columbia, Canada. Revelstoke is a small town surrounded by high mountains and gets snow about four months in a year. Klaus works with people with special needs in this mountain community to create work opportunities for them. As a result of their work, cardboard and paper is recycled and a home recycling pickup service is planned.

Mother of All

Real love exists in the heart. This love cannot be spoken and cannot be put into words. Words are in the intellect. In words, there is no love, only ego. Go beyond words and language, to the heart.

– Amma

In May 1995, I was in Tokyo one day for some work. As I was walking to catch a train to go back home, a young woman approached me and asked me the way to the station.

"I am also going there; you can walk with me, if you like." I replied.

As we started walking together, she told me about a program in Tokyo the next day. "You will enjoy it, Indian people will be playing Indian music," she said. "You should come."

I couldn't really understand what she was talking about or why she was telling me this. It was unlikely that I would come to Tokyo on two consecutive days from my home in Chiba, a good two-hour ride by train. I just smiled back at her without saying anything. We parted at the station and I never saw her again.

The next day, I felt very restless. I wanted to go to the concert, but I could not understand why. I left everything and caught a train to go to Tokyo again. I asked many people on the streets and in the shops, before someone finally gave me the correct directions. I arrived at the hall after four hours!

The concert had already started. On the stage, a woman and five or six men were singing and playing some musical instruments. They were all dressed in white. Suddenly, the woman looked up at the ceiling with arms open upwards and burst into laughter.

> Suddenly, the woman looked up at the ceiling with arms open upwards and burst into laughter. I was startled.
> – **Mituko Noguchi, Japan**

I was startled. The woman's behavior seemed a little strange. "The Japanese people are very shy and reserved. I wonder what they will think of her," I thought to myself. I did not even know the woman's name and it was not until I met her again, four years later, that I found out that she was called Amma.

Soon the music ended and the woman began to hug people, one by one. She had a big smile as she took each person into her arms, pressing her cheek against theirs, as if she really loved them. I watched, trying to understand what was going on. After some time, I noticed tears rolling down my cheeks. I felt blissful and the tears came from the bottom of my soul. I was moved to see the Indian lady loving my friends, the Japanese people, so much.

As she was about to leave, I stood at the back of the hall not sure about what to do. I had not gone for a hug. As she walked towards the exit, she gave candies to everyone. I received a candy too as she walked past me. She went all the way to the exit and then turned around to come back and give me another candy. Then she was gone.

On my way back home, I kept thinking about her. The great love, sweetness and beauty with which she hugged everyone filled me with respect and gratitude towards her. I had been interested in spirituality for some time and something told me that what I had just experienced was divine. However, there were many questions in my mind. "Was it really possible to experience inner growth by singing Indian songs that I didn't know the meaning of?" I would surely get frustrated, I thought. "I should learn how to clean my mind but in Japanese." I did not realize then that Amma's love surpasses all barriers of language. My heart was attracted to her , but my mind held back. Deciding that she was not right for me, I soon forgot about my encounter with her.

Four years later, in 1999, my family moved to Yomiuriland, Kawasaki from Chiba. Amma was visiting Yomiuriland in those days but I did not know that. One day I saw a poster on an electric light pole announcing her impending visit. I was surprised and delighted and I remembered my brief encounter with her four years ago. I decided to meet her.

On May 28, 1999, the first day of Amma's program in Yomiuriland, my husband and son dropped me off at the hall. I felt cheerful and did not really understand why. Amma was sitting in the front, hugging people in the same manner as four years before. When I saw people petaling flowers, I joined them not knowing this was blessed work called seva. After some time, someone else asked me if I had received a hug. When I said that I had not, she explained that I could join the queue to receive darshan.

Feeling a nervous excitement, I joined the queue. When I reached Amma's arms, she whispered something into my ear and pressed her cheek to my cheek. She was talking with a man next to her at the same time and I was put off by this seeming lack of attention.

"You should do your job with more sincerity," I thought to myself. I was disappointed. Of course, I did not know that Amma could pay attention to many people at the same time, giving each one exactly what was needed.

Something made me attend the program again the next day. As I sat waiting for the singing to start, I noticed a very bad smell in the air and felt sick. When the singing started, I got into the mood and clapped my hands in rhythm. After sometime, I noticed that the bad smell was gone. I knew that Amma's power had purified the hall.

The next year, I decided to travel to India to Amma's ashram. During my last darshan in the ashram, I wanted to tell Amma that I was leaving. In broken English, I said, "Tomorrow Tokyo go back. Good-bye."

To my surprise, Amma answered in Japanese! "Come back, come back," she said, repeating the same words many times. I was very touched by Amma's love and very sad to part.

After leaving the ashram, I traveled to Cochin to participate in the *Amritakuteeram* project with twenty-five Japanese college students who were helping to build simple houses for the poor and destitute. I was very impressed to see them working very hard every day, carrying heavy blocks, sand and water. For six days, I cooked for the students with the local people. This was a time to think of God and Amma, in the daytime under the dazzling tropical sun and at night under the stars.

In May 2001, I received a spiritual name from Amma. I am now also known as *Lavanya*, which means Goddess or beautiful thing.

When I first met Amma, I did not understand Her greatness. But today I understand Amma's real power. Today I know that Amma can purify everything, not just the environment. She is here to especially purify people like you and me. Today I can say that I am Amma's daughter. I wish I could give the love I receive from Her to you. I feel that Amma's great love will expand over the entire earth, wrapping everyone in its light. It will be so wonderful when all my brothers and sisters from all over the world will feel this ever lasting love. Om Namah Shivaya!

Translated from Japanese by Inagaki Naoko

Mituko Noguchi is 60 years old. She has been married for 38 years and currently resides in Chiba, Ichihara city in Boh-Soh peninsula, Japan with her husband and two grown sons. Her daughter lives nearby with her husband. Mituko currently leads a retired life after raising her family and working long hours without any holidays at many different jobs at a time when Japan was very poor.

Blue Tattoo

*Everything is pervaded with Consciousness.
To worship everything, seeing God in all,
is what religion advises. None of us would
consciously injure our own body because it
would be painful. Similarly we will feel the
pain of other people to be our own when the
realization dawns within us that everything is
pervaded by one and the same Consciousness.*
— *Amma*

It was a very rainy evening in the winter of 1990/1991. The cold, wet weather was no surprise, not in the Pacific Northwest…and especially not in Vancouver, Canada. We have beautiful, big trees here and they need lots of watering. I ducked my head against the onslaught of rain as my brother-in-law, his friend and I scurried to the shelter of Heritage Hall on Main Street. We were all interested in hands-on healing and my brother-in-law's friend had told us of a woman saint from India who would be giving a program in Vancouver that evening. I went thinking that she would give a presentation about energy healing. Well, she sure did!

As we entered the hall, I was appalled to learn that the women were to stay to the right, and the men to the left. At the time, I was studying law at the University of British Columbia, and was very active in my protests against biases in favor of men. To say the least, I was very, very prickly about the seating arrangement in the hall.

Seething, I sat down as directed at the back as close as possible to the center as I could. I looked up at the stage. A big-boned Indian man in orange, seated behind his harmonium, seemed to be the lead singer. A small Indian woman in white was singing with him and was

> *To say the least, I was very, very prickly about the seating arrangement in the hall. Seething, I sat down as directed at the back as close as possible to the center as I could.*
> *– Jill O'Carroll, Canada*

seated slightly behind him. The music sounded strange to my ears. The Indian man seemed aloof and arrogant.

Suddenly, the Indian woman in white arrested my full attention. She was moving her tiny brown hand in a smooth, circular motion from the wrist. I became aware of an overpowering change in the energy in the room. It felt as though the consciousness of all beings in the room had united! I felt as if I was floating in a sea of compassion and warmth! I sat in this kind of stupor until the music ended.

I thought I might faint from the intensity of this experience, so I broke my gaze from the stage at the end and looked around the room. People were shuffling to get to the middle to line up to the stage. The next thing I knew, the little woman was hugging people from a fancy chair up front.

It was obvious that it would be hours before my companions and I could go up for our hugs. I believed, given the obvious attitude towards women in the hall that I would have to wait for all the men to go up before my turn. This wasn't true, of course, but I didn't know it then. My daughter was very little at the time and I was anxious to return home to her.

I beckoned my brother-in-law to leave. He was very understanding and after he found his friend, we all left. But not before I noticed a lot of tacky Indian souvenirs for sale at the back of the hall. I was shocked to see these trinkets and it wasn't until much later when I read one of the pamphlets about Amma's charitable works that I understood their use.

I remember getting home that night and going in to look down at my little daughter in her crib. I was overcome by a feeling of incredible love and gratitude. I picked her up gently in her sleep and held her close for a long time. My marriage at that time was very painful and dysfunctional and yet, that night, the hell of it seemed to have lifted slightly.

I did not see Amma again until four years later. She did not come back to Vancouver and I did not know then that she visited the U.S.A. regularly. In May 1994, a friend who lived in Arizona, U.S.A., told me about her. When he informed me that she would soon be in Seattle, a four-hour drive from my home, I scrambled to take time off from my law practice so that my daughter and I could go to see Amma. By this time, my marriage had failed.

When we arrived at the little hall at Fort Flagler, it was raining (again!). My daughter and I waited, a little breathless and quite damp, for Amma to enter the hall. It was so wonderful to see her again. She created the same beautiful feeling of unity that I remembered from my previous meeting with her. I was entranced!

My daughter was only seven, so we were eligible to go up for darshan in the shorter family line. Strangely enough, however, my daughter bought flowers for Amma and wanted to wait in the adult line. We waited until midnight for our darshan. Amma gave my daughter a shining smile, took her into her arms and then turned to me. She appeared to glow and my heart felt as though it would explode in my chest.

Time stood still. There was no one in the world but Amma and me. I forgot everything and everyone, including myself. I heard her voice chanting "Ma, Ma, Ma," in my ear. I felt her warmth and smelled her beautiful scent. I felt my body melt and dissolve in a vast sea of loving presence.

Suddenly, I became aware that I was sitting back on my heels, looking into Amma's face. Her head was cocked to one side, like a little sparrow and she was smiling playfully. She wasn't dark brown anymore...she was blue! Her facial skin, her hands, her little foot sticking out from under her sari...were all blue!!

I knew very little about Hindu scriptures at that time, but I did know that the visages of many gods, goddesses and incarnations, such as Krishna, were depicted as blue. I understood that blue, the color of the ocean and the sky, was symbolic of the infinite consciousness of these beings.

In that moment of divine darshan, a feeling of wonderment, love, and awe were branded into my heart. I do not know how to explain it any other way. The feelings of warmth, strength, and unwavering support were tattooed on my inner being.

From that day on, the terrible disruption, confusion, and turmoil in my life began to ease. When we returned home, I put Amma's pictures throughout the house. Next year, we went to see her in Boston and I received a mantra. We saw her every year thereafter when she came to the U.S.A. in May and June. My daughter and I were in love.

Four years later, in September 1998, I attended a healing conference in Ireland where I met a long-time Amma devotee. Joe had been seeing Amma in Europe when I had been seeing her in the U.S.A. We took to each other immediately. I returned home after nine days, having agreed to meet him in Amsterdam nine weeks later during Amma's European tour, to ask her if she would bless our union and marry us.

We went to see Amma with great hope and trepidation. She took Joe in her arms and gave him a beautiful darshan. He nervously asked her if she would marry us, but she pretended not to understand him. Instead, she took me into her arms and while giving me darshan, whispered into my ear, "Marry you, marry you, marry you!" She released me, then looked at the two of us and burst out laughing. Joe, still unsure, asked her again. She looked at him, waved her hand in dismissal, and said, "Yes, Yes, Yes!!" Our delight was unbounded!! We stumbled away, blinded by tears of joy.

We were married in San Ramon, on the night of Devi Bhava, in June 1999. Amma has graced our home in every way ever since. When I spread Devi Bhava flowers in the garden, even the natural pests and blight disappear!! Her loving presence is always with us. Her abiding compassion helps us live in harmony with each other and deal with problems, confusions, and frustrations gracefully. It is very difficult to describe the changes that Amma has brought into my life and my family's life. All I can do is live in gratitude of Her endless blessings.

To sum up…my experience is that my first darshan never ended…it was and is a continuous embrace by the Divine.

Jill O'Carroll (Visala) currently lives in North Vancouver, B.C., Canada with her husband Joe (Hari Das) and daughter Emma (Rasa). She has a degree in law and practiced law until 1998 when she changed her career to pursue a lifetime interest in energy healing. She now works from her home with her husband. Jill likes gardens, animals, and children.

Refuge at Mother's Feet

*The experience of oneness with the inner Truth
is the goal of all religions.*

– Amma

Many people I talk to wish that they had met Mother sooner than they actually did. Whenever I read about or hear stories of the early days, I also feel envious of the intimate settings and beautiful experiences that people could have with Amma when the crowds were small. However, I know that everyone comes to Amma when the time is right and the circumstances appropriate.

I spent a lot of time setting the stage for my Guru's wonderful entrance into my life. I was first exposed to Indian spirituality during high school when I read about Gandhi and realized that his philosophy mirrored my own innate ideas about reality. I continued an academic study of Hinduism and Buddhism during my undergraduate education at the University of Virginia. The academic community there was very strong in Tibetan Buddhism and eventually I started identifying myself as a Buddhist. After graduation in 1994, I moved to Austin, Texas, in order to work with Tibetan refugees for the Tibetan Resettlement Project. This gave me an opportunity to spend much time with spiritual people from all backgrounds.

A woman I met there, Zana, was an Amma devotee. I agreed to accompany Zana to Dallas to meet Amma, more out of interest in spending time with a friend than anything else. When we arrived in Dallas, Zana was very determined to be there the moment Amma came and to stay until Amma left. I remember feeling out of place and being uncomfortable with people bowing and

> *A dilemma was created, however, when, while waiting for the mantra, I was asked my chosen form of worship.*
> *– Tony Stupski, U.S.A.*

touching Amma's feet. The crowd was big and the darshan line incredibly long. I waited for a long time until someone came up and asked if I could come back during the evening program to have darshan. I felt a little disappointed. Between programs, I couldn't relate to Zana's or her friends' enthusiasm for Amma.

At night, I joined the darshan line again. The closer I got to Amma, the more I began to sense the spiritual energy near her. When I was finally in Amma's arms, I just felt peace and a sense of timelessness. After getting darshan, I felt strangely happy as I walked around. A smile was on my lips from an inner feeling that I could not quite pinpoint. It was as if someone were tickling me from inside. The music contributed to my blissful state and little snippets of bhajans lodged themselves into my consciousness.

I woke up the next morning to the tune of *Teach Me the Language of Your Heart* playing in my mind. Strangely I felt just as enthusiastic as Zana to see Amma. During Devi Bhava, I knew inside that I had to get a mantra. A dilemma was created, however, when while waiting for the mantra, I was asked my chosen form of worship. Even though I felt very affected by Amma, I was not ready to make her the focus of my worship. I still felt as though I was a Buddhist so I requested for a mantra for Buddha.

The greatest part of my entire initial experience with Amma was the unbelievable darshan I received at the airport. I accompanied my friend Zana to see Amma off. When Amma finally walked up to where we were standing, a friend called out, "Amma, here is a new person for you!" pointing at me.

Amma turned and gave me the most beautiful smile I had ever received. She took me by the hand and proceeded to walk down the airport with me. She said, through helpful translators, that actually I wasn't new to her at all and that we had known each other in a previous life. I felt completely and utterly blown away.

I realized that all the things I had read and studied about mysticism and religion were indeed true. They were now being manifested in this beautiful Guru of mine. The magic of the moment really overwhelmed me. I waited until the plane actually took off and left with a sad but sweet feeling in my heart. I remember thinking how odd it was that I had waited for the plane to actually leave. I had taken so many people to the airport in my life, but had never lingered on for a good-bye for as long as I did that day with Amma.

After Amma left, I relished her feeling in my heart. The feeling lasted several weeks as I listened to the bhajan tapes I had bought, chanted my mantra, and meditated every day. I planned to go to India soon to teach English in a Tibetan refugee camp and figured that I could also spend time at Amma's ashram. After some more time passed, I became less consistent with my mantra and started becoming confused. Which religion was I following? Was I a Buddhist or had I become a Hindu? Was it right for me to chant a mantra to Buddha when I thought of Amma as my Guru?

After I went to India, my time became consumed with Buddhist practice in the Tibetan refugee camps, temples, and monasteries. I no longer felt any rush to go to Amritapuri. Eventually I made the trip to Kerala.

Once again I was blown away by Amma's spiritual power. My sense of connection was so strong that it felt other-worldly and magical. I realized that I had been foolish to not have gone there right away. Still, the question of my religious identify bothered me. I felt that I needed to clear it up.

I decided to ask Amma if the mantra she gave me was right. I thought to myself that if Amma said yes, then it meant that I was a Buddhist and that if she said no, I was a Hindu. When I got darshan and asked Amma that question, she gave me a strange look and burst into a great big laugh. I frantically asked the translator what her answer was, but he said that Amma did not say anything.

At first, I was incredibly disappointed not to receive an answer. After thinking about it for some time, however, I concluded that Amma actually did give me an appropriate response. She did not want to indulge my silly mind game of labeling the religious paths. What was important was that I did my spiritual practice, used my mantra, and tried to grow. The label was not important at all.

The other big question in my mind during this time was whether or not I could become a brahmachari. If spirituality is ultimately the only thing that was important in life, should I not just give everything up in the pursuit of enlightenment?

It didn't take me long to figure out that I was not ready to be a brahmachari. With great guilt, I realized I still looked at women even while I was at the ashram of my Guru attempting to dedicate all my time to spiritual practice. I understood that I wasn't ready to live the life of a monk. But I also knew that my partner had to be someone committed to spirituality and open to Amma.

I had met Sajeda while I was living in Texas. We had a great connection with very easy free-flowing conversation and similar interests. Her parents had come from Bangladesh to the United States in 1970, and were very traditional Muslim parents. Her father, an extremely devout Muslim, was the president of the Muslim association for the Bangladesh community. I appreciated his utter devotion to God but was very concerned about how they would react if Sajeda and I got married.

Sajeda started coming to Amma satsangs with me and really learned to love bhajans. When she met Amma for the first time the following summer, she took to her immediately. We had a great time following Amma's tour from San Ramon to Washington DC.

When we decided to get married, we were very relieved when her parents agreed to the marriage. Sajeda and I had the great blessing of having Amma conduct our wedding ceremony. This wedding ceremony was followed by a traditional Muslim wedding also. Whenever we visit my in-laws, I go with them to the mosque to pray. I sense the same universal presence of God there as in the presence of my beloved Amma.

Amma is a big part of our lives today and we are constantly striving to follow Her amazing example of selfless love for all of humanity.

Tony Stupski lives with his wife Sajeda and their daughter, Hana, 3, in Texas, U.S.A. Currently a medical student at the Texas College of Osteopathic Medicine, Tony is looking forward to starting work as a doctor soon. The family is expecting their second child in a few months.

7

Something, Not Sure What

> If Mother's words and deeds are contem-
> plated, not a single scripture need be studied.
> — Amma

Interviewing Amma

While doing one thing, your full attention should be in it. Only then will shraddha or loving awareness come. Actions done with shraddha will lead us to God.

— Amma

On Friday, July 14, 2000, I was just finishing up my work for the week when I received a telephone call about 5:45 p.m. My bureau chief at *People Magazine* was calling to ask if I would do a story about a woman who would be in Boston the following Monday "giving out hugs all day".

My response was, sure. How hard an assignment could that be? I figured the woman to be some sort of therapist. I received the assigning wire from *People* which gave the woman's name as Amma, without much more information. I didn't know if Amma was the woman's first name, last name or only name. I didn't know where she was going to be in Boston, or how to get in touch with her. There was no one left in the *People* office in New York to ask either. All I knew was that on Monday, someone named Amma was going to be somewhere in Boston giving out hugs and I was supposed to do a story about her. But how?

I went to the web and through a search, found her website at www.ammachi.org. There I found out that she wasn't a therapist at all. In fact, she wasn't even an ordinary human being. This woman Amma was considered a living saint in India. She fed fifty thousand hungry people a month in India and had built schools, hospitals, orphanages, and hospices. She neither proselytized nor espoused any dogma, only that people should be of service to the world. And she toured the world giving out hugs as an expression of compassion and caring. Most importantly, I learned that she wasn't going to be in Boston at all.

She was going to be in a suburb twenty miles north of Boston at the Rolling Green Ramada Inn. I called the hotel, but they had no one registered under the name of Amma and hadn't a clue regarding what I was talking about. I emailed

> *In all the years I have been a reporter and the thousands of interviews I have done, I have never ever had an experience that even came close to this one. It was transcendent.*
>
> *– Anne Driscoll, U.S.A.*

the contacts listed on the website, explaining who I was and what I wanted. I checked my email all day on Saturday but did not hear back from anyone connected with Amma. I began to panic. I needed to set up a photographer to be there first thing on Monday morning and even as late as Sunday, I had been unable to contact anyone from Amma's organization. What was I going to do?

I finally decided that I would drive up to the hotel Sunday night and see if I could find out anything there. I got to the hotel about 7:30 p.m. that night, entered the lobby and stood there wondering. I did not have to wonder for long. Let's just say, the saris were a dead giveaway. I approached two women wearing white saris and asked them if they were connected to Amma. It turned out that they were. One had been with Amma for about twenty years and the other for about five years. I interviewed them both and learned about Amma's humanitarian work and her early life growing up in poverty in a village near the backwaters of India. I left with a three-hundred page biography and two of her videos.

When I got home about 11:00 p.m. that night, I was like a college student at finals. I had to cram for the next day and cram fast. I found myself watching the videotape while reading the biography at the same time. Even while I was doing this, I could see the folly of my ways. I often tried to do several things at once, like watching *Charlie Rose*, reading the newspaper, flipping to another news program, and so forth. I knew that this did not help me retain much of what I wanted to absorb. In this case, however, I had to be ready by the next morning to interview Amma and I couldn't really help myself.

The next day I reached the hotel ballroom bright and early. There were about two thousand people who had come to see Amma and receive a hug from her. I sought out one of the Swamis and asked if he would arrange an interview. Since Amma does not speak English, the Swami asked me to write down seven or eight questions for Amma, which he would then translate to her.

I thought to myself, "How do you interview God? What exactly do you ask?" It was intimidating, to say the least, but I quickly scribbled down my questions and handed them to the Swami. He and I knelt beside Amma's chair on her right. He asked my questions and translated Amma's answers, while a continuous line of visitors kept approaching one at a time to receive Amma's hugs.

We finally came to my last question. "What do you hope for the world in the future?" I had asked.

"That people will be fully alert and present. Because when you are building the blueprint for a bridge, you should focus on the blueprint. And when you are building the bridge, you should focus on the bridge," she replied. Then she added, smiling, "And you shouldn't really watch television while you are conducting your studies."

I felt as if someone had kicked me in the chest. I sort of started half-crying and half-laughing, collapsing a little bit. I couldn't help it. She laughed a little. I smiled and thanked her and then kind of fell away from her chair. I spent some more time interviewing other people who were there. I heard some incredible stories, strange, miraculous stories that could not be explained.

In all the years I have been a reporter and the thousands of interviews I have done, I have never ever had an experience that even came close to this one. It was transcendent. I would have been a doubting Thomas myself were it not for my own experience. Amma returned to the same hotel this July. I was there. This time, though, not as a reporter.

Anne Driscoll, LCSW, is an award-winning journalist. She is a freelance writer and correspondent for People Magazine and the New York Times. She has published several books for pre-teens and is an adjunct professor of journalism at North Shore Community College in Boston. Anne lives with her husband and her three children, Maura, 17, Marisa, 15, and Colin, 12 in Swampscott, Massachusetts, U.S.A.

Vision of Forgotten Joy

Saranagati (complete self-surrender) is not something which can be taught verbally. Like love, it cannot be studied or learned from books. Self-surrender comes as love grows. In fact, the two grow simultaneously. The more you love a person, the more you surrender to him or her. This is what happens in a normal love affair between a man and a woman also.
— Amma

In February 1983, when I was in my early twenties, I was in Kathmandu, Nepal, attending a Buddhist seminar with my girlfriend. One day I met a lady who told me about Amma. She said that Amma was a young, saintly Indian woman who lived in Kerala, India. I had studied many different spiritual traditions and had met many saints but had never met a female saint. I asked her to tell me more about Amma.

"She lives in a fishing village near the sea," the lady said. "A few foreigners and a few Indians live with her. She embraces people as a form of blessing. You can be with her all day and ask her anything you like if only you can find someone to translate."

"I was able to meditate in her presence for a very long time," she added.

I did not feel very interested. The lady took out Amma's photo from her handbag and showed it to me. She explained that this was a picture of Amma in Devi Bhava, a special mood of identification with the motherly aspect of God. I examined the photo closely. A dark skinned woman in a red sari and a crown holding a trident and a sword in her hands, wearing many nose rings. It looked like a carnival costume to me!

> *The weaver of my fate was sitting right in front of me but I was not aware of it at that moment.*
> *– Lutz Domitz, Germany*

"Those Indians are funny," I thought to myself. "What does this have to do with my search for the deeper meaning of life?"

The lady looked at me and said, "You should go and experience for yourself how wonderful it is to be with her."

Hmm…I was not convinced.

"She will embrace you and touch your heart!"

"Ah, but I love my girlfriend…I don't need that," I responded with a wry smile.

As if making a last attempt, the lady said, "She will touch your third eye and reconstruct your inner being!"

Huh, what was that? Something in me responded. "That sounds interesting," I heard myself say.

"Perhaps I will go and see her. I can later tell my friends in Europe about the exotic woman I met."

I told my girlfriend about Amma but she was not interested. The lady's magic promise had me hooked however, and I decided to make the long journey from Nepal to Kerala, India, alone. After a short flight to Patna and several days in crowded trains, almost one full week later, I finally found myself on a small peninsula near the backwaters of Kerala. Only a few people were around. I noticed a tiny temple, a cowshed and a few palm leaf huts. A skinny Australian woman served me some tea and explained that Amma would come soon to sing and pray to God.

Soon a small dark woman in white appeared and sat down near the entrance of the small temple. The number of people had grown to about one hundred. There were only a few westerners. Everyone sat down on mats or on the sand in front of the temple. Some people went up to Amma and prostrated to her.

When Amma started singing, I had no clue what she was singing about and was not very impressed. "An Indian woman singing in a local language," I thought to myself. "What is so special about that?"

The weaver of my fate was sitting right in front of me but I was not aware of it at that moment.

The singing went on for an hour. Amma then went inside the temple and the doors closed. Someone told me that she would soon manifest her Oneness with Krishna. Although I had seen a few pictures of Krishna with a flute and a cow and had read a little about him in the *Bhagavad Gita* where he was described as God in human form, I had no clear idea of who he really was.

"And this woman can show her Oneness with him at will?" I silently wondered. "How does that really work?"

Soon the doors opened and I was invited to enter. Since I had come such a long way, I was given the privilege of entering soon after a worship ceremony called arati was performed. Not knowing what to expect, I stepped over the threshold into the tiny temple room filled with humid warm air and a pleasant incense smell. Pictures of Jesus and various Indian gods and saints greeted me.

There she was, the same Indian woman now wearing a small crown decorated with a peacock feather. A white sari with colorful scarves complemented her attire. One foot was resting on a small pedestal shivering almost constantly as if her body could not handle all the energy. My gut feeling was that something was not normal there.

Music and singing were interwoven in the hot, humid air. An almost tangible bright Presence, emanating obviously from her, permeated everything. Puzzled, I sat down on the bare ground and watched. Gradually my mood changed and my ever flowing thought stream calmed down. In this tiny temple, something had changed me without anyone uttering a word. It was as if I had just awakened from a dream. Or was this a dream?

Amma seemed to notice me and beamed a smile at me from across the room. The smile struck my heart. I looked at her somewhat bewildered. Another smiling look followed. A light flowed into me enlivening every cell in my body making them dance in joy. The vision of a young, fearless, deathless boy sprang from my heart. Was that I? Or was that she?

I forgot about myself and not knowing whether to cry or laugh, I just let go and allowed the flow to happen. My common sense, thoughts and doubts were all flushed away by the stream of life bubbling from within. My heart was bathed in joy.

Deep down in my heart of hearts, I already knew that what seemed to be normal life was not the entire truth of human existence. I sensed that the living proof of my faint comprehension of the Divine was standing there in front of me. I continued watching the scene quietly.

Amma in her Krishna Bhava stood in the corner of the temple effortlessly receiving person after person to bless them. People would wait outside and enter in small numbers to receive their blessings. Amma pressed her index finger on their third eye. Occasionally she looked at me. I asked her inwardly if I could come and get the magic touch, too. After a short while, I joined the queue and finally came right in front of her.

My heart was beating fast when our eyes met. Amma embraced me gently. She pressed her index finger between my eyebrows and I expected that a lot would happen. But I felt nothing, no miracle, no mysterious vision, nothing at all! With a mischievous smile, she looked at me and gave a gentle push gesturing for me to go back to my place.

She continued receiving people until the last person was seen. Stepping out of the temple door with everyone else, Amma then began to dance in blissful ecstasy with her hands raised high above her head and a blissful smile on her face. It was just a marvelous sight and I watched spellbound! Finally, she entered the temple and the doors shut behind her.

After about half an hour the doors opened briefly to reveal Amma praying inside to the Divine Mother. Then the doors closed again. Suddenly a wildly dancing Amma stormed out of the temple and danced, swaying her trident and sword. I watched in awe. I was torn between admiration and an unease about such raw, untamed display of female power.

After blessing people outside the temple, Amma entered the temple again and sat down on a little stool. Arati was performed to her and people were again allowed to go for darshan. I was still recovering from my darshan with Amma in Krishna Bhava and could not readily relate to her in this very different state. I watched until early morning when she finished blessing the last person.

I stayed with Amma for about three weeks. I totally fell in love with her and wanted to be nowhere else. Even with the rudimentary living arrangements, it was pure heaven! I returned to Nepal in about a month's time. I was so filled with joy! I talked about Amma to as many people as possible!

My girlfriend became very jealous and upset when she learned about my encounter with Amma. Later, she visited the ashram and had her first darshan with the blissful mother. Many visits followed over the years.

As for me, I decided to go to see Amma again. Soon I attempted to become a dedicated disciple under Her personal supervision. However, my ego revolted against the Indian dictum of "accept whatever it is as the leela of the guru." I found it difficult to completely trust and surrender my whole being to that mysterious Kali Goddess.

I was also simply scared of Her. I knew in my heart that having a close relationship with Amma would transform my being to the core but my fear of the unknown was greater than my trust and love for Her. After a few years, I returned to the west. In the material-oriented western world, I found it difficult to keep in tune with Amma and felt often pulled back and forth between India and Europe. For many years I was like a comet that was attracted by the sun but hurled away after a brief hot meeting.

My story with Amma has not ended. Almost twenty years after my first darshan, I feel an inner connection with Her which helps me to live in peace even though I may physically be far away from Her. I remember my first darshan with Amma in Krishna Bhava at times when life is not so bright. The Krishna-like boy I saw in my

heart then has not yet been born into this world. I pray daily for
him to come forth again.

---

*Lutz Domitz lives in Berlin, Germany, and works as CAD drafter and
IT consultant for small companies. He likes to hike and bike in nature.
He has travelled extensivly in Asia and has lived in Nepal and India
for extended periods.*

She Makes Me Cry

Children, tears wash away mental impurities.
Then we can smile with an open heart and
true happiness can dawn.

– Amma

I was seventeen when I first met Amma in July 1995. I was part of a youth orchestra and had just returned home after a two-week concert tour in Spain. On my return, my mother told me that she along with my father, sister and brother had met a very nice Indian lady saint the day before in Antwerp, Belgium. She wanted me to come along and meet her also. She said that the saint was very special and that it was really worth going.

I was not interested. Exhausted after my two-week long trip, all I wanted to do at that moment was sleep. Antwerp is at least a one-hour drive from our home in a small town in Belgium, but my mother insisted, so I reluctantly agreed to go.

Soon, my entire family got into the car and about an hour later, we arrived at the hall. We were not particularly spiritual people and I was feeling very tired, so I could not help wondering what we were doing there. There were a lot of people in the hall and it seemed to me that they were flaunting their spirituality with the white clothes, malas and bracelets that they wore. Up in front was the "nice lady saint" my mother had talked about. She was hugging everyone who went up to her.

There was no token system at that time, so we had to wait in a queue for our hug. I am the kind of person who is always observing everything very carefully in order to understand it. And here I was, queuing up, with no idea of what I was waiting for. I did not understand most of what I saw around me. I was also feeling

> *I did not understand what happened to me or what happened between us but the crying irritated me immensely...I could not help it, however, so I continued crying for sometime.*
>
> *– Hadelijn, Belgium*

self-conscious because I was wearing a really short dress that I had just bought in Spain. The wait lasted hours and hours and I became irritated, bored and very uncomfortable.

Something changed, however, when we were only about twenty meters from Amma. I suddenly became aware of her. The closer we went, the more she seemed to affect me, until when we finally arrived at her feet, I was crying uncontrollably. Amma looked at me, smiled and stroked my back a few times. Then she gave me a close hug and smiled again.

I did not understand what happened to me or what happened between us but the crying irritated me immensely. I felt very ashamed to cry in front of my parents, brother and sister and all the hundreds of people there. I could not help it, however, so I continued crying for sometime.

The next time we met Amma was one year later. During that year, I had read a few pages of an *Awaken, Children!* book that my parents had bought during our first trip, but I had not really thought very much about Amma. This time when we went for darshan, my only wish was that I would not cry. When we came closer to Amma, I again felt like crying but managed to hold it in and did not shed even a single tear. As soon as Amma let go of me, however, I could not hold it in any longer and ran to the toilet to cry and cry and cry.

Slowly, very slowly, I became close to Amma. Crying became an important part of my relationship with her. Over the years, I learned that it was not such a bad thing to cry in public. I learned to cry and enjoy the feeling.

Nowadays, if I see Amma and don't cry, I feel as if something is not right. A friend of mine who doesn't know Amma, once asked me what I do when I am with her. My father answered before I could say a word, "Oh Hadelijn, she is always crying when she sees Amma!" I was puzzled by his answer but in fact, he was right.

Crying has helped me release unknown burdens. By taking them away, Amma made me realise that I was carrying them. Crying is like a shower, which She turns on to clean the inner me. I hope that She turns on the shower many, many more times!

Today, Amma is the most important thing in my life. Before I met Her, I was just strolling around without any sense of direction. She brought me closer to my self and made me more confident. I am now slowly beginning to understand what I am doing here and why. Amma touched the rest of my family just as much as She touched me. All of us feel drawn to Her in our own ways, but with the same strength and intensity. She is the focus of the entire family!

Hadelijn, also known as Elisabeth Marie-Henriette, is 23 years old. She currently lives in Gent, a small, pretty, medieval town in Flanders, Belgium with her parents, younger brother Haiden and little sister Mangelamba. She has studied fine arts and is currently working as an art teacher in a secondary school. She enjoys playing the violin, visiting art exhibitions and travelling abroad.

Finally Found

Don't think that you are physically away from Amma. This is a doubt raised by your mind. Stop listening to your mind and you will feel Amma right there in your heart. Then you will know that Amma has never ever forgotten you and never will.

– Amma

In 1996, my wife and I, with our two children, Rune and Asger, then four and two years old respectively, had set out on a journey to India that would last six months. My wife and I both had an intense yearning for something other than the material and worldly and hoped to find it in India.

The day before New Year's eve, we found ourselves at Varkala, a tiny tourist spot in Kerala. We had already been away from Denmark for over two months by that time but felt greatly at home in India, and did not have any desire to return soon.

In the evening, while we were waiting for a meal at a restaurant, an American couple started playing guitar and singing. It sounded very American and country-like and had a western rhythm to it, but some words caught my ear and I started paying attention. They were, in fact, singing bhajans. I could recognise some of the melodies and the words. What joy!

Suddenly a fairly large man appeared at our table with some balloons. He was with the musicians and introduced himself as Ziggy. He started making hats and dogs and birds out of the ballons as fast as a magician. The kids loved him! We began talking to him about our travels in India. He told us about a woman avatar, Amma, who had a cosy ashram, not far from Varkala. We had never heard of Amma but he urged us to visit her ashram.

We had no set plans regarding where we would go next, so
we decided to follow his advice.
We took a taxi to Kollam and
then got on a backwater boat.
It took us about two or three

> *We outfitted the children with fine clothes for their first meeting with Amma…they found Amma quite funny.*
> *– Peder Rosenkranz, Denmark*

hours to reach Amritapuri. The boat was about to go right past the
place when we suddenly realised that this was it! We saw a thirteen-
storey apartment building still under construction, visible from the
backwater canal over the tops of the palm trees. Ziggy had told us
to keep an eye out for this landmark. The boat left us and went
away. We were all by ourselves and had no idea what to expect.

We walked for about twenty or thirty meters in the sand and
came to a small house with happy-looking people relaxing outside.
We asked for directions to Amma's ashram and they pointed the way.
We continued walking along a high wall and entered the ashram gates.

Lots of noisy construction was going on and many people were
moving about. Everybody seemed busy but calm. There was a
temple right in front of us. We were feeling a little lost. As we were
walking towards the temple steps, our feet bathing in the sand, I
had a warm feeling of coming home, a sense of belonging. On the
surface, we all felt quite confused and lost, but at the same time,
there was this feeling of coming to an oasis.

Before we reached the temple steps, a tall, thin and almost bald
fellow dressed in white came to greet us. He welcomed us to the
ashram. When he heard the children speaking in Danish, he beamed
and started talking to us in Danish also! His name was Christian
and he was from a tiny town in Denmark, north of Jutland. Leaving everything behind, he had come to stay in the ashram, hoping
to become a permanent resident. By this time, Christian had been
living there for more than two years.

He told us that he had just finished his meditation on the roof
when he noticed our small party of four landing at the jetty. Seeing that we looked confused, he decided to meet us, not knowing
that we were also from Denmark and that this was our first visit to

Amritapuri. We felt blessed by this unexpected hand of welcome. During our stay in Amma's ashram, Christian became our closest companion. He was a good teacher for our infant spiritual consciousness.

After we settled into our rooms, we decided that I would go alone for Amma's darshan. We felt that this was the most convenient way with the kids since we expected the familiar hustle, bustle and crowding of Indian masses at any gathering. However, when I went into the temple, I was amazed to find that people were lined up neatly and seated quietly. Most were dressed in white clothes.

From a distance Amma looked small, but I could sense something very powerful and energetic radiating from her. The air was rich with incense and the intoxicating music. I joined the darshan line. When I was only two or three metres away from Amma, my jungle of thoughts receded. The room and the people seemed to fade away and my focus was solely on Amma. No thoughts, no distractions...just a feeling of gentle contentment and child-like happiness.

Darshan was over all too quickly. I longed for more of that contented feeling. The next day, my wife and children also went for darshan. We outfitted the children with fine clothes for their first meeting with Amma. They sat fairly patiently in line and did not seem bothered by the heat or the long wait. When our turn came, they received big, warm hugs and lots of attention from Amma. They found Amma quite funny. My wife also felt very happy after the darshan.

We stayed for eighteen days in the ashram. Needless to say, we attended darshan as often as possible. We also participated in seva and helped to clean pots and pans and prepare food in the kitchen. We attended yoga and meditation classes, read spiritual books and had many deep conversations with Christian. There was this wonderful feeling of having finally found what we had set out to search for. We worried a little that we might not be able to recreate this peaceful and contented state once we were back home in Denmark.

We truly enjoyed being together as a family more than ever before. There were no worries, troubles or anger. The kids were happy, though they couldn't exactly tell why. During one darshan, my wife and I asked Amma if we should have one more child. Amma laughed and asked "Why? Isn't two enough?" She smiled affectionately at our boys and handed them some extra candy. As we got up, Amma added, "Wait for some time, then have a child." We felt utterly blessed, no matter what happened in the future. Today, our third son Johnnes is three years old.

We left for Madurai with hearts full of peace and joy and a fresh outlook on life. We felt so blessed by our meeting with Amma and our stay at the ashram. We travelled around south India for another three months, thinking almost daily about the ashram and trying to implement the peace and contentment we had felt there into our daily lives. It was not easy and at many times we felt the urge to return to Amritapuri. Returning home to Denmark was even harder because Amma was not there.

Next year, we saw Amma on her European tour in Sweden and Finland. These were times of bliss in an otherwise dark and cold world. For a long time, we had tried to live at home more or less like we had at the ashram but it had not worked out. We had returned to common worldly living with T.V., shopping, parties and vacations.

After our second meeting with Amma, I slowly started realising that Amma is always there showing the way, guiding and assisting. We need to go inside ourselves to find Her. Only then can She become more and more a part of us. Today, I think we are slowly being guided by Her in the right direction. My family and I have been rewarded with a greater serenity and a greater sense of meaning in our lives. With love, from Peder, Janne, Rune, Asger and Johannes.

Peder Rosenkranz lives with his wife Janne, and their three children Rune, 9, Asger, 7, and Johannes, 3, in Kalundborg, 100 kms west of Copenhagen, Denmark in a country house together with a cat, some chickens and a lot of rabbits. Both Peder and Janne work as physiotherapists. They love travelling around the world.

Searching for Love

*If you have faith, you can leave everything in
the hands of the Guru, whatever the situation
may be. The Guru's hand will be there to
protect you.*

– Amma

My first darshan with Amma was in October 2001 in Muenchen.
I had known about her for three years. My yoga teachers, Rolf and
Cora, spoke of her again and again. They had told me that she is a
holy mahatma and had described the darshan she gives. Each year
they had asked me to drive with them to see Amma. I didn't like
being in gatherings of several hundreds of people and the thought of
having to stand in a long line had held me back from accompanying
them. Perhaps the right time had not yet come.

In October 2000, I ordered Amma's biography in German from
Verein Amrita e.V., Amma's organisation in Muenchen, to learn more
about her. After reading the biography, it became clear to me that I
wanted to see Amma the following year, no matter what! Soon after
this, I met Beate. Beate was moving to Amma's ashram in India and
was winding up her affairs in Germany. She told me many beautiful
stories about Amma and how wonderful it is to be with her. Soon I
found myself ordering all Amma's books available in German. I read a
few volumes of *Awaken, Children!* and *Eternal Wisdom*. To my surprise,
I found that other books didn't interest me anymore.

My inner connection to Amma was developing. My thoughts
were often with her and I started impatiently waiting for her next
visit. I wanted to meet Amma personally and lay in her arms. I
started attending bhajans and learning the auspicious mantras.

Slowly my life began to change. The changes grew from day
to day. In February 2001, I totally changed my diet to vegetarian
food. I stopped drinking alcohol and watching T.V. I had no interest

in meeting friends who didn't know Amma. I voluntarily started waking up every morning at 5:00 a.m. to practice yoga, pray, chant and meditate.

I felt as light as a feather. It seemed to me as if I had just woken up.
– Saskia Schulz, Germany

And I eagerly awaited Amma's visit in October.

Finally the day came. I drove in a rented bus to Muenchen with Cora, Rolf and six others from our bhajan group. We left early in the morning and arrived around 1:00 p.m. As we entered the hall, my heart suddenly began to pound wildly. At first, I couldn't see Amma at all, because so many people were in the hall and so many impressions were bombarding me. Then Rolf pointed her out to me. She was sitting in a chair in the front giving darshan. I felt like breaking into tears as soon as I saw my beloved Amma. Somehow I controlled myself.

I longed to run up to Amma and just throw myself into her arms. The others in our group decided to go for darshan that evening. In a way, I was relieved because I would have surely cried in Amma's arms and I didn't really want to do that in front of everyone. After just a short time, I saw Beate. I couldn't believe it! I was very happy to see her again as I was not even sure whether she was in India or Germany. Beate found me a seat right next to Amma. I sat there for many hours observing Amma and the people who lay in her arms. I felt the love and warmth that they experienced. My mind was completely quiet...it was just indescribable...

In the evening we picked up our darshan tickets and waited in line with other devotees. I was a little anxious. There were flyers with information about how one should approach Amma and support one's self, so as to not physically burden Amma's body. I was hoping in my heart that I would remember everything when my turn came.

As we slid closer to Amma, my anxiety slowly disappeared. I became peaceful as I watched Amma hugging person after person. Then it was my turn and my head was pressed into Amma's arm. I felt her hand on my head and heard a rushing sound as she said something into my ear. I could have stayed in this position for hours but it went by quickly and I stood up.

I felt as light as a feather. It seemed to me as if I had just woken up. I don't really know how to explain this. I could still smell Amma's fragrance, even hours later as I lay in bed that night…it was just heavenly…

We stayed in Muenchen for three days. I experienced a peace and inner tranquility I had never known before. I also saw something new every day. There were tables with jewelry, audiotapes, books and Amma dolls. There was an astrologer and lots of information about Amma's charitable projects. I helped with some seva, which was fun. It was strange but the big crowd did not disturb me at all. During these three days, I hardly slept. We always stayed until the end of the program and were back again the next morning, but I did not feel tired at all.

During Devi Bhava, I asked Amma for a mantra and received it. This was a very, very beautiful and moving experience. After these three days, instead of returning home with my bhajan group, I decided to follow Amma to Bonn. I spent two days with her there, and was able to lay in her arms again each day. Every hug was special.

My husband and I had separated in June 2001. Right after this meeting with Amma, I was to finally move into my own apartment. The move went smoothly. I did not take much with me and trusted that Amma would help me handle everything. She did. Today my life is slowly getting back into order. I feel that Amma has been very generous with me. I really thank Her for the blessing of being close to Her. I can't quite put my feelings for Amma into words, in the way that I sense them, but I can only bow in deep humility before Her.

Translated from German by Dania Edwards and Jake Urech

Saskia Schulz is 40 years old and currently lives in Nordrhein, Westfalen in Germany. After being a housewife and mother, she recently started working as a secretary in a notary public office after separation from her husband. Her daughters Melanie and Mauela are both grown and live in their own apartments. She also has a son Patric from an earlier marriage who lives with his father and often visits his mother.

8

Slowly, Over the Years

Love just flows. There are no terms or conditions. All who are willing to take the plunge and dive in, will be accepted as they are. If you are not willing to dive in, what can it do? Love remains where it is. Love never says no. It is only constantly saying yes, yes, yes...

— Amma

Amma's Mritasanjeevani AIMS

There are hundreds of educated and experienced children who have come to join the ashram. This is how so many institutions have come up. When children who were doctors joined, the ashram began to run hospitals. This is not just work for these children, but part of their sadhana. Amma will say that even the breath of one who serves the world forgetting oneself, is beneficial in every way.

– Amma

We had always been a traditional God-fearing temple-going family. We had heard of Amma from relatives and friends but had never met her. I remember that in 1996, one Sunday morning, I watched a TV program about Amma. This was the first time I saw her giving darshan, hugging perhaps hundreds of people, one after another. I was impressed to hear her simple words of advice and felt drawn to her. I still remember the first bhajan I heard her sing, *Amriteswari, Jagadeeswari, Surapoojithe Saranam.*

At that time, we were a small family of four, my wife Sreedevi, son, daughter and I. I had just retired after working for thirty-four years in a private sector company in Mumbai. We were planning to move to Kerala, our native state, in November 1996 to settle down in Ernakulam. After seeing the TV program and learning that Amma's ashram was only about two to three hours away from our new home, I decided to surely visit her after moving to Kerala.

Amma's glowing face remained vivid in my memory for many days after the TV program. Sadly, however, with the passage of time, I forgot all about her. In November 1996, the move to Ernakulam in Kerala happened as planned. Soon after, my son left for the U.S.A. to work for a company there. My wife, my daughter and I became busy with trying to settle down in a new place. Life went on as before and the thought of visiting Amma did not occur to me.

Over one year passed. In December 1997, my wife lost her father. My mother had passed away about two years earlier while we were still living in Mumbai. These two incidents so close together made us very sad. Instead of leading a peaceful and retired life, our minds were agitated and we led a restless life.

> *"Did you lose everything, my daughter?" Amma asked her in Malayalam after listening to the entire story.*
> *– K. Jayadevan Nair, India*

In February 1998, we went to a nearby town to visit some relatives. When we returned, we were shocked to find that our home was burgled. The thieves had mercilessly ransacked the entire house and had made away with a number of valuables. It was a heart-rending scene and my wife felt completely shaken. Never before had anything like this happened to us. We felt helpless and forlorn.

At this time, a neighbor suggested that we visit Amma to calm our troubled minds. He offered to take us to her ashram in Vallikkavu. I instantly remembered the TV program I had seen almost two years ago. My wife and daughter agreed to go with the neighbor to meet Amma. I decided to stay back as we did not want to leave the house unattended again.

On Thursday, February 12, 1998, just a week after the burglary, my wife and daughter met Amma for the first time. It was a Devi Bhava night. When my wife's turn for darshan came, Amma embraced and kissed her. My wife broke into tears in Amma's lap. She narrated to Amma everything that had happened. Exuding kindness and love, Amma listened to her and consoled her.

"Did you lose everything, my daughter?" Amma asked her in Malayalam after listening to the entire story. Without waiting for an answer, Amma beckoned to her to sit nearby.

Mother's simple words often carry profound meaning. By asking my wife whether she had lost everything, maybe Amma had meant to remind her that not all was gone. Life was much more than just material possessions.

My daughter also felt very happy after meeting Amma. She bought many books from the bookstall to learn more about Amma and her teachings.

I was amazed to see the transformation in my wife when they returned home. She seemed completely recovered from her shock. She seemed to have off-loaded her burden by telling Amma everything and Amma's soothing touch and endearing words seemed to have worked like magic to heal her bruised mind.

None of the stolen items were ever recovered and we slowly bought and replaced some essential things. About a month later, Amma's senior disciple, Swami Poornamritananda Puri visited our house and performed a puja. He suggested some alterations in the house according to *Vastu Shastra*, the ancient science of construction in tune with the universal prana. Accordingly, we shifted our kitchen and puja room to the correct directions.

After making the alterations, it was my turn to meet Amma for the first time. On Thursday, April 9, 1998, I went to Vallikkavu to see Amma during Devi Bhava. Upon arriving, I felt as if I had entered a different world altogether, the abode of the Divine Mother Herself! Devotion pulsed through the atmosphere as holy mantras were loudly chanted and devotional songs were sung. The whole atmosphere was so enchanting. I sat in the darshan hall and watched Amma from a distance.

Around half past midnight, I reached near Amma after standing in the queue. I kneeled and lay in her lap. She held me in an embrace and said something in my ear, which I did not understand. I requested Amma to give me a mantra. She agreed and asked me to sit nearby.

Meanwhile Amma continued to give darshan to others. I was in no great hurry to receive my mantra and almost ten minutes elapsed when she suddenly turned to me, almost apologetically, and softly whispered the mantra in my ear. Such humility! Here was *Jagatmata*, the Universal Mother, apologising to me for making me wait for a mere ten minutes!

After receiving my mantra, I continued to sit beside Amma for some more time. Then I came back to the hall and spent the rest of the night watching her and listening to bhajans. Even though I had booked accommodation in a nearby building, I did not go there at all.

After meeting Amma, life was not the same for us. A feeling of normalcy returned soon and the theft was forgotten. Our loneliness also vanished as we started attending Amma's bhajans regularly and feeling one amongst her large family. Slowly we began to understand the great truth behind Swamiji's words.

"Now that you have come to Amma, don't worry. Everything will be all right."

A month after my first darshan, on May 17, 1998, we attended the inauguration of the Amrita Institute of Medical Sciences (AIMS), Amma's super specialty charitable hospital in Ernakulam. This was a very big event for the entire state of Kerala and the Prime Minister of India came to inaugurate the hospital. Inspired by Amma, my daughter who was already working as a doctor in Ernakulam, had applied for a position at AIMS. The day after the inauguration she started working as a Resident Medical Officer in the Internal Medicine Department.

Over the next two years, she happily put in long hours at her job. She daily narrated to us many cases where patients were brought without any hope for recovery and yet, just in a few days, were brought back to stable health. The magic seemed to be the nourishment provided by human kindness and love and the intensive care. She reluctantly quit her job, when in July 2000, she was married with Amma's blessings and left to join her husband in the U.S.A.

In September 1998, when my son came to visit us, we took him to Amma's ashram. He was very excited to meet Amma who left an indelible imprint on his young and receptive mind. In February 2001, his marriage was arranged with Amma's blessings. He and his wife were recently blessed with a newborn son.

After our children's marriages, my wife began working as a volunteer at AIMS in its pediatric ward. The pediatric ward has, at any given time, about forty or fifty children suffering from various ailments. Amma's devotees have donated many toys and books from all over the world that are used to cheer up these kids. My wife's role is to support the nursing staff by spending playtime with them as well as by talking to parents about their concerns.

A few months later, I also started volunteering at AIMS. My first assignment was to hand out visitors' passes in the Outpatient Department. I was amazed to see the large number of people from different backgrounds, many of them very poor, coming every day to receive state-of-the-art treatment. Never had I imagined that such a thing was even possible! Highly specialised treatment, but given totally free to those who cannot afford it!

After some time, I began working in the pharmacy stores conducting inventory. Volunteers at AIMS are not necessarily given work related to their past work experience. In this huge hospital complex plenty of odd jobs are available that can be done well by elderly and retired people without over-burdening them. This is no doubt Amma's Grace and my wife and I are very grateful for this opportunity to perform selfless work. We get immense satisfaction even though our contribution is very meager.

AIMS is Amma's *Mritasanjeevani*, a mythological herb said to resurrect the dead. Amma's unseen hands are at work behind each and every task accomplished here. Today, this hospital stands as a towering monument of Amma's love and compassion for the suffering millions.

K. Jayadevan Nair lives in Kerala, India with his wife, Sreedevi. The couple have two children, Dhanraj, 32, and Jayashree, 28, and were recently blessed with their first grandson, Avinash. Jayadevan worked for 34 years in an engineering company in Mumbai, India, as a Purchase Executive before retiring in 1996. He spends his spare time reading books and writing poems.

Returning Home

Life is a mystery. You cannot understand it,
unless you surrender, for your intellect cannot
grasp its expansive and infinite nature, its real
meaning and fullness. Bow down low and be
humble, then you will know life's real meaning.
— Amma

I lived in Austria for twenty-five years before I met Amma. For the first seven years, I studied Catholic theology, where I filled my head and heart with information about Christ, Christianity and the Church. I was convinced that only Christ could be called *Son of God*. He was a unique incarnation of God in this creation.

After finishing my degree, I turned to psychology. After completing my studies, I started working as a psychotherapist. One day, in 1987, I heard my co-workers talking about a young Indian saint who was coming to Austria for a few days on her first world tour. Spirituality generated a lot of interest among us as we always tried to see whether it could help our therapy. However, arrogant as I was, I firmly stated that our work aimed to free people from all dependencies, so I did not see any point in going to see another one of those gurus.

One of my co-workers was a nice, young man named Hans. He went to see Amma with some other people. When they came back, Hans shared with me his belief that Amma was God incarnate. Hans had undergone the same training in theology as myself, so I expressed my doubts to him.

"How can you really trust that Amma is one with God? Even to go as far as to say that Amma is God incarnate?" I asked him.

> *I planned to see Amma and then return home quickly…Returning home, however, turned out to be a bit different.*
> *— Yvonne Lanners, Luxembourg*

Hans responded that he had no intellectual proof, but that he knew this to be true in his heart. He said that he felt a peace of mind that he had never felt before, and also saw this for other people.

"What about the concept of reincarnation?" I continued. I knew a little about eastern spirituality and its beliefs. "As Christians, how can we accept that we are reborn again when we believe that Christ will redeem us from all our sins?"

Hans answered again in his quiet way that this had also bothered him at first, and that he did not want to betray his first great love, Christ.

"But," he continued "Christ did not say that we will grasp His message all at once. Maybe we need to put forth more effort and time to be one with Him, to understand what He was talking about and to receive His love fully in our lives. I can say that Amma has claimed me. Now I just have to respond to her call, get on my feet and move into action."

I continued questioning Hans and he replied with unending patience. I processed his answers within the frame of my western psychotherapist mind. I did not find anything to kick me out of my normal way of thinking and feeling. But my interest was awakened and I had to agree that Amma's teachings did not harm people.

As I look back today, I can clearly see that this was when Amma started to pull my soul and body towards her. However, with my attitude, I was not open enough to visit her and as a result, missed the very intimate moments during the earlier world tours. It was not until 1997, nearly ten years after I first heard about Amma, that I finally met her.

In August 1997, I decided to go to the program in Munich, Germany. This was the closest city that Amma was visiting. I am not sure what made me finally decide to go but I just told myself that I did not have much to lose. I knew some of my co-workers were on tour with Amma, but I was not sure whether I would see them there. I chose to go on Devi Bhava night because I knew from them that this was the last program. I would not have to stay long, I reasoned. Little did I know that Devi Bhava was a special ceremony that many people loved. I planned to see Amma and then return home quickly.

Returning home, however, turned out to be a bit different. As I walked into the entrance of the hall, people were being seated for some puja. I immediately started to cry. Within seconds, I found myself in a different state of mind, and was confronted with another person inside me, one I had sought all my life. I had studied Catholic theology to get clear answers about God and had been disappointed. Then I had turned to psychology, but the answers I had found were all for my intellect. Here, in the entrance of the program hall, my heart already felt its hunger satisfied. My mind stopped functioning. I sat there with my tears, completely defenseless, open and overwhelmed.

When I finally got up to Amma, I just collapsed and surrendered. Deep in my soul, I knew that I had finally returned home and that my wandering, searching soul could now rest in Amma's motherly arms. In this very first meeting, I asked Amma for a mantra. When she said yes, I felt deeply grateful to become part of her blessed family.

After that night, when Amma accepted me as Her darling daughter, my life changed and my attitude at work changed. But that is another story, one that is in full progress.

Yvonne Lanners was born and raised in Luxembourg. She later moved to Vienna, where she studied and worked for over 25 years. She married an Austrian man and they had two children, but later divorced. After the death of her ex-husband five years ago, she moved back to Luxembourg and currently works and lives there with her family.

From Judgement to Devotion

Children, when we see a lawyer's garb we
are reminded of our case and its success.
When we see a postman we are reminded of
letters. Mother's dress is to remind us of the
Supreme. The visual appearance of Mother
in Devi Bhava is to release us from our limited
perception of our Self and remind us of the
Supreme which is our true nature.

– Amma

My very first impression of Amma had formed in 1989 when I was visiting my friend, Lalita. Lalita had a fancy altar with many photos of Amma and flowers, incense, candles. I remember having shaken my head in firm judgement.

"How can anyone give their power over to another person?" I had wondered. "You, my friend, are just empowering another religion of dogma and followship."

I had quickly looked away.

Eight years later, in 1997, after I had failed at every single attempt to "help the world's poor and hungry" and had ended up in material poverty myself, I was visiting another friend, Noella, who had met Amma the previous year. She had a photo of Amma hanging on her wall. Amma's smiling face gazed at me, her hand on her cheek.

Suddenly, in a split second, it appeared as if the face came right out of the frame, becoming much larger and seeming very alive. My heart opened…in awe!

I was familiar with this phenomenon, yet it startled me. The previous year I had seen Paramahansa Yogananda's photo on his autobiography book cover. That picture had also jumped out at me and had seemed quite alive.

Both experiences lasted only a few seconds, but were very real to me. Perhaps after having experienced so many failures in the material world, I was becoming more open to looking deeper at life.

> *"Why do you allow this display of glitter?"* My eyes darted out disapproval at her, even while my heart begged to understand.
> **– Dania Edwards, Canada**

Two months later when Noella was preparing to drive down from Vancouver Island to Seattle to see Amma, I was unable to go with her, but requested that she bring a photo of Amma back for me. She returned with a photo identical to the one I had seen in her house; she had also taken it to Amma to have it blessed. Noella told me that when she said to Amma that the photo was for me, Amma had laughed with delight! Once again, I felt awed. I became intrigued to find out who Amma was.

Since Amma was still in a living human body, unlike Yoganandaji, I felt that I had to go and see her at the next possible opportunity. By this time I was convinced that she was someone special, maybe even the living saint I was longing to personally meet. "After all, why should all saints be dead?" I had thought to myself.

The following year I was prepared. I even registered for the retreat to give myself enough time to observe her carefully. One spring weekend in June 1998, nine years after I first heard of Amma, I drove with Noella, her husband and two friends to Fort Flaggler near Seattle. The small intimate retreat site seemed somehow familiar. We were in the midst of nature, by the ocean, in buildings with meadows between them, with the aroma of the ocean air all around! We camped in tents in a forested park within walking distance of the retreat hall.

My friends and I made our way to the hall early in the morning. I caught my first glimpse of Amma in the midst of what at that time seemed like a large crowd of people to me, but was actually only about three to four hundred. Most were wearing white and all were focused on one person, Amma.

"She is so small! And so wonderfully dark-skinned!" I thought to myself.

I remembered my friends I so loved while living in West Africa where I was the only white woman in the village. "Does she feel similarly now, surrounded by mostly white-skinned people?" I wondered.

The first hug from Amma holds one clear memory. I remember thinking, "At last I have found a sister! A sister who loves life and is so full of joy!" Today I cringe at my naivete. Calling the Mother of the Universe my sister! But Amma embraced me anyway. Of course, for me it was like a normal embrace from a sister. Little did I know what it actually meant.

In between programs, I followed Amma, along with many others, across the green meadow to her cabin. Amma was singing a simple, delightful bhajan, and we were all echoing her chants. It delighted my heart to watch and hear her sing with so much passion.

The memory is very strong. Amma swaying and dancing back and forth, clapping her hands, singing *Amba Bhavani, Jaya Jagadambe*. Everyone else was singing and walking in rhythm behind her, barefoot on the soft grass, with the ocean in full view. Children of all sizes, following their Mother! It reminded me of the picture of Jesus, surrounded by children coming to sit in His lap. That was perhaps one of my many interactions with Amma that weekend, which developed my impression of her from that of sister to mother.

Another time, I caught a glimpse of Amma's car. My eyes followed the car from a distance. A few small children were playing in the meadow near the road and they started waving to Amma as the car approached them. Her car stopped. Amma just snapped up one of the little children and the car drove away. I remember thinking, "How I would love to be abducted by Amma like this!" I learned later being invited by Amma to come up to her house was a very special treat that all small kids craved.

I learned to trust Amma in her simple white sari and her simple, sweet ways. She was approachable as a mother, and not like a big shot guru on a pedestal. Then came the evening of Devi Bhava. When the curtains opened, up on the stage, decorated with glitter and lights, sat Amma dressed in sparkling silk garments, glittering golden jewelry and even a large silver crown! This was a shock for me. My mind raced.

"What kind of a show is this, Amma? How could you betray the poor, dressed in this lavish way?"

I felt disappointed. As a citizen of a wealthy western country, even I could not afford to dress like that. Was this not exactly how Hollywood dressed its movie stars? In glitter and pomp?

"Why do you allow yourself to take on the role of the rich and wealthy?" I asked Amma in my mind. "Is it to please them? Why would you want to please them? They are the exploiters of the planet and of the people of this world. They torture for power, murder for gains, plunder to rule."

I remained sitting with my friends, stunned, but not saying a word. I continued watching with mistrusting eyes. Even as a child, I had noticed the big differences between the rich and the poor. I had grown up with a little more than most kids around me and had always felt awkward about this imbalance. I could still see quite vividly the many bare-footed, shabbily dressed, dirty children from the tiny house with broken windows next to my big white house.

In 1984, I lived with semi-sedentary folks in the Sahara desert in Mali, West Africa for a year. That year I saw one of the worst droughts in Mali that was created in part due to the western "donated" dams, upstream along the Niger river. I was witness to thousands of villagers fleeing to faraway towns and many dying of starvation, dehydration, and cholera along the way. Tens of thousands of survivors made cardboard or tin dwellings and lived in refugee camps on the outskirts of towns. People were sick and starving and very weak without food.

This was all in my mind as I watched Amma. She represented wealth gained from and used for the exploitation of land and people. I planned to just get up and leave.

"Why do you allow this display of glitter?" My eyes darted out disapproval at her, even while my heart begged to understand.

Suddenly something changed before my very eyes. My familiar Amma started becoming visible to me within the garb of Devi. I saw her compassionate smile, the sparkle in her eyes, and the loving way in which she held each person to her chest. My heart melted and my mind shattered. My eyes overflowed with tears, which started rolling down my hot cheeks.

"Please forgive me, Amma," I silently implored.

There she sat dressed as a queen, embracing all sorts of people, shedding tears with the sorrowful, laughing with the joyful, playing with the children with the same love and compassion for all. Slowly a question came into my consciousness.

"How many people in my life have I judged in this same way just from their appearance? What if there was a compassionate core within those people too?"

"Do I blind myself with judgement, like I just did with Amma?"

I sat there thinking. "I thought you had deceived me, Amma. But it is my very own mind that is the big deceiver." The understanding was slowly dawning.

Amma was revealing to me my judgements about the rich and wealthy in this world. She had burst through the walls of prejudice in my heart to begin healing me from those destructive thoughts. My judgements had kept her away from me for so long. My judgements had kept unconditional love and perhaps many people in my past and present away from me as well. It was as simple as that.

Two years after my first darshan, Amma gave me a spiritual name. Her eyes twinkled as She looked at me, smiled, touched my arm, and said *Sreemayi*.

"She who is permeated with the bliss of Lakshmi, the Goddess of material prosperity and spiritual liberation!" Swamiji translated the meaning for me. Yes, both at the same time!

It is funny how things change so much around Amma. Some of my favorite satsangs today are with Lalita, whom I had judged over ten years ago as a fool for "giving up her power" to Amma. Today, I am so grateful for having become another such fool. Today I know of the dozens and dozens of charitable projects for the sick, the poor, the widows, orphans, children, and students that Amma has initiated and blessed. Amma is manifesting my planetary dream of helping the whole world.

Today I am begging Amma to teach me what it means to surrender to Her, to surrender the ego to Divine Love. I still discover judgements within me that shock me. It is not easy to change core negative programming. But Amma is here to help!

> "Awaken, Children," You call to us. Oh, how we
> need Your help, Amma! So full of judgements
> of others and even ourselves. What a miracle
> that You are here, walking Your talk, living from
> Your Heart, showing us how it is really possible to
> be here on Earth with no ego and how to serve
> people selflessly.

Dania Edwards currently lives in rural Canada with her partner, Jake, their 7 goats, 3 cats, and a small flock of chickens. She is building a private practice in acupressure in Nelson, British Columbia. She was raised on the Canadian prairies, then moved to Munich, Germany, where she studied pedagogics and worked with children and youth. Her main interests are singing, chanting, and playing guitar and drums.

Paras

*Mother is not a guest. She is your mother.
There is no need for any elaborate preparations to receive her. Your love for her is more
than enough. Whatever you offer with your
own hands is like ambrosia to Amma.*

— Amma

In India, we believe that a piece of iron brought into contact with the fabled *Paras* gem can be transformed into pure gold. To me, Amma is like this *Paras* gem, transforming the lives of so many people. But at first, this was not how I saw Amma. I was the type of person who never wanted to see her, as I did not believe in God in human form. Moreover, Amma is from Kerala and I am a native Maharashtrian living in Mumbai, so I did not feel much interest. The first time I went to see Amma was out of pressure from my bank officer, Mr. Dayakar Karkera.

In mid 1993, when the previous officer retired, Mr. Karkera was transferred to my department. He was a masterpiece of devotion. He had intense love for Amma and always talked about her during his spare time. I did not really like him and would get fed up listening to his stories. I preferred to chat about films, dramas and household affairs. Today, I understand that it was only due to Amma's sankalpa, that I was forced to work under Mr. Karkera so that I could become drawn to her.

One day I asked him why I should pray to God when I did not have any miseries. He replied that I should pray to express my gratitude for not giving me any miseries. He tried his best to convince me that Amma was none other than the Almighty God. I still disliked the idea of God in human form as I thought that such a person was an agent between God and me.

One day in May 1994, I received a telephone call at my office informing me that my husband had collapsed on his way to work due to low blood pressure and was admitted in the Intensive Care Unit of a

> *Amma, I am not Shabari, but you are Prabhu Ram; Amma, I am not Radha, but you are Shri Krishna. Please come and bless my house...*
> **– Mangala Gokhale, India**

nearby hospital. I frantically rushed to the hospital. Mr. Karkera's words came to my mind and I remembered that he had said that Amma was an incarnation of God and the most loving mother in this world. Without even realising what I was doing, I started praying to her to give me the strength to handle this situation.

Both my sons were writing their final exams and I was alone in the hospital. I kept praying. After forty-eight hours, the doctors declared my husband to be out of danger. After this incident, my attitude towards Amma changed somewhat and I decided to go for her darshan the next time she visited Mumbai.

Nine months later, in February 1995, Amma was visiting Mumbai for five days. On February 7, the first day, I went to her program at the Leela Penta Hotel in Andheri, a suburb of Mumbai. I went after work and reached the hall after the program had begun. The hall was very crowded and I could not see Amma clearly. Darshan did not start until after 10:00 p.m. In the meantime, my husband had come to pick me up and we returned home without taking Amma's darshan.

My husband did not know anything about spirituality, so I was very surprised when I saw that he had bought a cassette of Amma. He had arrived just in time to listen to a part of Amma's satsang and had liked what he had heard.

"She is not telling us to just sit with a japa mala, but to also do work," he said.

The next morning I went to Partkar Hall, Churchgate, another suburb of Mumbai, for Amma's second program with my younger son Anil, who was then seventeen. A big crowd was already waiting in a queue by the time we arrived. Announcements were being made that we should come for darshan without breaking the queue and that Amma knew who was breaking the rules. I thought to myself, "Let her know and punish me. After coming here, I cannot wait for too long." So I pushed forward and reached Amma. In my heart of hearts, I was praying that she would forgive me for breaking the queue.

Amma hugged me and whispered something in Malayalam. I did not feel anything special from her touch. I was just happy that I could now tell my officer that I had taken Amma's darshan as per his wish.

I saw my son silently standing in the gents' queue with folded hands. It took him almost two hours to get his darshan and I had to wait until his turn came. When we came back home, he showed me two small acrylic frames that he had bought. One was of Amma in Devi Bhava and the other was a padam. He told me that when he purchased a car he would keep these photos in it. I was surprised. What had made my son feel that Amma was God just after one darshan?

The next day, for some unknown reason, I felt like going to see Amma again. This time her program was in the M.A. Math in Nerul. The *Brahmasthanam Prana Prathishta*, where Amma installs a murthi in a temple, had taken place the previous day. When I arrived, *Lalita Sahasranama* archana had just finished. A lady asked me to help remove the archana flowers from the hall. I started picking them up when I found Amma's padam photo inside some flowers. I treated this as a good omen and thinking that it was Amma's prasad, kept it near my heart. I took Amma's darshan and without having any other special feelings, returned home. I kept the padam photo on my altar.

The next year when Amma was visiting Mumbai, I asked my husband to take me for Amma's darshan. At first he refused because he was very busy at work trying to get approval for an electric connection for an important project. But when I told him that if he took me to the Math, Amma would surely help him complete the project, he reluctantly agreed. In reality, I did not have much confidence in Amma, but I wanted to see her. The very next day, my husband received the required approval. Amma had shown me that if we had faith in her, even if it was not one hundred percent, she would reward with her grace.

In December 1996, Mr. Karkera became a resident at Amma's ashram in Kerala. Earlier I used to dislike hearing stories about Amma from him, but now I missed them. I started attending satsang every week. During bhajans, I would close my eyes and listen whole-heartedly, forgetting the world around me. I also started reading Amma's *Awaken, Children!* books. Slowly, very slowly, I was coming close to her.

In 1997, Amma appeared in my dream. She was in my puja room and I was doing her pada puja. When I woke up, I did not give much importance to the dream because the area I lived in was not very prominent and I thought that it was not likely that Amma would really come to my house. I treated this as an ordinary dream and soon forgot about it.

A year later, when I heard that Amma's public program was being arranged at Borivali, a five-minute drive from where I live, I could not believe it! I remembered my dream. Perhaps, she would come to my house after all! I started praying to Amma constantly. "Amma, you are coming to Borivali for the public program. Amma, I am not Shabari, but you are Prabhu Ram; Amma, I am not Radha, but you are Shri Krishna. Please come and bless my house, make this *grihasthashram* into an *anandashram*." For months, I prayed to Amma in this manner, crying in front of her photo to fulfill my wish.

Every day I imagined decorating Amma's seat and washing her feet. I made full preparations with the hope that Amma would indeed come to my house. I continued to pray, "Amma, if not in this birth, at least in the next birth please come to my house. Till that time I will cry at your lotus feet, so that I become eligible to receive your blessings."

On March 9, 1999, the scheduled day of Amma's program, I got up at 4:00 a.m. and cleaned the house. Neighbours asked me whether Amma had promised that she would come. I told them that Amma had not said anything and that if she did not come, I would do more bhakti in my life, so that at least in my next birth she would visit my house.

At 5.30 a.m., some of Amma's brahmacharis came by to rest. I did their seva and made them breakfast. In the afternoon, some senior Swamijis also came by to rest awhile. They asked whether Amma was visiting the house. My son replied that his mother had full faith that Amma would indeed come and was preparing for her visit.

It was now evening and Amma had still not come. My son insisted that Amma had already visited in the form of her brahm-acharis and Swamijis and that we should not trouble her by asking her to come herself. He took all the offerings kept aside for her to give them at the program. With a heavy heart, I did Amma's manasa puja and prostrated at her feet. I prayed that Amma makes me purer, so that at least in my next birth my Bhagwan would come to my house. I then left for the program.

At the end of the program, Amma, who is omnipotent, omni-scient and omnipresent, told the co-ordinators that she would visit my house. When I was informed, my joy knew no bounds. I ran home barefoot. Within twenty minutes, Amma came. I did not even have time to think. Amma came and sat exactly in the same seat where she had sat in my dream.

My condition was like that of a mad person and I was not in my normal senses. I kept clinging to Amma and saying, "Amma, You are my Krishna, You are my Rama." To which she replied, "No, Amma is just a crazy child of God." For months and months, I had waited for this moment. I had made elaborate preparations to receive Amma. Amma, the all-knowing one, knew about my plans and had expressed her decision to visit only at the last moment. She had not wanted to give me any time to do elaborate rituals as she did not want any unnecessary pomp and show.

The next day, when I went to Nerul Math for darshan, Amma did not even look at me. I knew that Amma was behaving like this so that I would not become egoistical thinking that Amma had come to my house. At the Math, devotees had heard about Amma's surprise visit and I gave Amma's prasadam to everyone.

After that day, Amma made a lot of changes in my life. My attitude towards my fellow human beings changed. For example, if someone insulted me, I tried to remember that I was Amma's daughter and that I needed to be loving towards all. When I became tired from housework, I recalled how Amma did everything herself, even though She was an incarnation. Then could I not work for my family? Thinking like this, I would become fresh and energetic and have a smiling face most of the time.

Amma is not a human being, but a phenomenon, no less than *Tretayugi* Ram or *Dwaparyugi* Krishna. In *Tretayug*, Prabhu Ram built setu bridge with the help of *vanarasena* (army of monkeys), who did the work, chanting *Ram Naam*. In the same manner, Amma has many brahmacharis, sanyasis and grihasthashramis, who are doing service in Her name. As a result, Amma's great projects like the super specialty charity hospital, colleges, houses for the poor and needy and Brahmasthanams have taken shape. In *Dwaparyug*, Krishna Bhagwan used to play the flute to attract the gopis, cows and other elements of nature. In the same manner, in this *Kaliyug*, Amma is attracting the whole world by Her soul stirring bhajans.

I pray that Amma will make me an instrument in Her mission. I know that I have to become very pure at heart for this to happen and that it is possible only with Her Grace. I pray that my Satguru's Grace flows towards me and that She gives me the strength for one-hundred percent surrender at Her Feet.

Mangala Gokhale lives a retired life with her husband in Mumbai, India. She served as a bank employee for 30 years. The couple has two sons, Sunil, 27, and Anil, 25, both working as engineers. Mangala spends her free time participating in various service projects.

I Wasn't Looking for Anything

Never look back and grieve.
Look forward and smile.

– Amma

In 1993, I was living in Sydney, Australia. I didn't know I was looking for anything. In fact, if you had asked me I would have told you I didn't want a spiritual teacher. I had been there and done that.

Two years before, I had been very disappointed by my earlier spiritual teacher and had left his group. Although I had gone to this teacher more out of curiosity than anything else, leaving had been very hard for me. I had made a decision to not look for anything for at least two years and probably not at all. I knew that it would take me that long to sort out my life after having been involved with a teacher who did not practice what he preached. I wanted to sort out my thinking and beliefs. As a part of this, I had stopped meditating because I didn't want to use the mantra that I had been given.

A friend told me about Amma and suggested I come along. I was very suspicious. I did not want to join anything, or be part of any group. I certainly did not want more dogma, more teachings, more empty words. I was very resistant. I wasn't in the mood for a big crowd. But finally, I told myself that it might be worth going in order to get a new mantra because I might want to start meditating again. So I decided to go.

My background is Jewish and at first I was quite disturbed by the different forms of worship. In Judaism, there are no graven images, no kneeling and no forms of God other than the one, invisible, unnamed God. I was very uncomfortable with any form of worship that seemed to be in direct conflict with the teachings I had grown up with. I knew nothing about Vedic teachings and I did not want to know anything about them.

The singing started. My friend had not warned me about this. I hated the music. It seemed to go on forever. I chuckle now while I write this. One of my favorite things today is to sing Indian and other devotional songs at our weekly satsang gatherings. Even more wonderful is to sing Indian songs to Amma when she comes to Australia.

> *I was relieved when I heard Amma speak. The teachings were simple and I wasn't being asked to do anything, or join any group, or think in any certain way.*
> **– Nitya Rona, Australia**

I was relieved when I heard Amma speak. The teachings were simple and I wasn't being asked to do anything, or join any group, or think in any certain way. Amma spoke about love and how we say that we love each other but often don't really mean it. She used the example of a cow. She said, we say that we love our cow but if she stops producing milk we don't love her any more. I remember thinking that this was a funny example to use here in Sydney, Australia, where all the milk came from a supermarket.

Once at the program, I decided that I might as well line up for darshan and did so, feeling quite grumpy. The line moved slowly, the floor was uncomfortable, the incense was too strong and my back hurt. I wondered about kneeling down in front of Amma and how I would feel about this, being Jewish. All those thoughts disappeared as I approached her.

About halfway up the darshan line I started to think again. I thought that my heart felt closed and that I would love it if it were more open. Strange that I had not noticed this before. Amma took me into her arms like she did everyone else. She whispered something into my ear that I didn't understand and pushed a sweet into my hands.

I was disappointed. The earth did not move; I hadn't even understood what she had said. As I was about to stand up and move on, Amma pulled me back and started stroking my chest quite firmly. I experienced a strong pulling sensation as if my chest was being ripped open. Suddenly tears started pouring down my face. I managed to stagger to the nearest chair.

I cried for the next couple of hours. Between my tears, I carefully watched to see if Amma did this with anybody else. I couldn't quite believe that she had known that I had wanted my heart to be more open. To my surprise, she did not rub anybody else's chest that whole night. Perhaps she did really know what I had wanted. This seemed extraordinary.

I went home that night feeling as though a great weight had been lifted from my heart. I told myself that I would return the next day to get a mantra. It never occurred to me that I was going back to see Amma. Only that I wanted a new mantra, so I could start meditating again.

With my previous teacher, getting a mantra required years of commitment, apparent spiritual progress, and quite a substantial amount of money. You had to write to the teacher for permission and then continually write and report back your spiritual progress. I remember being amazed that after a small talk explaining the commitment I was making, I could just line up to get a mantra from Amma. The only criteria seemed to be agreeing to take it seriously. No fee, no forms to fill out, no record of who I was.

Even though I was told about the seriousness of the commitment, I didn't really understand the implied connection to Amma. My only thought was that I could now meditate again. How naive I was! I had not understood what an incredible blessing it was to be initiated by Amma.

At the end of the evening's program I was stunned to see Amma helping to clean up the hall. In my previous group, the teacher never did any work. This night Amma powerfully showed me that she was different. She didn't tell me to be of service, she demonstrated service.

My relationship with Amma developed slowly, seemingly without any desire on my part to have a relationship. The next year when Amma was in Sydney, I decided to go to see her only at the last minute. I had not thought much about her during the previous year. I carried on like this for three or four years, enjoying her visits but not thinking much about her in between.

I can't say exactly when my attitude changed. I remember being very surprised at myself when in a few years, after a couple of days with Amma, I found myself signing up for a retreat the following day. I was teaching at that time and had to miss class to attend the retreat. I couldn't explain to myself why it was suddenly so important to attend. All I knew was that I could not miss the retreat. Such was also the case in 1998, when I decided with two weeks' notice that I would go to Amma's ashram in India.

I wasn't looking for anything the day I met Amma. But I sure found something. Today, I cannot imagine a life without Amma. She is my constant source of inspiration, love and comfort. Amma brings meaning and purpose to my life. The time I actually spend with Her is the highlight. The time in between seems like just marking time.

Nitya Rona is a longtime resident of Sydney, Australia. She has a masters' degree in counselling and works as a psychotherapist in private practice. As a senior therapist, she also supervises and trains other therapists as part of their ongoing professional development. She enjoys reading mystery novels, going to the theatre and spending time with her family.

Turning Point

My children, sing from the depths of your hearts. Let the heart melt in prayer. The joy of singing the Lord's name is unique. Bhajan singing is for us to pour out all our hearts' accumulated dirt. Leave aside all shyness and open your heart to God.

– Amma

To understand my journey to Amma, it is necessary to tell you a little about myself. I was only nineteen when I first became interested in spirituality. I had joined military service out of pressure from my father. I did not like the discipline and refused to march and fire. They put me in prison. Actually, it was much better for me to be in prison than to go to war and be a soldier. Here I discovered Jesus and the Bible. "The Sermon On The Mount" fascinated me and I read it over and over.

Fortunately, my stay in prison was not too long. After my release, I continued reading the Bible and began attending church services. I did not, however, find what I wanted. One day I watched "Gandhi," the film about the Indian non-violent freedom fighter made by Richard Attenborough. Watching the film was a revelation to me! Gandhi seemed like the true example of the teachings of Christ. I read all the books I could find about him.

This is how I discovered Indian culture and yoga. For the next four years, I attended yoga classes. In 1989, when I was twenty-four, I joined a yoga center in Paris. With people from that center, I went for a yoga teachers' training course in India not very far from Amma's ashram in Kerala.

I first heard about Amma while doing the yoga course. After it was complete, I went with a friend to her ashram. Everyone who had told us about her spoke in very laudatory terms. I wanted to meet this great soul. The meeting turned out to be the most beautiful experience of my life. Tears of joy come even now as I write this.

> *Because I had somehow become perfectly quiet inside, I had this feeling of seeing Amma in everyone.*
> *— Jean Claude Reig, France*

When we reached the ashram, a devotee told us to hurry because Amma was just finishing darshan. We rushed into the darshan hut.

I had brought fruit to offer to Amma. In the excitement, the fruit fell down and went flying everywhere but I was not conscious of it. I only knew that I was in Amma's arms, in God's arms. I felt sure about that. Tears of joy started overflowing.

Amma finished hugging me and my friend and left. We were perhaps the last ones to receive darshan that day. I could not leave the darshan hut but sat there for a very long time. I felt a deep peace inside me. Amma's darshan had given me a profound experience of unconditional love. My friend also had the same feelings of being absorbed in divine love. He had met other masters also, but had not met anyone like Amma before.

We spent three days in Amma's ashram. It was a marvelous time. I dreamed of Amma each night. Because I had somehow become perfectly quiet inside, I had this feeling of seeing Amma in everyone. It was so powerful! I even had the feeling that the ashram was Amma, that everything was pure presence of unconditional love. I felt a great joy inside and no conflicts to disturb my peace.

Three days later, I returned to France. I knew that I had touched the deepest spirituality of India. I now had absolute faith in the Divine nature of human beings. I had seen God, I had experienced His Love. Not just in books but from heart to heart, from soul to soul. A part of me wished that I had gone to Amma's ashram earlier, then I could have stayed with her longer. Yet I also knew that the yoga class was my preparation for the first meeting with Amma.

Back in Paris, I practiced yoga and meditation at the yoga center. I taught some classes and wanted to become a professional yoga teacher. When I spoke to people about Amma, the resident Swami explained that in the Indian tradition, the relationship with a master was very precious and that one should not change masters. I felt very confused. I loved yoga but I also loved Amma. The inner struggle went on for almost two years.

The turning point was in July 1991 when I helped prepare for Amma's program in Paris. After the program was over and everyone was at the airport waiting to see Amma off, Amma called me to sit next to her. She said something in Malayalam that was translated to me.

"Amma knows that you have been working very hard for Amma's program. Amma wants to thank you for your help."

I was in tears. I had not done much, yet Amma was thanking me! When Amma left on the plane to go to the next city, I decided to follow her tour.

From program to program, my love for Amma grew. During Devi Bhava in Zurich, I bought an old photo of Amma in Krishna Bhava. She no longer did Krishna Bhava. I remember saying to myself, "Amma I would have been so happy to meet you as Krishna…"

She looked most beautiful when I went for darshan. After darshan, I sat down in front of the stage looking at her. Suddenly Amma looked at me and smiled. She looked younger and even more beautiful. Her look was full of love. As I watched, the colour of her skin turned blue! I understood in that moment that I was seeing Amma as Krishna. I started crying. It was obvious to me that Amma knew everything about me.

In 1993, I went to live in Amma's ashram in India for six months. I started to learn how to play the harmonuim there. Earlier, I did not sing much even though I enjoyed Amma's bhajans. Slowly my passion for yoga gave way to my enthusiasm for bhajans. As my bhajan practice blossomed, I came closer and closer to Amma in my heart. Today, singing bhajans every day is my main sadhana.

In 1995, Amma married Sabine and me in Etampes. Today we have two daughters, Amarilys and Pauline, who like Amma very, very much. I try my best to live a spiritual life with my family and with Amma's help.

Translated from French by Danielle Cherel

Jean Claude Reig lives with his wife Sabine and their two daughters, Amarilys, 8, and Pauline, 3, in a small, happy village in the south of France. He works at the local post office.

9

Leading to Renunciation

Ashrams and gurukulas are the pillars of our spiritual culture. If we do spiritual practices according to a Satguru's advice, we need not go anywhere else. We will get whatever we need.

— Amma

In My Mother's Arms

Spiritual life is something that happens spon-
taneously. Nobody can force spirituality onto
someone else. It happens out of an urgency.
In this state of urgency, a person cannot do
anything but choose spirituality. There is no
explanation for this; it just happens.

— Amma

Meeting Amma

I lived in Baltimore, near Washington DC, U.S.A. when I first heard about Amma in 1994. A man I had met only a few days earlier told me about her.

"…this Indian saint is here and I am going to see her…"

"Really, what is her name?" I asked. Not that it made any difference to me as I did not know any saints from anywhere.

"Her name is so and so…" he replied.

I did not understand a single word he said. Incredibly, however, my whole being went into a frenzy! I started shaking and no words came out. He gave me the phone number and the address for Amma's program in New York. I was barely able to write this information down.

I knew I just had to go to New York to see her. No questions asked. "This is crazy," I thought. My behavior stunned me. It was as if I had no control.

I called a good friend and asked him if he would come to my house so that we could leave for New York at 4:00 a.m. the next day, which was a Sunday. Surprisingly, he agreed without even asking why. Half way to New York he finally asked the purpose of the trip. I told him the little that I knew.

"Lord!" he said. "They are going to preach to us and hit us up for money. Are you crazy?"

I told him that they would not preach to us nor would they hit us for money. As if I knew!

> *There is not a day that Amma is not there with me, guiding, chiding, being my conscience.*
> *– Harsha Carley, M.A. Center*

We arrived at the church in Manhattan and were guided to the eighth floor. I saw many people dressed in white bustling around. The church windows were open and a beautiful breeze came in. A chair in front was being adorned with flowers.

"What is this?" my mind asked. "I thought she was a saint. So why all this pomp and circumstance? Oh! Oh! Have I been had? Is this some charlatan I have come to see?"

We sat down on the floor right in front of the chair. After some time, people started chanting something incomprehensible. Before I knew it, everyone was standing up and crowding around the short, plump, Indian woman who was walking by with a smile on her face.

She came to the front and sat down. Soon she started receiving people, taking them in her arms for a minute or so. Since we were seated right in the front, we were ushered up to her right away. Amma hugged me and said something in my ear that made no sense whatsoever.

What a disappointment! Nothing happened! No feelings, no emotions, no lightning bolt! Nothing! Had I been conned?

I was standing in the middle of the crowd, when I heard right inside my head, the most incredibly divine music my being had ever experienced. I looked around to see where the music came from. I saw a group of people in orange and white singing and playing musical instruments. The music they were playing, however, had nothing to do with the music I had heard in my head. One was angelic and the other one sounded like heavy metal compared to it!

The hours went by and finally around 3:00 p.m. Amma left. A lady approached me and said, "You are from Baltimore, aren't you?" Imagine my astonishment! How on earth did she know? Before I could properly respond, she had told me that she held satsangs at her house in Baltimore every Saturday. She gave me her address and invited me to come.

My friend and I left. I was shaking my arms and legs and pinching myself. My friend was bewildered and asked me what I was up to.

"I am trying to understand what is happening to me. I feel like I have no body…no weight…like I am lighter than air…yet I can see me, I can touch me. This is so bizarre!"

My friend did not feel anything special after Amma's darshan. Our trip back to Maryland was uneventful.

Back in Baltimore

A week later, I attended satsang at that lady's house. I was looking through some photographs to find one I had seen at the bookstore at Amma's program. I had wanted to buy it then but was told that the photo was very old and out of print, therefore not for sale. I looked carefully through the collection of photographs that the lady had but could not find the one I wanted. Disappointed, I went to the bathroom.

When I returned to the table just a few moments later, the photo I wanted was lying on top of the heap in plain view! I was utterly surprised! There was no way I could have missed it earlier, no way! I asked the folks talking a few feet away if they had moved or touched the photos. They had not even been aware of my presence!

Transformation Begins

At that time, I was the Vice President of a company that oversaw the housekeeping department of about ten hotels and hospitals. I was known for my fiery temper. A couple of weeks after meeting Amma, I had a meeting with my employees and ample opportunity to explode. Instead, I found myself talking very calmly and thinking, "This is not me talking. These are not my words." Deep down, I knew who was responsible for this sudden change in me. Amma!

A Longing Arises

Somehow the idea of moving to Amma's ashram in California got slowly implanted in my head. Myriads of questions came from

friends. What about your work? What about your beautiful collections of art and glass? What about your three dogs and six cats? No
one thought I could part with my beloved animals, least of all me.

It took me several years of "getting ready" to move to the ashram
before I was finally able to give everything up. It was an intense
process. Finally, there was nothing left for me to do but to move. I
loaded up my little car and grabbed my friend who had driven with
me to see Amma that first time. We both drove from Maryland to
California where he handed me over to Mother…

Now…

I've been at the ashram now for three and a half years. How time
passes by! Life with Amma has been a roller-coaster to say the least
but I have always experienced a peace and a strength I never knew
before. After meeting Amma, I volunteered to attend a ten-week
hospice training course. Now I am a full time care giver. The joy,
the lessons, the gifts I receive from this work are endless. There is
not a day that Amma is not there with me, guiding, chiding, being
my conscience.

My life has not been the same since that day in July 1994 when
I first met Amma. I cannot even imagine life without Her today
and wonder how I possibly managed all those years before I met Her.
But then again, who says I was without Her? I truly believe She
was always with me, only I did not know it. Meeting Amma was
the very best thing that happened to me. I cannot even remember
how I was a few years ago! I am counting my blessings!

---

*Harsha Carley was born in Alexandria, Egypt and grew up in Greece.
She moved to London in the early 1970s where she lived for 12 years
before moving to the U.S.A. Currently she works as a hospice care-
giver and lives in Amma's San Ramon ashram. Animals are her great
love. She enjoys the outdoors, walking on the beach, reading, meeting
people, and traveling.*

The Destiny of the Dove

*Selfless service and utter dedication are the
two things that will make one fit to receive
the Guru's Grace.*

– Amma

<u>You are my Son!</u>

I was born and brought up in Lebanon, a country constantly immersed in violence and civil wars. My family provided a sense of security and emotional support, which gave me a positive and happy view of life. When I was eleven years old, I started writing poems. The very first poem I wrote described a white dove, happy and carefree, and playing freely with the wind. The dove saw an elephant near a pond and without knowing why, came and sat right beneath the elephant. It remained there in the shade of the elephant, peaceful, silent and serene until nightfall. It then looked at the elephant with innocent eyes and asked, "Will you be my father?" The elephant gazed back into the dove's eyes and replied lovingly, "Yes, you are my son! From now on you will remain with me."

I continued writing poems until the age of seventeen. Finally, living amidst the never-ending violence, I gave up my inner life of poetry and spirituality and took it as my duty to do what the outside world expected me to do, strive for a respectable position in society. I always remembered, though, a 'promise' that a last poem held.

Oh Mother of Nature and Life!
Remember well, tomorrow a day will come
when I will leave everything and come to your kingdom.
Having completed my duties towards the world,
I will answer your call and let you,
and you alone, guide my life.

> *During the following two days, I picked small yellow flowers from the bushes outside the darshan tent and offered them to Amma each time I went up to her.*
> *– Priyan Fouad Nassif, Amritapuri*

I graduated from law school when I was twenty-three and started working as a trainee lawyer with a respected law firm in Beirut. By 1991, I was a fully qualified lawyer. In front of me lay a promising worldly career of wealth, prestige and success. But I did not feel attracted to it. I felt that I had learned what was to be learned in the material world and that it was enough. I did not need to prove anything else to others or to myself. I did not want the endless pursuit of money and the bondage of family ties to define the rest of my life. My interests turned slowly towards reading spiritual books and recollecting my earlier poems and writings.

Beirut as a Starting Point

It was at this time that I first heard about Amma from some friends living in Paris. They told me that Amma was a great Mahatma like Ramana Maharshi and Anandamayi Ma. I had read books about these renowned saints of India, even though they were relatively hard to come by in Beirut. My friends sent me Amma's biography and her 1992 Europe tour program. Reading about Amma's life reminded me of the devotion I had felt when reading about Ramakrishna Paramahamsa's divine moods. What attracted me to Amma was the fact that she was in a living body and still young. I decided to travel to Assisi, the holy land of St. Francis, to see Amma just *once* in my lifetime!

A few days before my journey, I had a very beautiful dream. I was among many people waiting to see Amma. When she arrived, dressed in white, she was quickly surrounded by everyone. An irresistible force pulled me towards her. When I reached her and lay my forehead on her right shoulder, an indescribable feeling of bliss entered my body. Sensing my touch, Amma turned back to me and said, "Ah, you! Yes, I know who you are. You have come!" I woke up at that instant. My forehead was burning with fire and my body was drenched in such a powerful and blissful energy that I was unable to move for a long time. Amma was waiting for me!

The First Darshan

My first darshan took place on July 20, 1992, in a majestic white tent set in the beautiful hills surrounding the city of Assisi. I felt completely captivated by Amma's charming presence and divine beauty. I remember that when I was in the line moving towards Amma's lap, she spotted me and gave me a long and precise gaze. I felt that she was studying me deeply.

She held me tight in her arms for a long darshan. She placed my head on her shoulder and murmured soft words into my ear that I couldn't understand. My eyes were closed and I repeated the sacred syllable *Om* in my mind. As the embrace ended, I moved aside and sat down close to Amma. I stayed there for a long time, first with my eyes closed and then staring at her, feeling mesmerised. Every now and then she looked at me and smiled. I was happy just to be there. My mind was silent and at peace and my heart filled to the brim with innocent love.

During the following two days, I picked small yellow flowers from the bushes outside the darshan tent and offered them to Amma each time I went up to her. This was a silent ritual in which only the eyes and the heart communicated.

When the three-day program was over and Amma left Assisi, I returned to the deserted darshan tent. Uncontrollable emotion welled up in me and tears of love and gratitude flowed down my cheeks for a long time.

The Dove Finds its Father

Back home I realised that all my spiritual energy had become con-centrated on Amma. All my thoughts and activities were shared with her subtle presence. I could clearly feel her grace with me. Whenever I felt sad or missed Amma, she sent abundant and clear signs to cheer me up and keep my faith high. Whether it was finding a bush with the same yellow flowers I had offered to her in Assisi, or experiencing incredible events of synchronicity, or being blessed with vivid dreams of her, Amma let me know that she was close at hand.

Some ten months later, I travelled to San Francisco to see Amma again. As I went up for darshan, Amma looked at me with amusement and asked, "Italy?" She continued, "The first time Amma saw you, Amma knew you were her son!" Hearing this, my whole being was stunned with emotion.

Such a straight and direct affirmation was a real shock to me. I was not ready to accept such a final Guru-disciple relationship so soon. I wanted to remain free. For the next three days, I remained shaken. I cried and told myself, "No! I don't want a tie with the outer Amma. I just want more inspiration to experience the inner Amma." I felt that the perceptions I had had as a child and the poems I had written in my childhood were somehow more profound than my meeting with the outer Amma.

On the fourth day of Amma's programs I gathered my courage and with determination went to "challenge" her. I came straight through the question line, showed her the notebook with my poems and said, "When I was a child I wrote poems and many of them had you in them. Do you know about that?" For me it was a way of telling Amma that the writings meant more to me than her physical presence.

Amma's answer was immediate, clear and calm. "Yes, Amma knows." She then repeated what she had said earlier. "In Italy, the first time Amma saw you, Amma saw that you were her son. Your link with Mother comes from previous lives!"

There was no longer any room for doubt. Everything had been said. I was left with no choice other than to completely surrender. My soul had found its eternal guide. The dove had found its father elephant.

Images of that poem came clearly back to my mind, and with tears in my eyes, I sat in a corner of the hall rewriting the lines, trying to remember the innocence I had felt as an eleven-year-old boy, and the exact words I had used then.

"Always Remember!"

During Devi Bhava, Amma initiated me into a mantra. Nine months later, I journeyed to India for a two-month stay in Amma's ashram in Kerala. The following year I was back again for a five-month period. In 1996, I became a resident at Amritapuri and a member of Amma's ever increasing family.

In the ashram, I have had the opportunity to learn the value of selfless service and this is what all my time is dedicated to now. Often I go to Mother to report some "serious" matters related to the work She has entrusted me with. She uses these opportunities to remind me, "Always remember your original innocence. That is the most precious thing in one's spiritual life."

Could the dove ever forget the loving gaze and the very first words of its father elephant? How could a heart nurtured by the love and the care of the Divine Mother not keep its innocence alive?

"Yes, you are my son! From now on you will remain with me." All is Hers. Truth! Love! Peace!

Priyan Fouad Nassif, has been a permanent resident of the Amritapuri ashram since 1995. He is a Lebanese citizen and holds law degrees in Lebanese and French law. After meeting Amma in 1992, he gradually gave up his law practice in Beirut and London to be with Amma. At Amritapuri he has worked at the Foreigners' Office, the Seva Desk and the Information Centre. He also helps organize Amma's tours in India. Priyan writes and sings devotional songs to Amma in English and Arabic.

Finally Home

A real guru is one who is endowed with all the Divine qualities, such as equal vision, universal love, renunciation, compassion, patience, forbearance, and endurance. Such a guru is like a huge ship which can carry thousands of passengers. The guru's mere presence will give a feeling of protection and safety and an assurance to the disciples that they will reach the goal.

— Amma

The friend who dropped me off at Heathrow airport left and I was all alone. A huge wave of pure joy filled my whole being. My excitement was both quiet and bubbling. Many months earlier, while I was attending a service at a Spiritualist Church, a sweet old clairvoyant lady had told me that I would soon go on a journey, after which I would never be the same. As I waited, I felt that her words were indeed coming true. A deep part inside me knew that something glorious and beautiful was about to happen. Life was wonderful, God felt near and I was going to India!

Later, somewhere over the desert in the Middle East, with the setting sun painting the most beautiful colours I had ever seen, I was still trying to contain my excitement. I was cautioning myself that I should not have too many expectations, because they lead only to disappointment and sorrow. Yet I could feel that God was about to bring magic into my life.

I landed at Trivandrum airport, and took a taxi to the yoga ashram where I would attend a teachers' training course over the next several weeks. The ashram was located on the hills just outside the city. During the taxi ride I saw scenes that felt familiar, even though I had never been to India before. The humidity in the air, the red soil, the thick vegetation, cows, dogs, rickshaws, little children playing half naked on the streets, young women carrying water pots on their hips, old men smoking by the sides of the road...everything seemed so heartwarmingly sweet.

> *It was clear that God had a grand plan for all of us, and that Eternal Joy was our final destination. Amma was there to help us all.*
> **– Sivani Banchio, Amritapuri**

I got to the ashram, pitched my tent, and lay down to rest awhile. The yoga course started the next day. It was intense and fascinating. One day an Italian boy told me he had just come from another ashram, where he had met a lady who was Pure Love. Her name was Amma and she hugged everybody who came to her. Later that day, an Israeli girl approached me and asked me whether I knew Amma. She said that she had just spent the most beautiful Christmas holiday at Amma's ashram.

By the following day at least six people had asked me whether I knew Amma. Coincidences? By this time I knew that I was meant to go and see her. Initially I thought I would visit her ashram after the yoga course ended. Imagine my astonishment when the very next day, someone came up to me and told me that Amma was giving a program right there in Trivandrum! At that moment, it became crystal clear to me that this saint was sending me a message, "Come!" And to make sure that I did not miss it, it had been repeated again and again from different mouths.

I grew incredibly restless. I had to see Amma and I had to see her immediately! Luckily, I found an Indian man who was going to her program that same night. I begged him to take me along and he agreed. He asked me to wear white if I could.

After a long bus ride we got to the program site as the bhajans were just starting. In India, men and women sit separately, so I found myself sitting in the sand at the back of the huge tent that had been erected for the occasion, surrounded by thousands of beautiful Indian ladies who were singing and clapping their hands. Amma was just a little dot far away. I could hear her voice over the microphone though; it was deep and unusual. She would burst out laughing in the middle of a song. I didn't quite know what to make of it all. I was a little worried because I couldn't feel anything.

"Is this right?" my mind asked. "Why don't I feel any major earthquake within?"

Darshan started. I somehow managed to join what seemed to be the queue, though it looked more like thousands of bodies just pressed together. Although I usually felt very uncomfortable in large crowds, I was very relaxed and ready to wait all night if needed to meet Amma. A western lady saw me waiting and came up to me to tell me that westerners, because they come from so far away and also because they are not used to waiting for long periods of time, are allowed to join the line further up. I however did not mind waiting, so I remained in the queue. When she came back the third time asking me to come up front, I followed her closer to where Amma was sitting.

Now I could see Amma very well. She was talking to and hugging and kissing each person who came up for darshan as if they were the only thing that mattered to her at that moment. It was the sweetest sight I had ever beheld! Amma seemed so totally focused and present in the moment. Tears came to my eyes. I tried to stem them, but I just couldn't stop crying. Was she for real? Was this Love really real? Or was this just a dream?

When my turn came, Amma looked at me with the deepest, most glowing eyes I had ever seen, then kissed me, hugged me and whispered *Om* many times into my ear. She took my hand and kissed it before letting me go. I immediately kissed her hand also. It felt very intimate. Later I was amazed at how natural the whole thing had seemed; there I was, embracing and kissing a complete stranger! Amma told me to sit on the stage. I sat there for a while, trying to figure out what was happening to me.

My whole life had been full of restlessness. Things would generally be interesting for a while, as long as they were new and kept the mind busy. Then boredom, disillusionment and restlessness would set in, and I would act, generally by bringing about a complete change in my outer environment. The same pattern repeated itself again and again, as I first left my home country, Italy, family and studies, and then other countries, friends and jobs, in a never ending sequence of outer changes. After coming to spirituality my restlessness had decreased, but there was still an inner disquiet that surged in waves and made it clear that my quest was far from over.

Most of all I felt the lack of love in my life. Love was my main concern and focus. I would think, "Oh, if only God sent me a true example of love, so that my heart could open." I needed to see, feel, experience love. And now...

Could it be that Amma was what I had been looking for all along? Was this it? I somehow felt like I had reached God's own home. The sweet fragrance of jasmine garlands, the colorful saris of thousands of women, the heavenly notes of devotional songs, all this created a whirlpool of beauty that merged into Amma's physical form.

When my time on the stage was up, I met my Indian friend again, who suggested we eat something. They were serving delicious dosa and sambar in the canteen. Every single detail of that night is forever etched into my mind.

Afterwards, as I was standing by the side of the stage looking at Amma, a western lady asked me if I would like to give prasad to Amma. I did not understand what she meant. Later I learned that in India, Amma gives a packet of blessed ash, wrapped around a candy, to each person who comes to her for darshan. The westerners travelling with Amma have the good fortune of handing those packets to Amma. This gives them the opportunity to be near Amma for some time. My friend had asked me to wear white so the lady must have thought that I was a part of Amma's group. I couldn't believe that this was really happening! I joined the prasad line.

As I slowly got closer to Amma, my excitement grew exponentially. A children's dance was being performed on the stage behind Amma. Even though she could not see what was going on behind her, she was the first one to turn around and clap after the performance was over. She seemed so totally aware of everything!

Finally, it was my turn to give prasad. Words cannot express what I felt at that time. Only the heart can understand. Time stopped for me as I felt transported to a place where there was only Love. Amma's Love towards humanity; full, unconditional and eternal.

So many people came to Amma's arms while I gave prasad to her. I could see their expressions. Even though I could not understand their words, I could sense their feelings. Many had tales of sorrow. I could see their tears and hear their prayers. Amma comforted each one in her own way. How incredible, to love everybody in the same, yet special way!

Not even in my wildest dreams, had I imagined that anyone like Amma could exist in this world! She was Divine! She was pure Grace, pouring out over the whole of humankind! Looking at Amma for what felt like a never-ending moment in time, I suddenly realised that all was well. For the first time in my life, everything made sense. All questions stopped. The mind fell silent. I felt taken care of, safe and loved. I felt that every being in the whole of Creation was God's most beloved child. It was clear that God had a grand plan for all of us, and that Eternal Joy was our final destination. Amma was there to help us all.

After that most beautiful experience of my life, I went and sat at the back of the stage, and cried uninterruptedly for three full hours. The shell of a lifetime's accumulated dirt, as Amma refers to it, was beginning to crack.

The search was over. The adventure had begun.

Sivani Banchio was born in Italy in 1968, where she studied foreign languages at the university. Afterwards she moved to England, where she lived for a few years, working as a restaurant assistant manager. In 1998 she went to India to study yoga, where she met Amma. She has been living in Amma's ashram as a renunciate since 1999. Her current sevas in the ashram include baking, ordering supplies for the western canteen and translating Amma's books and satsangs into Italian.

From Holland to Amritapuri

A sadhak should not eat much tasty food. The attraction towards taste will make it difficult to overcome many other desires also. No matter how tasty a thing is, it is not possible to know the taste once it goes down the throat. Both tasty and tasteless food should become the same. Practice eating bitter things. Not only the tongue but all the sense organs should be overcome

– Amma

Holland, Summer 1996

I went into a vegetarian restaurant one day and joined two of my friends at a table. They had just returned from India and were talking about an ashram they had visited.

"Yes, the climate is terrible, so hot and humid. And the food is also horrible, always rice and much too spicy."

I was a little surprised. You don't go to an ashram for this kind of comfort.

"And there are so many mosquitoes there. The beds are so hard, its like sleeping on the floor."

Without intending to, I blurted out, "Well, in that case, I will just take my air mattress with me."

"Gee, what did I just say?" I thought to myself. I did not even know which ashram my friends were talking about.

They told me that the ashram they had visited was that of Amma, the hugging guru. I had heard of her but did not know much about her. I had been practicing Transcendental Meditation for many years. When my friends told me more about Amma, I liked the idea of a loving mother and guru.

> *I feel that now there is someone standing behind me and that a new period in my life is starting.*
> *– Henk Maas, Amritapuri*

Shortly thereafter I borrowed and read one of Amma's books, *Awaken Children – Volume 1*. I felt very happy to read the book. I found out that Amma was visiting Paris a few months later. I decided to meet her then.

Paris, November 1996

I don't remember much about the way I felt when I saw Amma for the first time. I do remember that after my first darshan, one of my friends asked me about eating or going to the hotel. I just did not understand him. I was so elated by Amma's bliss that I was not even thinking properly. Only after a half hour went by was I able to come back to earth and become interested in mundane things like eating again.

Devi Bhava was very special. I don't think I had ever experienced such joy and happiness. During the final ceremony, Amma showered flowers on everyone. I was overjoyed with Amma's love and her beauty.

I remember having a conversation with my friend on the way back home. "I feel that now there is someone standing behind me and that a new period in my life is starting." I had said. Later this turned out to be completely true.

Amritapuri, December 1996

I was in Amma's ashram in India just one month after my first darshan. I had taken an air mattress along, just in case. But I found no problems adjusting to the austerity of ashram life. For me, Amma's love provided fulfillment in such a way that those outer things did not matter at all.

After only a short stay, I desired to become a permanent resident at the ashram. During darshan one day, I whispered this desire into Amma's ear. I spoke in English but I am sure she understood. Amma said nothing in reply.

Holland, Summer 1997

After my return to Holland, my desire to live permanently at Amritapuri only increased. It was such a unique opportunity to live with a Guru. I did not want to waste it. During Amma's European tour, I asked Her if I could come to the ashram and stay for three months to see if I could live there forever.

"Amma feels happy if you come," Amma replied beaming a smile at me.

Amritapuri, Today

After Amma's summer tour, I stayed in the ashram for three months. It was a very happy time. Long before the three months were over, I asked Amma if I could move there permanently and she agreed readily. I did not want to go back to Europe but had to wrap everything up. As it turned out, I had no difficulty in taking leave of everyone and closing all my affairs in Holland. I did not have the feeling that I was giving something up. Instead, I knew I was getting closer to God.

I became a permanent resident at Amma's ashram in December 1998. I have lived at the ashram now for over three years. Living here has been a continuous training to get rid of all negative tendencies and desires. I have been confronted with situations where anger, suspicion, desire for food or lust arise. I have seen how these tendencies bind one and obstruct one's life. I have found that the solution is to remember Amma always and keep the goal clearly in mind.

The challenge is to live always according to Amma's teachings and instructions. I pray that Amma gives me devotion and strong faith and that She always keeps me at Her sweet Lotus Feet.

Henk Maas, 53, has lived in Amritapuri since December 1998 as a permanent resident. He works in the western canteen cleaning, serving, supervising, cooking, and baking bread. He also translates Amma's books into Dutch.

In Mother's Sacred Land

You may see a person who really wants to sur-
render and become a disciple undergoing a lot
of difficulties and problems. This is because
such a person is going through a process of
purification. The sufferings and problems that
you witness in their life are actually speeding
up the exhaustion of both the seen and the
unseen vasanas and karmic bondages.

– Amma

What is Life?

While I was still very young, I wondered about the meaning of life. I did not believe in God's existence. If He existed, He had to be good. Then how could He allow all the suffering we saw in the world? If I asked myself what makes life beautiful, the answer was arts, nature and the love that existed between human beings. I loved music, ballet, literature and poetry.

In June 1985, when I was twenty-seven years old, I was waiting at a train station in France one day, when I heard someone say, "So according to this book, we are the Absolute Incarnate, but we do not know it." That one sentence struck me deeply. I went up to the stranger and asked what he was talking about.

The man was waiting for the same train to Paris as I was. We talked at the station and on the train for the next hour. The book he had referred to was *I Am That: Conversations With Nisargadatta Maharaj*. He lent me the book to read even though I had just met him and he did not know me. I started reading the book the very same day.

The book was a revelation to me! It changed my life! Nisar-gadatta Maharaj was a Self-realised soul who lived in India in the

twentieth century. He left his
body in the 1980s. Though I
did not fully grasp the meaning
of his words, I knew that this
was the Truth. In his writings,
I found an explanation for the

> *I wanted to say, "Come, come!*
> *In Amma's heart, there is room for*
> *everybody."*
> *– Amritapriya, Amritapuri*

suffering one saw in the world. People suffered as a result of their
past actions. The book talked about the Self and the divine nature
of human beings. This was beyond anything I was familiar with.
Really, who could fully grasp the meaning of those words, except
another Self-realised soul? This was my first experience of faith.

The book became my constant companion for the next two
years. I learned that the teachings were actually *Vedanta*, the
thousands of years ancient wisdom contained in the *Upanishads*,
the scriptures of India. I read the treasure of the *Bhagavad Gita*. In
the second chapter, I was thrilled to read Sri Krishna talking about
the Self, which could not be burnt by fire or cut by a sword. I also
wanted to explore other religions, so I read the *Koran* and the *Bible*.
I found that the basic values of compassion, humility, detachment
and service to others were the same in all religions.

By July 1988, I was asking myself, "So I have faith now, but what
can I do practically?" It was then that I met Amma, in a small city
south of Paris. Amma says that we don't need to search for a Master. The Master comes when our heart longs for Him. I went to
see Amma out of curiosity, after reading a few lines in a magazine.
Little did I know that this meeting would change my life completely!

My First Darshan

I still remember that I felt quite nervous before Amma came. I was
not used to being with many people (at that time, one hundred
seemed many to me!). We left our shoes outside and I wondered
if the floor was clean. When Amma came, I felt powerful waves
of love and serenity radiating from her. I somehow knew that she
was a true Master, a God-realised soul. I had never experienced
anything as powerful before.

When I went for darshan and was in Amma's lap, someone nearby started crying very loudly. At that moment, my heart was so expanded that I lifted my arm, as if to invite the crying person to come to Amma. I wanted to say, "Come, come! In Amma's heart, there is room for everybody."

Amma laughed heartily and tapped me on the head. When she left the program, she smiled at me and gestured as if to say, "We will see each other again." I wondered how that could be. I had my work, I wanted to marry and have children. I did not know when I would see her again.

A Deep Longing

Within a few months, I was thinking of Amma regularly, even contemplating a one year visit to her ashram in India. I did not know anything about her ashram, not even where it was located in India. I felt very scared to go to India. Where did the thoughts of going to the ashram come from? I pushed them away, thinking I would never really want to go. I loved my country where everything was pretty and convenient. Materially, I had a comfortable life. Still the thoughts about Amma and her ashram kept recurring.

In June 1990, two years after I first met Amma, I decided to ask her if I could go to her ashram for a year. I still remember that darshan. We camped on top of a hill in the middle of unspoiled nature in Provence. The Mediterranean light, the trees, the enchanting smells! And under ancient chestnut trees Amma giving darshan in her simple white sari, radiating love and purity. I had felt this must be similar to the time when Christ was alive and wandering in the Holy Land sharing love and inspiring His disciples.

When I asked Amma if I could go to India, she immediately said, "Yes" and gave me a very happy glance. That was a turning point in my life.

The Journey Begins

In September 1990, I rented out my apartment, took a one year leave from my job and left for India. The same man who had given me the book at the train station, now a dear friend, came to see me off at the airport. When the plane took off, I was so scared that I had tears in my eyes. I had Amma's photo with me and held it close. Her love had moved me to make this journey into the unknown. From now on, she was my only support.

I opened a book I was carrying with me right to the passage where a saint described his decision to leave home to become a sannyasi. Reading this felt very comforting to me. Somehow, I was doing something similar, even though I did not know how long I would stay in India.

During the rest of the journey, I was guided by Amma's invisible hand in every way. When I landed in Cochin, some people I had met on the plane invited me to stay at their home. I gratefully accepted the offer. The next day they dropped me off at the boat jetty in Vallickavu. In the boat, a simple Indian lady showed me what to give to the boatman and then led me to the entrance of the ashram.

There I was, on the sacred land of Amritapuri. I did not know then how holy this place was, but I remember feeling very happy. I did not also know that this would become my home for many, many years.

A brahmacharini welcomed me lovingly and took me to the darshan hut where Amma was still giving darshan. When I saw Amma, her face beaming love and compassion, I started crying.

"The journey is over. This is home. This is the end of suffering." Those were the thoughts in my mind.

Amma took me into her arms. I was still crying. After wiping my tears, and giving me a sweet hug, she got up. Darshan was over. I had been the last one to go into her arms. It was as if she knew that I was coming and was waiting for me.

One week later, I asked Amma for a name. I was starting a new life where Amma was my Mother, so I felt that she had to give me a name. I wanted a name with Amma's name in it. I also wanted Amma to tell me that she loved me.

When Amma gave me the name Amritapriya, meaning "darling of Amrita" I could not believe it! Amrita is part of Amma's name,

Mata Amritanandamayi. Before giving me my name, Amma put her foot on my head when I bowed down. This was very special because in the scriptures, it is said that the Grace of the Guru flows through the feet.

My Path Unfolds

I stayed in the ashram for the full year. It was just heaven! Granted there were many difficulties with irregular water and electricity supply and the spicy Indian food, but still there was so much joy. Amma's presence gave so much happiness! I loved bhajans. I loved Devi Bhava. I loved working for Amma. Amma often worked right along with us. During those days, Amma also meditated with us on the beach. Amma created so many enchanting moments to make Her children happy.

All was not a festival, however, and many difficult situations also arose. Those were hard but helped me grow spiritually and make me strong. Amma says that the ashram is a Kurukshetra; that is the battlefield where the war between the Kauravas and the Pandavas was fought in the Mahabharata. The Kauravas represent our bad tendencies and the Pandavas our good tendencies. While there may be a hundred Kauravas, and only five Pandavas, Krishna is with the Pandavas and victory will be theirs in the end.

Since Amma wants us to be happy, She shows us the obstacles to real happiness that we carry within us. By Her grace, this awareness comes to us slowly. Then hand in hand with our beloved Mother and Master, we can work on removing these obstacles. Like warriors, we learn to be alert, but also relaxed. Self-effort is absolutely essential in spiritual life but tension from anxiety is not good. A warrior has to unstring his bow to keep it in good shape. That is why Amma likes to laugh and joke with us so much.

After the one year in the ashram ended, I went back to France to get a new visa. It took me about a month to complete all the tasks required. During this time, I was not happy at all in my old world. The pleasures I was earlier used to were tasteless and empty compared to my life with Amma.

Living in the Sacred Land

When I returned to Amritapuri, I asked Amma if I could stay in the ashram for good. Amma responded affirmatively. Since then I have been blessed to stay with Her. I have experienced many beautiful and truly blissful moments in Amma's divine presence. I have also gone through much struggle and pain. But it has been worth it. By Amma's grace, I have gained strength to face challenging situations when they arise. Today I feel more peaceful and contented within myself. I still have a lot to learn. But then again, what else is the purpose of this life?

Amritapriya, 44, is a renunciate in Amma's ashram. She is of French nationality. She taught at a high school until 1990 until she moved to Amritapuri at the age of 32. Her seva over the years has ranged from washing dishes to cleaning bathrooms to laundry service. Today, she mainly does translation work for Amma's books and CDs and also assists with making Amma dolls.

Epilogue

You are the ones who have to soar high into the vast sky of spirituality. To do that, you need the wings of self-lessness and love. We should be able to do everything with sincerity and love. The opportunity to serve others should be considered a rare gift, a blessing from God. We should be happy and thank God for providing such opportunities.

– Amma

"This book must be another one of Amma's clever ideas to keep Herself alive in the hearts of Her children," said a longtime devotee helping with this project. To all of us, over a hundred of Amma's children involved in the making of this book, working on the book was a beautiful journey with Amma and a lovely way of remaining connected with Her. Please allow us, dear readers, to share a little from that journey.

How the Book Came Together

A book like this one, with contributions representing nearly thirty countries of the world would have been impossible to conceive even just a decade ago. Our lives have become so shaped by the omnipresence of computers and email and Internet, that we take instant worldwide communication for granted today. A person on our team compared email to telepathy and the Internet to a fantasy land called Computer Land. If we stop and think about it, these descriptions certainly seem apt.

It was the e-seva or tele-seva of many, many of Amma's children that made this book possible. Stories were collected using a website. Two online discussion groups devoted to Amma (http://amma.hindunet.org/amma-l and http://groups.yahoo.com/) became wonderful resources to connect not just with storywriters but also with many sevites. Over ninety percent of the stories were collected during the months of January and February 2002.

A Word About the Writers

While many people worked hard for this book, the greatest contribution is surely that of the writers who lovingly contributed their stories. Theirs was the blessed but difficult seva of sharing Amma's impact in their lives with the world at large. Without exception, each one wrote about their shortcomings and their learning with brutal honesty in order to illustrate how Amma's love is slowly transforming them and helping them become better individuals. They did it as service to their beloved Amma and in the hope that their stories might help readers understand more about Her. We bow down in front of these children of Amma who shared so openly and generously. They shine as examples of true selfless service.

Satsang Coordinators

Right alongside the writers' contribution is that of the satsang coordinators in the different countries and cities of the world. They believed in this project and whole-heartedly supported it. From encouraging devotees in their countries to write, to penning their own stories, to providing whatever other help was asked of them, these children of Amma were truly a joy to work with. Many have all but given up their worldly lives to serve their beloved Mother even while still living in the world. They work as instruments of Mother to organize the worldwide programs, the main means for Amma's children to come to Her. Their example of service is very inspiring.

Other Sevites

Many, many people helped contact writers within specific groups and regions. Stories received in other languages were translated into English by sevites. Teams made of both Amma's devotees and those new to Her read the stories to provide feedback. Writers most willingly incorporated this feedback to revise their stories if needed. The stories were then edited. One of Amma's younger children, a fourteen-year-old girl, suggested titles for many of the stories. A team searched for Amma's quotes to go with every story. Many people shared their collections of Amma's pictures to be used in the book. Amma's children did the book and cover design as seva. It was the dedication and the tireless efforts of all these people who worked together as one large family that made possible this offering of love.

Om Amriteshwaryai Namah

Glossary

Abhishekam	The ritual of bathing a deity in idol form with pure substances such as milk, curd, ghee, honey, and rose water as a form of worship
Advaita	The philosophy of non-dualism which teaches that the Supreme Reality is one and indivisible
Amritapuri	The home where Amma was born. Now it is the ashram, headquarters of Her worldwide mission and the spiritual home of over a thousand residents, and where thousands flock to have Amma's darshan.
Anandamayi Ma	Bengali woman saint who was the contemporary of Paramahansa Yogananda
Arati	The ritual in which light is offered to a deity in the form of burning camphor. This act of worship represents offering one's ego to the Divine. Camphor burns without leaving behind any residue. This symbolizes the total annihilation of the ego.
Archana	Chanting the different names of a deity, usually 108 or 1000. Also the offering for worship.
Asana	Postures in Hatha Yoga. Also a small mat on which one may sit during meditation.
Ashram	A place where spiritual seekers and aspirants live or visit to lead a spiritual life and practice sadhana
Ashtotharam	108 names of a deity
Avatar	Divine incarnation
Ayurveda	Ancient holistic health system wherein medicines are prepared from herbs and plants
Balakendram	Spiritual classes for children
Bhagavan	God, Lord

Bhagavad Gita	Bhagavad = of the Lord; Gita = song; Song of the Lord. The epic song in the Mahabharata, consisting of a dialog between Krishna and Arjuna, carried on in a chariot drawn up between two opposing armies. Symbolically the chariot represents the body, Arjuna our ego, Krishna the Supreme Spirit, and the opposing forces of Kauravas and Pandavas the higher and lower natures of man.
Bhajan	Devotional song
Bhakti Yoga	Union through devotion. The path of devotion. The way of attaining Self-Realization through devotion and complete surrender to God.
Bhava	Divine mood
Brahmachari	A male disciple who practices spiritual disciplines under the guidance of a Guru
Brahmacharini	A female disciple who practices spiritual disciplines under the guidance of a Guru
Brahman	The Absolute Reality; the Whole; the Supreme Being, which encompasses and pervades in everything and everywhere
Brahmasthanam	A unique temple concept that is ushering in a new epoch in the ancient tradition of temple worship. The aim is to mitigate human suffering and re-educate people about the true principles underlying temple worship, thus leading them to the realization of the Divinity within.
Brahmasthanam Prana Prathishta	Breathing pure life energy into the temple murthi or idol. Amma consecrates each one of these Brahmasthanam temples.
Brahmin	The highest intellectual caste of the four castes prevalent in ancient India

Buddha	Famous saint born in 2000 BC whose followers are known as Buddhists; one who is awake, intelligent and wise
Chakra	Wheel, discus, center in the body, centers of psychic energy, the weapon of Vishnu, symbolizing cyclic evolution, a cycle
Crown Chakra	Energy center on the head
Darshan	An audience with or a vision of the Divine or a holy person, commonly referred to receiving a hug from Amma
Darshan Token	The token number given to indicate the sequence in which one can receive Amma's darshan
Darshan Line	The line that is formed to control and maintain the flow of people to Amma
Devi	Goddess, Divine Mother
Devi Bhava	The Divine Mood of Devi. The state in which Amma reveals Her oneness and identity with the Divine Mother.
Dharma	That which upholds the universe. Dharma has many meanings, including the Divine Law, the law of existence in accordance with divine harmony, righteousness, religion, duty, responsibility, right conduct, justice, goodness, and truth.
Divine Mother	The universal mother who is the source of each and everything in this universe
Durga	A name of Shakti, the Divine Mother. She is often depicted as yielding a number of weapons and riding a lion. She is the destroyer of the evil and the protector if that which is good. She destroys the desires and negative tendencies of Her children and unveils the Supreme Self.

Dwaparyuga	The time period in which Sri Krishna incarnated on planet earth – the third of the four ages (Yuga)
Gopis	The gopis were cowherd girls and milkmaids who lived in Vrindavan. They were Krishna's closest devotees and are known for their supreme devotion to the Lord. They exemplify the most intense love for God.
Grihasthashrami	One leading a spiritual life, while leading the life of a householder
Gyana Yoga, Jnana Yoga	One of the yogic paths to God where one uses his intellect to realize God
Guru	Spiritual teacher, master, guide; one who removes the darkness of ignorance
Hatha Yoga	A system of physical and mental exercises developed in ancient times to make the body and its vital functions perfect instruments, in order to help one attain Self-Realization
Hindi	The official language of India
Jagatmata	Jagat = world, mata = mother; Mother of the Universe
Japa Mala	A necklace or mala used to keep a count of the number of repetitions of a mantra; string of beads
Jyotish	Science of predicting the future events based on the planetary positions and their effects
Kali	The dark one; An aspect of the Divine Mother. From the viewpoint of ego, She may seem frightening because She destroys the ego. But She destroys the ego only out of her immeasurable compassion.

Kaliyuga	The dark period of 432,000 years of mortals in Brahmanical computation. It is the present Yuga, the age in which we live, and is described in the Mahabharata as characterized by great material advance but spiritual darkness (see Yuga). Some of the characteristics of this dark age are people are much more extroverted, possess weak memory, and are unable to grasp spiritual truths. The greatness of the Kaliyuga is that by the mere chanting of the Divine names one can merge into the Lord.
Karma Yoga	Union though action. The spiritual path of detached, selfless service and of dedicating the fruit of all one's actions to God.
Kerala	Amma's home state in India located on the southwestern tip of India
Krishna	He who draws us to Himself; the principle incarnation of Vishnu. Born in a royal family, Krishna grew up with foster parents and lived as a young cowherd in Vrindavan, where he was loved and worshipped by his devoted companions, the gopis and gopas. Krishna later became the ruler of Dwaraka. He was a friend and adviser to his cousins, the Pandavas, especially Arjuna, to whom he revealed his teachings in the Bhagavad Gita.
Krishna Bhava	The state in which Amma reveals Her oneness and identity with Krishna
Lakshmi	Goddess of material prosperity and spiritual liberation
Lalita Sahasranama	The thousand names of the Divine Mother
Leela	Play. The movements and activities of the Divine, which by nature are free and not necessarily subject to the laws of nature.

Mahatma	Great soul. When Amma uses the word mahatma, She is referring to a Self realized soul.
Mahavatar	Maha = big and important, avatar = incarnation; an incarnation of the Supreme God
Mala	Necklace; rosary made of rudraksha seeds, tulsi wood, crsytal, or sandalwood beads
Malayalam	The state language of Kerala
Manas Puja	Manas = mind, puja = worship; mental worship
Mangal Puja	Worship conducted for the well being of everyone
Mantra	Sacred formula or prayer that is constantly repeated. This awakens one's dormant spiritual powers and helps one reach the goal. It is most effective if received from a spiritual master during initiation.
Mata Amrita-nandamayi Devi	Amma's name given to Her by Her children; Mother Goddess who is ever blissful with Divine Ambrosia
Math, Mutt	Spiritual place, ashram
Maya	Illusion. The Divine power or veil with which God, in his Divine Play of Creation, conceals Himself and gives the impression of the many, thereby creating the illusion of separation.
Meenakshi	Goddess worshipped in South India
Murthi	Idol
Om	Sacred syllable. The primordial Sound or Vibration, which represents Brahman and the entire creation. Om is the primary mantra and is usually found at the beginning of other mantras.
Om Amriteshwaryai Namah	Salutations to our beloved Amma

Pada Puja	The worship of God's or the Guru's feet. As the feet support the body, the Guru Principle supports the Supreme Truth. The Guru's feet represent the Supreme Truth.
Padam	Feet
Pancha Karma	Ayurvedic treatment to balance all five elements of our body
Paramahamsa Yogananda	Indian spiritual master who can to the west to spread the knowledge of scriptures
Patanjali Yoga Sutras	The science of Yoga as written by Patanjali, an ancient saint in India
Prabhu	God
Prana	Breath; the vital force derived form the sun, which is represented in humans by the breath
Pranam	Salutation
Prasad, Prasadam	The consecrated offering distributed after puja. Whatever a mahatma gives as a sign of his blessing.
Prema	Supreme love
Puja	Ritualistic worship
Radha	One of Krishna's gopis. She was the closer to Krishna than any other gopi and personifies the highest and purest love for God.
Ram	The Giver of Joy. The Divine hero in the epic, Ramayana. He was an incarnation of Vishnu, and is considered to be the ideal of virtue.
Ramakrishna Paramahamsa	A well-known Indian spiritual master who instructed Vivekananda to impart the knowledge of Vedanta in the west
Ramana Maharishi	A well-known Indian spiritual master who lived at the foot-hills of the Arunachala Mountains

Rishi	Singer of sacred songs; poet; one to whom the Vedas were revealed
Rudraksha	The seeds of the rudraksha tree, which have both medicinal and spiritual power, and are associated with Lord Shiva
Sadhak	A spiritual aspirant who practices sadhana for the purpose of attaining Self-realization
Sadhana	Spiritual disciplines and practices, such as meditation, prayer, japa, the reading of holy scriptures and fasting
Samadhi	Sam = with; adhi = the Lord. Oneness with God.
Sandalwood Paste	The paste prepared by grinding the Sandalwood with some water on a stone
Sani Puja	Worship conducted to nullify the effects of planet Saturn
Sankalpa	Used here to refer to resolve made by Amma; volition, strength of mind; thought, reflection
Sanskrit	The ancient language of India which is the basis for most of Indian languages
Sannyasi	A monk or nun who has taken formal vows of renunciation and wears a traditional ochre-colored cloth representing the burning away of all attachments
Sari, Saree	The traditional dress worn by Indian women
Satguru	Self-realized spiritual master
Satsang	Sat = truth; sang = in association with. Being in the company of the wise and virtuous. Also a spiritual discourse by a sage or scholar.
Seva	Selfless service
Shabari	A famous devotee of Sri Ram, her story is part of the Ramayan epic

Shakti	The dynamic aspect of the Universal Mother
Shankaracharya	An ancient spiritual teacher in India
Shiva, Siva	A static aspect of Brahman as the male principle; one of Hindu trinity (Brahma, Vishnu and Siva), the destroyer, or transformer
Shraddha	In Sanskrit, Shraddha means faith rooted in wisdom and experience, whereas the same term in Malayalam means dedication to one's work and attentive awareness in every action. Amma often uses the term in the later sense.
Sri	Luminous; Holy; An honorable prefix
Swami, Swamini	A monk or nun who has taken formal vows of renunciation and wears a traditional ochre-colored cloth representing the burning away of all attachments
Tretayuga	Name of the second of the four Yugas or ages. It contains 1,296,000 years of mortals (see Yuga).
Vallickavu	The place where Amma was born. Currently the site of Her ashram
Vanarasena	Vanara = Monkey, Sena = Army. The army of monkeys that was with Rama during the war with the demon Ravana
Veda	The ancient, sacred scriptures of Hinduism. A collection of holy texts in Sanskrit that are divided into four parts: Rig, Yajur, Sama and Atharva, they are among the world's oldest scriptures. The Vedas are considered to be the direct revelation of the Supreme Truth, which God bestowed upon the rishis.
Vedanta	The philosophy of the Upanishads, the concluding part of the Vedas, which holds the Ultimate Truth to be One without a second

Vedic Astrology	Also called Jyotish, science of predicting the future events based on the planetary positions and their effects
Vibhuti	Sacred ash
Vishnu	All-pervading. The second member of the Hindu trinity.
Yoga	To unite. The path through which one can attain oneness with the Divine.
Yogi	Someone who is established in the practice of yoga, or is established in union with the Supreme spirit

Book Catalog
By Author

Sri Mata Amritanandamayi Devi

108 Quotes On Faith
108 Quotes On Love
Compassion, The Only Way To Peace:
　Paris Speech
Cultivating Strength And Vitality
Living In Harmony
May Peace And Happiness Prevail:
　Barcelona Speech
May Your Hearts Blossom:
　Chicago Speech
Practice Spiritual Values And Save The
　World: Delhi Speech
The Awakening Of Universal Motherhood:
　Geneva Speech
The Eternal Truth
The Infinite Potential Of Women:
　Jaipur Speech
Understanding And Collaboration
　Between Religions
Unity Is Peace: Interfaith Speech

Swami Amritaswarupananda Puri

Ammachi: A Biography
Awaken Children, Volumes 1-9
From Amma's Heart
Mother Of Sweet Bliss
The Color Of Rainbow

Swami Jnanamritananda Puri

Eternal Wisdom, Volumes 1-2

Swami Paramatmananda Puri

Dust Of Her Feet
On The Road To Freedom Volumes 1-2
Talks, Volumes 1-6

Swami Purnamritananda Puri

Unforgettable Memories

Swami Ramakrishnananda Puri

Eye Of Wisdom
Racing Along The Razor's Edge
Secret Of Inner Peace
The Blessed Life
The Timeless Path
Ultimate Success

Swamini Krishnamrita Prana

Love Is The Answer
Sacred Journey
The Fragrance Of Pure Love
Torrential Love

M.A. Center Publications

1,000 Names Commentary
Archana Book (Large)
Archana Book (Small)
Being With Amma
Bhagavad Gita
Bhajanamritam, Volumes 1-6
Embracing The World
For My Children
Immortal Light
Lead Us To Purity
Lead Us To The Light
Man And Nature
My First Darshan
Puja: The Process Of Ritualistic
　Worship
Sri Lalitha Trishati Stotram

Amma's Websites

AMRITAPURI—Amma's Home Page
Teachings, Activities, Ashram Life, eServices, Yatra, Blogs and News
http://www.amritapuri.org

AMMA (Mata Amritanandamayi)
About Amma, Meeting Amma, Global Charities, Groups and Activities and Teachings
http://www.amma.org

EMBRACING THE WORLD®
Basic Needs, Emergencies, Environment, Research and News
http://www.embracingtheworld.org

AMRITA UNIVERSITY
About, Admissions, Campuses, Academics, Research, Global and News
http://www.amrita.edu

THE AMMA SHOP—Embracing the World® Books & Gifts Shop
Blog, Books, Complete Body, Home & Gifts, Jewelry, Music and Worship
http://www.theammashop.org

IAM—Integrated Amrita Meditation Technique®
Meditation Taught Free of Charge to the Public, Students, Prisoners and Military
http://www.amma.org/groups/north-america/projects/iam-meditation-classes

AMRITA PUJA
Types and Benefits of Pujas, Brahmasthanam Temple, Astrology Readings, Ordering Pujas
http://www.amritapuja.org

GREENFRIENDS
Growing Plants, Building Sustainable Environments, Education and Community Building
http://www.amma.org/groups/north-america/projects/green-friends

FACEBOOK
This is the Official Facebook Page to Connect with Amma
https://www.facebook.com/MataAmritanandamayi

DONATION PAGE
Please Help Support Amma's Charities Here:
http://www.amma.org/donations

www.ingramcontent.com/pod-product-compliance
Lightning Source LLC
Chambersburg PA
CBHW071211090426
42736CB00014B/2779